30349518

This book donated through the Courtesy of The North American Falconers Association

A Bond With the Wild

A Celebration
of American Falconry

A Bond With the Wild

A Celebration of American Falconry

Kenn Filkins, Editor
Doug Daniels, Illustrator

North American Falconers' Association
Berthoud, Colorado

Library of Congress Catalog Card Number: 93-85241

All rights reserved. No part of this book may be reproduced or utilized in any form or by any means, electronic or mechanical, including photocopying, recording, or by any informational storage and retrieval systems, without written permission from the publisher.

Published by:
North American Falconers' Association
820 Jay Place
Berthoud, Colorado 80513 U.S.A.

Copyright © 1993 by North American Falconers' Association

0
799.232
B711
c.1

Dedication

**To the wild hawks and falcons
for gracing us with their presence**

Table of Contents

Preface

A Bond With The Wild offers a unique glimpse into twentieth-century falconry. Falconers practice a sophisticated form of bird watching while hunting with their hawks. The trained hawk or falcon flies free during the hunt and returns of its own volition. Fortunately, these birds return often enough to make the venture worthwhile and depart often enough to make falconers cherish their gracious presence. No other group trains wild predators to pursue wild quarry. This book reflects on how falconers weave their passion for hawks into twentieth-century life.

No book of this scope occurs without the effort of many dedicated people. The original concept of this book began nearly a decade ago when Jim Weaver, then President of the North American Falconers' Association (NAFA), conceived a falconry book to be published by NAFA. Weaver sent a personal plea to several falconers, but even before those manuscripts arrived the book's focus had changed.

At first, the book was intended to be a "how-to book" of falconry techniques. But when Jim Weaver mentioned it to me, its focus had been changed to "a coffee-table book with lots of color and stories of falconry. A book from which non-falconers, outdoorsmen and congressmen could read to understand what falconry really is . . . Something like a hard-cover **Gray's Sporting Journal** of falconry . . ."

At the NAFA Field Meet in Cedar City, Utah in November, 1987, Weaver discussed the book idea publicly and suggested that all interested falconers meet to discuss the future of the work. That night Jim Weaver, Charles Schwartz, Doug Pineo, Ralph Rogers, and I brainstormed the "NAFA Book."

Over the next year the seeds from that meeting germinated and grew without much direction. At the 1988 NAFA Field Meet, in Amarillo, Texas, the new NAFA President Ralph Rogers scheduled an open meeting to discuss the NAFA Book, an introductory falconry video and a falconry equipment book. Many people attended. It became clear from the conversation that the NAFA Book was perceived as another "how-to" falconry book. The group questioned whether it was needed.

The NAFA Book idea was about to be squelched. If so, I thought, they might as well squelch the **real** idea, then they would be making an informed decision. So I explained that the vision of the book was not "how-to" but "why we practice falconry . . . ." As the discussion continued, they realized that the NAFA Book would be unlike any other falconry book in European, Oriental or American literature. They understood how this book could become a catalyst for the growth of American falconry literature.

As a result, the group endorsed the NAFA Book and President Rogers asked me to pursue this idea. In the months that followed, I wrote to everyone I thought had a specific interest in the project, especially Charles Schwartz and Doug Pineo. The idea kept growing . . . .

At the 1989 NAFA Field Meet in Kearney, Nebraska, I scheduled an open evening meeting for everyone interested in the NAFA Book. Nearly seventy people participated. Charles Schwartz and I spoke about the concept and purpose of the NAFA Book, and Jim Weaver, Ralph Rogers, and Ken Felix added their comments. Later that week I spoke with falconer and author Dan O'Brien, to gain his insight into the project. The result of those meetings was the creation of a mailing list of interested falconers/writers and a NAFA Book Task Force.

By the spring of 1990, Schwartz, Pineo and I had created a thematic NAFA Book proposal for those interested in submitting their work. It contained an explanation of the book's elusive theme and sample stories from outdoor literature. Basically it said, "Don't send us stories about birds, send us stories about why you hunt with a falcon, about your passions for the raptors, quarry, land, families . . . . We don't want a feature film, just one scene . . . one glimpse into why you practice falconry in North America in the 1990s . . . ."

President Rogers asked me to chair the NAFA Book Task Force, and I selected Charles Schwartz, Doug Pineo, Kent Christopher, and Joe Vorro. Schwartz, Pineo, Christopher and I handled stories and Vorro, a former **NAFA Journal** Editor, gathered the photo submissions.

Then we asked for manuscripts from North American falconers and sent every interested writer a copy of the NAFA Book Proposal. And the manuscripts began to arrive. At first we wondered if we would have enough material about "why we pursue falconry" to compile a book. At times some thought the NAFA Book was dying . . . .

More manuscripts were requested through the **Hawk Chalk** and when they came pouring in, the real work began. The Task Force reviewed the manuscripts and suggested revisions.

Finally in the spring of 1991, the Task Force selected the twenty-four stories that you will find in this volume. NAFA contracted with Steve Bodio to edit the manuscripts. And at the November 1992 NAFA Meet in Lamar, Colorado, I presented a production plan for this book to the NAFA Board at the open meeting.

The support from the NAFA Board and general membership was overwhelming. A pre-publication offer was mailed to NAFA members in January 1993. And in September, 1993 the NAFA Book — now titled **A Bond With The Wild: A Celebration of American Falconry** — became a reality.

As with any project of this nature, this book would not exist without the vision and involvement of many people. I gratefully acknowledge the NAFA Book Task Force, which dedicated a huge amount of time and effort without any financial compensation. Thanks to Doug Pineo for his insight into the theme of this book, especially in the early stages, and to Kent Christopher for his labors at encouraging writers and reviewing manuscripts.

My personal thanks to Charles Schwartz, who has become my cherished friend, and who *haggled* with me for long hours over the vision of this project, the book proposal, the manuscripts . . . . Without his intuition about the book's theme and his long hours of reviewing, editing and encouragement there would be no NAFA Book.

I'm especially grateful to Joe Vorro, the first falconer I ever met, for handling the laborious task of collecting the photo-support, gathering bids from the printers, copy-editing the final manuscript, and guiding the designer in the creation process, and for his friendship that endures in spite of this project. And I thank Joe for his wise words under a conifer tree one day while hunting deer. Without those words I would have thrown in the towel on this book. Like Charles, without Joe there would be no NAFA Book.

I extend my sincere appreciation to the three NAFA Presidents who have served during the years it took to create this book. My thanks to Jim Weaver for his original vision; to Ralph Rogers for his unfailing encouragement, for the book's subtitle (from one of his comments at the Amarillo Meet) and for "E-6"; and to current NAFA President Ken Felix for unwavering support of the book and for "The 'Falcontry' Expedition."

This project would not have survived without the support of the fine men and women who served as NAFA Board members and officers during the last several years. My gratitude to all of them.

On behalf of the NAFA Board and officers, I thank all of those who submitted manuscripts for consideration, and especially the twenty-four writers whose work appears here. In writing for love, not money, they shared something that money cannot buy. I thank all the photographers who, just as unselfishly, shared their talents with this project without any financial return.

My deepest thanks to Doug Daniels, the Art Director at The John Henry Printing Company of Lansing, Michigan, for illustrating this book, and especially for the sacrifice of time and energy he gave above any demands of the contract. Doug, I *will* take you flyfishing for steelhead. Thanks to the rest of the John Henry staff for their professional and personal interest in making this book into a "world-class case-bound book."

Now the real reason for this book — the stories. Their variety is great, like the falconers themselves, the hawks they fly, the quarry they pursue, and the passions they express. Stories of humor, tragedy, fiction, true adventure, personal essay, and reflections on the past. The twenty-one stories by falconers and three by non-falconers share a unique insight into *a bond with the wild.*

Enjoy your flight . . .

Kenn Filkins
June, 1993

Forgot My Pants, Lost My Mind

by Tim Cahill

Falconry, I might have written recently, is that extinct medieval sport wherein guys in metal suits threw birds to fish. I admit to a large measure of ignorance regarding birds in general and falconry in particular. Tragically, I am afflicted with the agony of ornithological dyslexia. But ignorance, if it is sincere and pure of heart, can sometimes function as a knowledge vacuum. Which, I suspect, is the most obtuse and metaphysical explanation of how I ended up attending the 1988 North American Falconers Association Field Meeting in Amarillo.

Not two hours after I arrived in Texas, I found myself creeping through a dusty field, sneaking up on a small pond in order to ambush some ducks. The sun had just touched the western horizon and a full hunter's moon was rising in the east. The colors of the setting sun, pastel oranges and reds, shimmered on the surface of the water. It was a clear, windless day, and the image of the moon also glittered on the water, so that it seemed as if all of heaven and earth was encompassed in this farmer's stock pond.

The falconer slipped his bird (released her from his fist) and the peregrine took a pitch above, several hundred feet over the pond. I was given to understand that the bells, little jingle bells that falcons wear, are necessary to locate a bird feeding on fallen quarry in high cover, although there is something the least bit anticipatory about them. A hunting falcon rising from the fist sounds a little like Christmas morning.

When the falcon had taken a pitch of about 200 feet, various humans charged the pond and flushed the ducks. And suddenly there she was, a peregrine falcon diving at perhaps 200 miles an hour. I now know that falconers call this power dive a stoop, as in "she stoops to conquer." (The female falcon is a third again as big as the male and most falconers fly females.) The peregrine's wings were folded in against her body, and the wind racing through her brittle feathers and the bell slits sounded in a rising whistle. Two lines of flight, one horizontal, one vertical, intersected at a moment of savage radiance above the sun and moon shimmering on the moon below.

And that, I learned, is falconry. It is a form of personally engineered bird watching.

From the outside, falconers themselves appear to be fairly odd ducks. There were more than 300 birds at the NAFA Field Meet, both hawks and falcons. On sunny days, most often in midafternoon, most of these birds could be seen out in back of the Amarillo Hilton, sunning themselves on blocklike perches (weathering) while the falconers stood around arguing proudly.

Falconers argue as a matter of course. A falconer argues, I think, because the sport requires him to bend his will to that of the bird. There is no disciplining an unmannerly falcon. A disgruntled bird will simply fly away next time it is released, so falconers take out their frustrations on other people and bicker endlessly over the fine points of their sport.

They are, I'm obliged to state, monomaniacal in their frenzy. Often they take their birds with them on social occasions, and invariably the bird will mute, which is to say, engage its impressive waste-disposal system. When this happens in someone else's house and the mutes are spread across the couch and new carpet like the contents of several tubes of toothpaste, the falconer does not discipline his bird. Nor is he likely to help clean up. Typically, a falconer in such a situation will examine the mutes and proclaim, with great satisfaction, *"Now* that *is a healthy bird."*

Perhaps the strangest characteristic of the falconer, however, is the complete lack of trousers on the male of the species. (I have not yet observed such conduct in the female falconer, although I intend to be patient in this regard.)

The male falconer often runs around without pants because he forgets them in his frenzy. There is, for instance, a falconer of my recent acquaintance who lives in Winifred, Montana, not far from the breaks of the Missouri River. I'll call this fellow, oh, let's say Ralph Rogers.

One day Ralph decided to hunt the breaks with his peregrine. He packed up the essentials for the bird, the food, the weathering block, the hood, the jesses, the lure, the bells, the electronic transmitter and receiver, all the paraphernalia necessary for the comfort and safety of his falcon. Being an experienced outdoorsman, Ralph packed quickly for himself.

It was a warm day and Ralph had worn running shorts, but by the time he got to the breaks, the weather had turned cold. The experienced outdoorsman then discovered that he had not packed any pants. His partner lent him the only conceivable thing he could wear to cut the wind and blunt the chill. Because the other man was about a foot shorter and not nearly so, uh, muscular, the thermal underwear Ralph now wore had that overstuffed, over-the-calf look that so fascinates clothiers. Inevitably, the bird rode a particularly strong thermal, rose out of sight, caught a whiff of the jet stream, and got lost. Ralph had fastened a small transmitter to the bird, and he was using a black box with an antenna (the receiver) to find her.

The signal — it always happens this way — took the falconer through a small town. Now, when a man is searching for his bird with a receiver of this sort, he must constantly listen to the beeping of the machine, and turn in a complete circle, carefully blocking one point of the compass with his body in order to isolate the signal.

Falconers understand such antics at a glance. The rest of us find it bewildering. Here's a man frantically running through your backyard, holding a little black box with an antenna on it and wearing what seems to be a pair of longjohns bursting at the seams. Every once in a while he performs a slow-motion pirouette, then gallops off hysterically in one direction or another. Naturally, seeing such a person whirling through your yard, you might be inclined to inquire as to the nature of his business.

"What the hell's going on here?"

"Sorry," your falconer in lingerie is going to reply, *"can't talk now. I've lost my bird."*

For the average outsider, this translates into: *"Can't talk now, I've completely lost my mind."*

The ancient field sport of falconry has been the subject of some controversy in the past few years. There are a number of people who simply can't stomach blood sport of any variety, and they are people of good hearts. But I think it is wise for falconers to point out that they've had a guiding hand in bringing the majestic peregine falcon back from near extinction. In 1965, there were less than 20 known pairs of peregrines in the wild. DDT was killing them. In 1970, the Peregrine Fund, a nonprofit organization supported by scientists, ecologists, hunters, and falconers, began raising peregrines in captivity and releasing the young. Today there are an estimated 350 pairs in the United States, not counting Alaska. It's difficult for those of genuinely good heart to take issue with these statistics. Hunting peregrines are not taken from the wild: all these birds by law must be captive bred.

Some observers feel that falcons are invariably successful in their hunts. This is not so. A man with a shotgun is a more effective predator than any peregrine.

Indeed, the point of falconry or hawking is not merely to take game; the important issue is the manner in which the game is taken. One bright Amarillo morning, for instance, I was out by a duck pond with some falconers and noticed that the man flying the bird had it *"wait on,"* which is to say, hover, several hundred yards from the pond. When we flushed the ducks, the falcon stooped, but she was far out of hunting range, and the ducks flew off unharmed. Later, I asked the falconer why he had set up his bird for certain failure. "I want her to learn that she has to take a higher pitch," he said. "If she had been over the pond, it would have been a simple slaughter."

I then understood that falconers, like fly fishermen, require a certain perverse elegance in their sport. They are rather like the sexually obsessed in this regard: *"Well, if I can't do it with whips and midgets, I'd rather not do it at all."*

Most hunters — all but the most doltish fringe — speak about respect for the hunted. But a falconer's concern for the quarry is legendary. Consider the story of an individual I met in Amarillo. He is a pillar of moral authority in his community and, for that reason, has asked me not to reveal his identity. Let's just say that one fall day, on his annual hawking vacation, he was out flying Harris' hawks with several friends. This was in Colorado, and the friends were flying their hawks from their fists.

Now Harris' hawks, I've discovered, are rare raptors in that they hunt in groups, using strategy. I imagine the scene was rather like the one I had witnessed out in the corn stubble near the Amarillo airport. I recall a rabbit being pursued by the hawks. Once again it had occurred to me that if game were the purpose, a shotgun would have served better here. We scared up a rabbit, shouted *"Ho ho hawk!"* and the hawks sprang from four fists as the rabbit bolted slow off the mark, but one of the pound-and-a-half birds came in high, another low. The rabbit — there were several ferruginous hawks cruising the field and my guess is that the local bunnies were used to this sort of thing — stopped short so that the high hawk over-flew him. The second Harris' came in only inches off the ground but the rabbit leapt a full four feet into the air. Then it disappeared in a series of sharp angles and lost itself in the corn stubble. There was, on the part of the falconers, some small grudging applause for the rabbit.

The scene was somewhat similar in Colorado that day: four men walking through a field, hawks on their fists. A rabbit broke, the hawks flew. The rabbit bolted toward the gravel road. Between the road and the field, however, was an irrigation ditch. The day was cold and turning colder. A thin skim of ice had formed over the water in the ditch.

The rabbit had no time for caution and attempted to run across the ice, which broke. Now we have four men standing around with hawks on their wrists, looking down into a ditch with some consternation. The rabbit was drowning. It attempted to crawl up on a ledge of ice that immediately gave way, plunging the rabbit back into the water. When it surfaced the third time, ice was forming on its head. The men were abashed.

It is true that only moments earlier these men had earnestly desired the annihilation of the rabbit, but this drowning wasn't nearly what they had in mind.

Someone, it was decided, would have to save the rabbit. The gentleman in question — a moral pillar of his community, remember — took the task upon himself. First he removed his boots and socks. Then it occurred to him that the water might be two or three feet deep. A man could spend the rest of the day wearing wet pants. No, best to take them off. But his shirt and parka hung down past his waist, and, for all he knew, the water could be chest deep.

The rabbit was weakening.

No time to waste. Get the clothes off and save the rabbit. Hurry.

Imagine the scene. Three guys standing around with vicious-looking hawks on their fists and one naked man shivering on the subfreezing, wind-whipped plain.

Which is precisely what greeted the elderly couple as they drove down the lonely road that paralleled the ditch. There was a slowing of the car and our falconers had the enduring impression of two pairs of eyes, feeling much of what a driver feels when a deer is frozen in the headlights.

"Geez almighty. Madge, it's some of them devil worshipers Geraldo was talking about."

The squeal of tires, a spray of gravel.

The postscript here is that the rabbit was saved. It trembled in the men's hands, badly chilled. If they released it, this rabbit was going to die of hypothermia. The hunting trip was cut short, the hawks were hooded, and the rabbit was driven back to the motel, where it was warmed and dried by a blow-drier. It was later released in a large field where — if the coyotes haven't gotten it, if the wild hawks or foxes have somehow missed it — it's still alive, fat and sassy.

Nonetheless, I have a persistent vision of the maids in that motel gossiping: *"Don't know who they are, but they come here every year. Capture rabbits and style their hair. I think they're mad hare-dressers."*

The man who swam naked for the rabbit was finally foolish enough to tell his wife about it. And now, every time he comes home from a hawking expedition with some matter of grave or amusing import to relay — "Honey, guess what happened today?" — she replies in the world-weary tone of one who has experienced much in life and is not often surprised, *"You didn't get naked again, did you?"*

So yes, a week in the company of avid falconers has considerably broadened my horizons. Falconry, I can now confidently state, *'is that flourishing contemporary field sport in which frenzied, monomaniacal men (and some frenzied, monomaniacal women) soil their neighbors' living rooms with bird droppings and run naked in the snow.'*

Assateague Island

by Alva Nye

"The fishing was lousy, so we cruised the beach, shooting hawks with the scope-sighted .22 rifle. There were hawks sitting all over the beach on the sand. Incidentally, those hawks looked exactly like the ones you have tied out in the back yard on perches." These were the incredible words of fisherman Roddy Gascoyne, who had just returned from a surf fishing expedition to Fox Hill Levels on Assateague Island, Maryland on that September day in 1938. Who ever heard of the lordly peregrine of inland mountain cliffs sitting ignominiously about on the sand like seagulls or sandpipers? But Roddy insisted such was the case. We decided to check it out. What we found drastically altered the course of American falconry.

The time was September, 1938. Falconry was just beginning in America. The number of falconers practicing the sport was very small. The few peregrines that were used were all eyases, nestlings taken from inland cliffs. From what limited experience we had had with other hawks, plus what we had read in British falconry books, we knew that passage peregrines (those trapped on the first migration southward in the fall) were far, far superior birds to eyases. But what we didn't know was where passage peregrines could be trapped. So, when Roddy spoke of the many hawks on the beach, "just like the ones you have on perches in the back yard," our ears really perked up. We were excited!

A few weeks later, we made the first exploratory trip to the island. We found a long, thin, sand island extending some 40 miles along the coast of Maryland and Virginia. It was then, and remains today, a typical coastal barrier island with a large ocean beach, stretching back to rolling sand dunes and generally becoming a great marsh area on the inner or bay side. Scattered over the island were huge flat areas, or levels, caused by abnormally high tides flooding the island. The levels, we learned, were favorite landing and resting places for migrating peregrines.

The only human beings on the island were the occupants of four manned Coast Guard stations about ten miles apart, with only an occasional visiting surf fisherman or duck hunter. The island was forty miles of almost virginal, unspoiled coastal wilderness. The main reason it was so unspoiled was its almost total inaccessibility.

To get to the island required hiring a boatman to ferry you over. The ferry consisted of driving a car onto a flat-top barge, and then having a boat push the barge across an inlet of the bay. Once over the bay and on the edge of the island, the car was driven off to the sand shore on makeshift ramps. It was a hazardous experience. Then came the most trying thing of all — driving on the soft sand. There were no four-wheelers in those days, only conventional cars. So we had to let the air out of the tires until they were half-flat. With the air gone, the vehicle could be driven reasonably. It was poor going and we got stuck often, but somehow we managed to dig out and move on to some harder sand. It was almost frightening, especially when we got stuck trying to drive on the packed sand near the water's edge and hit soft spots with the tide coming in. But we were driven by the thought of peregrines being there, so we pushed on in spite of many hardships.

I can recall our excitement at the sight of the first peregrine sitting like a seagull on the sand of the front beach. She was a passager with dark plumage and heavy cheek patches. She bobbed her head up and down as we stopped to glass her with the binoculars. What a thrill it was! By the end of the run down the beach, we had seen five birds.

It was on this first trip that we tried a "pit" method of trapping. From previous bow-netting experience for inland migrating hawks, especially red-tails, we knew that it was not unusual for a hawk to tenaciously bind to the suspended lure pigeon and hang from the lure line. So we reasoned that if we could hoist a lure pigeon into the air, let a passing peregrine bind to it, and then lower the bird down to the top of a pit which had been covered with burlap and sand, we could then carefully reach up through a crack from our underneath hiding place and grab the falcon.

So we dug a pit and tried this idea. But it did not work. No peregrines were attracted in. This effort concluded our first and only trip to the beach in 1938. But one thing we did learn — there were migrating peregrines on Assateague!

For the next year, I don't believe a day went by without my thinking of the peregrines on the beach and some way to catch them. I felt that the big shortfall in the "pit" method of trapping was that we were sitting in the pit waiting for the peregrines to come to us. What we needed was to be able to drive on the beach to where we saw a peregrine and then set a trap to catch it. It was these compelling thoughts that ultimately generated the "head-set" method of trapping.

The headset method was simply this. A headpiece, made of chicken wire netting, and about the size of a bushel basket, was woven loosely with hay and long grasses so that it looked like a big clump of grass. When you placed it over your head, it was easy to see out through the grasses, but impossible to see into. The use of this headpiece was simple. We would drive down the beach until a peregrine was seen sitting on the sand. The car was stopped broadside to the bird, and we would exit the car on the lee side. Then we would dig a shallow trench in the sand and put a man in it with only his head protruding above the surface. Then the headpiece would be put over the man's head and the rest of his body would be covered with sand. A pigeon was then given to the one in the sand, whose hands were only slightly covered. By holding the pigeon's legs, a fluttering bait for the falcon resulted. To the falcon or any outsider, the scene was absolutely natural. Only a big clump of grass was apparent, and next to it was a fluttering pigeon. However, the man in the headset was fully aware of everything around him, and indeed had unlimited vision through some of the largest spaces between the grass. This, then, was the headset method that ultimately revolutionized peregrine trapping.

The first test of this concept came on September 30, 1939, when Richard Hufty and I went to Assateague. We arrived on the island about midnight, and immediately began to erect a blind and set up a bow net. As I recall, there was a bright moon. When it was completed, we drove down the beach a few miles to help another falconer, Bill Turner, and a friend, to erect their blind and set up a bow net. All of this was prior to dawn. Then as the sun began to rise in the east, Hufty and I began driving back up the beach to our blind and the bow net setup a few miles away.

In the back of the car was a woven wire headset that we had brought to the island to try if an opportunity presented itself. It surely did. We hadn't driven a mile or so up the beach when there on the sand sat a beautiful immature peregrine tiercel!

I turned to Richard and said, "Let's try for him in the headset!" We were almost in a panic with excitement as we swung the car broadside to the bird that was only about a hundred yards away. We slipped out of the lee side, grabbed two shovels, and began digging a shallow trench. When it was large enough, I lay down in it, and said to Dick, "Put the headset over my head, and cover me up. Be sure nothing shows, then hand me a pigeon." Dick did this, and then drove off down the beach from whence we had come.

I looked through a crack in the straw headpiece, and I could easily see the black form of the peregrine still sitting on the beach. As the sound of the car's engine faded away, I rocked the pigeon back and forth. It fluttered violently. My chest was thumping. Through the grass, I saw the peregrine launch into flight and head straight toward the headset. My heart pounded! A moment later, there was a whirring sound, as pigeon wings and falcon wings commingled in a mass of confusion. And then suddenly, sitting on the pigeon on my hands, eighteen inches from my eyes, was a wild, beautiful, glorious peregrine falcon! What a thrill! My chest thumped so, I was sure the peregrine was going to hear the pounding. What to do? Make a sudden grab — or use slow, careful movements of the hand up through the pigeon's feathers to the falcon's legs? I pondered it a moment, and then chose the latter. Slowly, my fingers crept up. My eyes were almost closed, for fear the falcon would see the whites of my eyes. No blinking, no movement. Then I felt the stiffness of the falcon's legs on the pigeon. I tightened my grasp. I had her!

I threw back the headpiece and sat up. Surprisingly, the falcon did not make any great effort to bite or fight, but seemed to accept her capture with reasonable calm. I stood up and waved to Dick, who was in the car watching the whole affair with binoculars. A moment later we both marveled at the in-hand beauty of a freshly caught, passage peregrine falcon. Little did we realize at the time how very much this capture would mean to the sport of falconry in this country in the years to follow.

Driving back down the beach to where Bill was operating his bow net, I stopped near his blind and yelled, "Any luck?" "No, nothing doing," he responded. I then asked him to come out a minute, that I wanted to show him something. As he approached the car, I handed him the socked-up peregrine. His eyes about popped out as he added incredulously, "How did you get him? You haven't been gone an hour!" So, as we admired the peregrine, I explained to Bill the technique and showed him the headset. Without a moment's hesitation, he took a pair of pliers, and cut a piece of his grass-woven bow-net blind and fashioned an improvised headpiece. Shortly thereafter, he took off down the beach, and we turned northward up the beach to begin trapping.

So effective was this method of trapping that by noon we had caught twelve peregrines. When we were having lunch, we had socked-up peregrines all over the place. Turner had a golden tiercel that, believe it or not, fed freely bareheaded on his fist. Our total captures were four haggard falcons, five passage falcons, and three passage tiercels.

We left the island about mid-afternoon and were back in Washington that night. When I called Captain Luff Meredith (the dean of American falconers) and told him of our luck, he would not believe me at first. Thus ended our memorable trip to Assateague, the first on which peregrines were captured. Incidentally, the haggards were all banded and released. I chuckle each time I think of how Luff at first disbelieved our captures, but then how quickly he showed up the next day in Washington to claim a couple. A few days later, Luff and I made the second trip of the year to Assateague, October 6, 7, and 8. On this trip, Luff caught his first headset bird, a haggard falcon, which we banded with the usual Biological Survey Band. Late in the afternoon, he caught a beautiful passage falcon. Our total captures for the trip were one haggard falcon, one passage tiercel, and three passage falcons.

The word about peregrines on Assateague spread quickly among the relatively few falconers practicing the sport in the late thirties. A total of twenty-two birds were trapped in 1939, the great majority of which were banded and released there on the island. In the five years 1940 through 1944, an average of sixteen birds per year was captured, again with most of them being banded.

The banding procedure was most interesting. When we were finished trapping, we would go to the middle of one of the huge levels or flats. Then we would take the falcon to be released, band her, and toss her high in the air. At the same time, we would release a pigeon. We reasoned that since we had deprived the falcon of food all day, she was entitled to her daily sustenance. Almost always, the moment the pigeon started out over the flat, the falcon would turn and give immediate pursuit, usually catching her quarry without too much effort.

Interestingly, one of the spin-offs of the headset trap was the development of the "harnessed-pigeon" or "throw-out" trapping method. Here's the way it came about. Frequently, when we had located a peregrine on the beach and were "digging in" for the headset, the peregrine would take off and leave the area. Then one of the early trappers hit upon the idea of serving the falcon a pigeon to "pin" her down, and keep her in the area while the headset was being set up. So a pigeon with a large tennis-sized ball of cord was thrown out of the car window for the peregrine. Handicapped by the weight of the unraveling ball of cord, the pigeon was dragged to the sand. The peregrine, seeing one of its favorite foods, would almost always go to the pigeon, dispatch it, and begin plucking. While this was going on, the falconers would quickly stop the car nearby and dig a man into the headset. When the man in the sand was ready, the car operator would drive slowly back toward the peregrine, and flush it from its quarry. Then he would quickly pick up the pigeon carcass, which the falcon could not carry away because of the cord attached to it, and drive rapidly away. The falcon, in the meantime, looking for her quarry, would suddenly see the flapping pigeon in the headset, go to it and be caught.

Then in the late forties, Brian McDonald hit upon the idea of making a leather jacket or harness for the pigeon that was thrown out to "pin" the peregrine. This jacket was ingeniously made so that the pigeon could use his wings and legs in a normal fashion. Then the harness was covered with strong nylon nooses so that the peregrine would entangle its talons when grappling with the pigeon. When entangled, it could not fly away because of the weight of the pigeon and the drag of the long ball of cord. This trapping technique became known as the "harnessed" or "throw out" pigeon method. It was very effective, so effective, in fact, that it ultimately replaced the "dig-in" headset. After all, it was a lot more comfortable to serve a peregrine with a harnessed pigeon (repeatedly if necessary) than to immerse oneself in the sand. Today, a great federally approved banding effort takes place each fall on Assateague. The trapping method is the throw-out harnessed pigeon exclusively.

As the number of falconers grew in the late forties and fifties, so did the popularity of Assateague, until it reached a point where sometimes three or four parties would be attempting to trap the same falcon. At that point, many of the old-timers abandoned the island as a source of peregrines, and moved to other coastal areas, such as Virginia Beach and Cape Hatteras. All trapping on Assateague and other coastal areas ended in 1973 when the *anatum* peregrine was being considered as an endangered species.

In retrospect, many significant things came about as a result of the discovery of Assateague. First, there were the peregrines themselves. Early on, it became clear that the peregrines that we were trapping were *not* the dark Appalachian or "anatums" that we had been taking from the inland cliffs; rather, the beach birds were smaller and generally lighter colored. For example, inland anatum birds usually weighed thirty-eight ounces for the falcon, and twenty-eight ounces for the tiercel. Beach birds weighed twenty-eight ounces for the falcon and about twenty ounces for the tiercel. It was clear to us that the peregrines of Assateague were different subspecies from the anatum. It remained for Clayton White years later to describe the new species as the arctic peregrine *(Falco peregrinus tundrius).* However, somehow those birds will always be known to those of us who trapped and trained them as "beach birds" or "tundras."

Another very significant effect of Assateague was the great lessening of pressure on the anatum eyries as sources of peregrines. Relatively few eyases were even taken after Assateague Island became known. After all, who would want an eyas if he could get the far superior passager? As Simon Latham, an early falconer, wrote in 1615 and so aptly put it when asked to compare eyases to wild-caught hawks (including passagers), "But leaving to speak any more of these kinde of scratching Hawks, that I did never love should come to neere my fingers, and to return unto the courteous and faire conditioned haggard faulcon, whose gallant disposition I know not how to extoll, or praise so sufficiently as she deserves." Falconers today believe that Latham's use of the word "haggard" was a reference to any wild-caught hawk, including passagers as they are known today.

In making passage birds available to falconers, Assateague also altered the direction of the sport in this country by focusing on the value of passage hawks, irrespective of species. It deemphasized the value of eyas birds and directed attention to fall migration flyway trapping sites, with the result that fewer and fewer eyases of any species were taken from the nests.

It's been half a century now since the first capture of a migrating peregrine falcon on Assateague, yet it all seems like yesterday. The smell of the salt marshes, the cries of the gulls and shorebirds, and the absolute, totally pristine beauty of that unspoiled wilderness will remain in my memory forever. Above all, however, is the dark, bobbing head of the magnificent peregrine falcon sitting on the crown of the front beach with the foaming surf of the Atlantic ocean pounding close by.

The Inspiration of Falcons

by Morlan W. Nelson

When I was growing up on a ranch along the Cheyenne River in North Dakota, I saw things that amazed me every day. I had a tall old racing horse named Slim and when I rode him, I could see his shoulder muscles flow in beautiful coordination as he jumped a ditch or a gopher hole. His ears would turn back as I gave him orders, no matter how fast we were going.

My big dog Buster could leap into the air and catch a ball with the grace and coordination of a tiger making its kill. He would follow me on my horse going downhill, leaping into the air, his front paws tucked under his chin as he sailed in a graceful arc balanced by his tail. Almost every day I saw some form of marvelous action.

The teal that lived on the ponds where I herded cattle were another form. On many occasions, these birds would drop in at high speed from great heights with their wings folded back and falling fast, but just before landing they would level out, brake with their wings and skid into the water. At that time in history, it was one of the fastest actions on the planet. It was 1928 and I was twelve years old.

One day, to my surprise, my youthful evaluations of speed were changed forever. I was watering my horse at a pond where seven teal lived. It was a cool morning in late

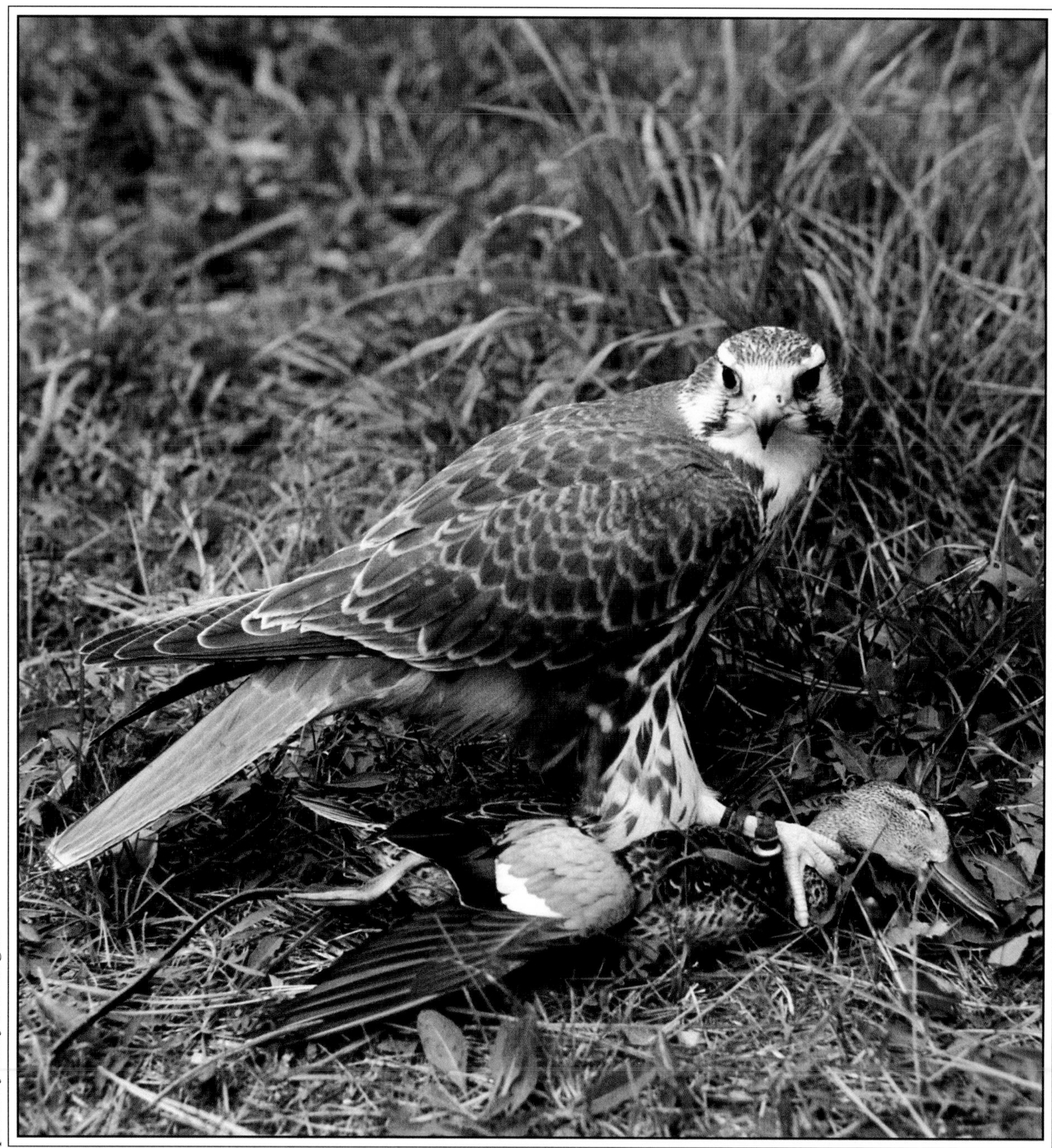

photo by Gary M. Cargile

summer with a light north wind blowing. The grass sparkled as the sunlight struck the dew-drops held between the stems and leaves. My attention was on this beauty when Slim splashed, flushing the teal from the pond. As usual they circled and climbed, but seemed to spread farther apart than usual.

Then my eyes glimpsed something I had never seen before. It was a bird in the shape of a bullet, fired from the sky straight at the earth. The clouds behind it gave me some idea of its speed, which was way beyond anything I had ever experienced. The air hissed as the bird leveled out to strike one of the teal. The other ducks scattered, but the struck one fell, spinning through the air. The falcon rolled onto its back after going straight up from the strike, folded its wings again, and in a steep dive took the teal out of the air and flew straight into the north wind and out of sight.

For several minutes I stood on the edge of the pond and marveled at what I had seen. It was difficult to believe that there was anything that could go several times as fast as a teal duck! It was a sight that I have never forgotten and never will. The stoop of that falcon was probably faster than any airplane then in existence, and to this day it is still the fastest single action under natural power.

The inspiration of that sight began my determination to have a hawk like that for hunting rabbits, birds, or maybe gophers. A hawk could not be any worse than the young, wild-eyed colts who kicked, bucked and reared back during training. My father, who was a lawyer and historian, told me that there had been falconers in the Middle Ages but that humanity had forgotten how to train hawks. After discussing with my father and grandfather my hopes to take a young hawk, they finally agreed but only if I could feed it and take care of it. They would decide when to return it to the wild if the bird was unhappy. We shot rabbits and gophers every day, so there was no difficulty obtaining food.

While working in the breaks to the river, I had observed a big hawk nest with young in it. My father said to be careful because the old birds might attack, and to take a big glove to hold the hawk. Also, I should let them know when I was going and exactly where so they could come and find me if necessary.

The nest was in a coulee with big trees on the north slope, only two or three miles from the ranch. The trail was one we used all the time with the cattle, so I did not worry about getting lost. When I rode under the trees the hawks screamed, but it wasn't until I began to climb the tree that they swooped down close.

Just below the nest, one of the adults hit my cowboy hat and knocked it off. It was obvious that they meant to keep me out of the nest. The nest itself was my protection as long as I stayed under it. Lacking the courage to go any further, I put my glove over the edge and one of the young hawks flew. It was almost as big as the adults. It made a very sloppy landing and just stood there on the ground as I hurried down the tree.

It would not stand on my gloved fist, but it would cling to a limb that I held in my hand. Whenever I made any fast movement, it would hiss and open its wings, trying to frighten me. The young hawk would stay on the limb, but Slim was very leery when it hissed and flapped its wings.

The only way to mount my horse with the hawk on the limb was to climb up on a steep cut where I could step over the saddle from a high position. Slim would not stand still even under those conditions, so I built a fence of limbs and brambles around him next to the cut. When I picked up the hawk on the limb and stepped over the saddle, the hawk opened its wings and Slim bolted, galloping for the barn with the reins up in position on the saddle.

When my horse arrived at the ranch, my younger brother and several hands rode out to find me walking home with the hawk on the limb. We shot some food on the way, and put the hawk in an empty stallion's stall that was completely closed in, as a stall has to be. It was ideal for the young hawk and, after supper, I went out to feed it a gopher.

The only training method I knew was to move very slowly, just as I would with wild horses. Much to my surprise, when I did this and sat down next to the hawk, it settled down too. I offered it a dead gopher and it bound to the food with great excitement, using its big feet and talons to hold it firmly. It did not eat, glaring at me with piercing eyes. Eventually it started to feed, and as long as I did not move, continued. When Buster came in, the hawk stopped eating, but did not back away from the food. The dog was sent away and the hawk resumed its meal.

Without any knowledge of falconry, I fed the hawk from my gloved fist in the stall to start with, and later merely went outside to feed and fly the bird with no jesses or gear. This worked fine, and as long as the hawk was hungry, she could be returned to the stall. If she was not hungry, she would fly off and land in a tree for the night. The next morning she would be ready to hunt again, but had to be put back in the stall while she was eating. It was a successful method and about the only one that could be completed without the jesses, leash and hood we use today.

The amazing thing about this experience is that I am doing the same thing today with a white gyrfalcon bred in captivity by the Peregrine Fund at Cornell University. Instead of a stall, there is a room with bars made for raptors. The gyr lives in the room and wears snap jesses that can be taken off or put on as needed. His name is Thor and he has been flying for me for about eight years now. Just as on the ranch, as long as we are close enough to his room to walk back and put him away while he is eating, he needs no jesses. Since he is flown every day near my home, no gear is required.

Following my first experiences with a hawk, we moved from the ranch into Fargo where I received some guidance in the art of falconry. This came from the famous Captain C.W. Knight and his eagle, Ramsey. In 1934, Knight gave me personal advice and some papers on falconry that were wonderful at the time. The papers were lost but never forgotten, and the advice was certainly used.

Captain Knight flew Ramsey in auditoriums on his lecture tours. His relationship with that eagle gave me confidence when I started to fly golden eagles after World War II and throughout my work with Walt Disney Productions. More than forty years later he came through the United States on his last trip here. He knew of my work in falconry and motion pictures, and other falconers had told him to be sure and stop at my home in Boise, Idaho. He called me one day and I asked him if he remembered 1934 in Fargo, North Dakota, and the time he started me down the right trail of falconry. He remembered, but did not realize that I was the same person. We had a great talk on the phone, but I was going to Arabia and could not see him. However, I have never forgotten him, nor have the many golden and bald eagles saved from the guns of the fifties and sixties when they were being shot by the government and sportsmen alike. Captain Knight and Ramsey remain alive for me, as they were the pair that demonstrated the potential of golden eagles on the field of action, as well as the depth of understanding necessary for their conservation.

My work in motion pictures began in 1946 when I was attempting to fly my falcons while still walking with a cane as a result of draining war wounds received in the mountains of Italy. So many people stopped to shoot at my falcon if it landed on a power pole that I carried a Colt frontier model six-gun to fire in the direction of anyone attempting to shoot my hawk. This action saved several falcons, but almost started a war in Utah where I lived.

The individuals involved always claimed that the chicken hawks, bullet hawks or duck hawks should be killed. Our arguments were fierce, because there was no law protecting raptors. Even the state and federal government programs were aimed at destroying hawks and eagles. Falconry was unknown, and the gun spoke with great authority. But I was compelled to stop defending my birds with my gun. The war was over and such actions had to cease. I had to agree, as the few times I fired my gun came close to ending in a shootout.

Drs. Bailey and Woodbury of the University of Utah invited me to present a

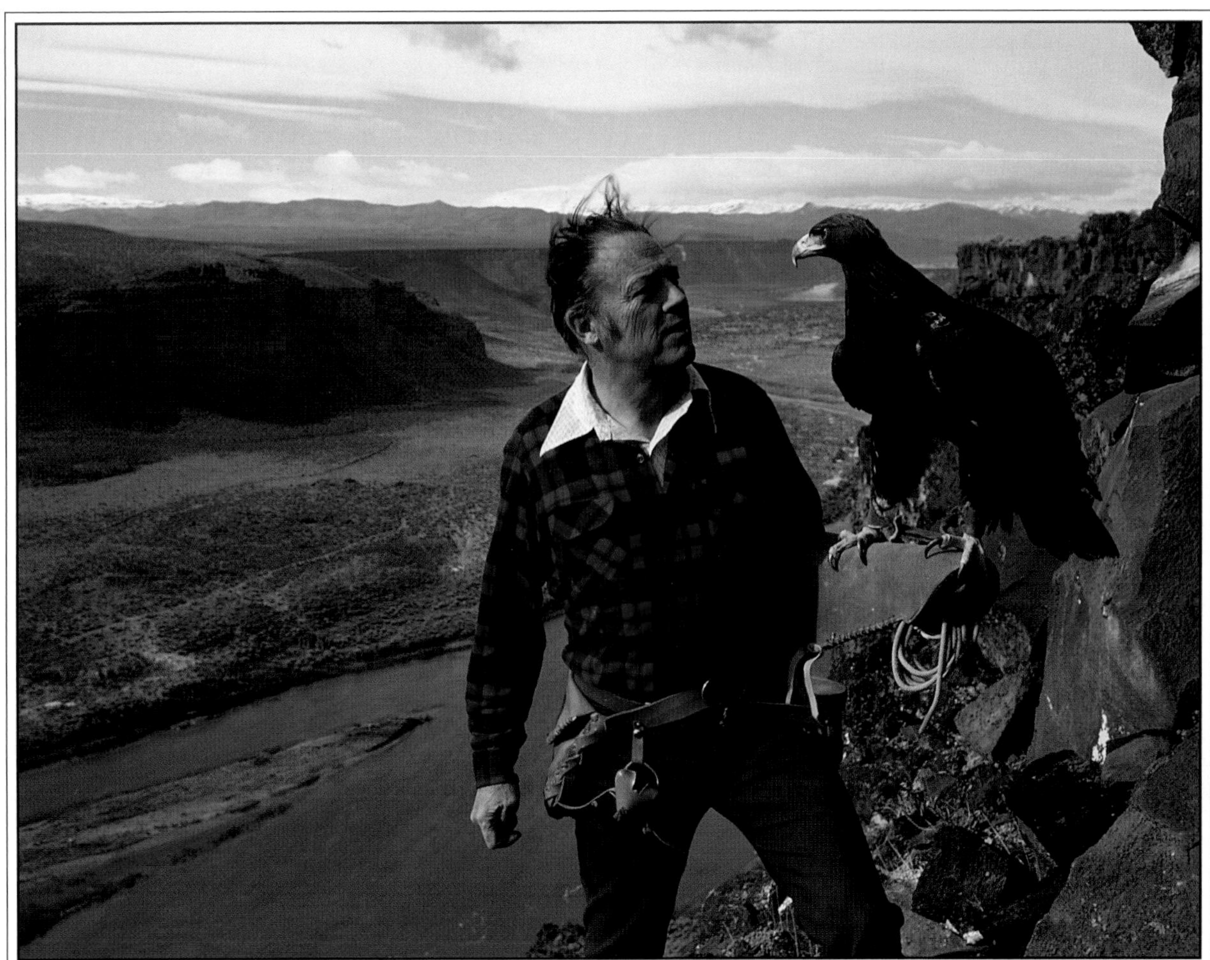

photo by Dave Boehlke

program using peregrines and prairies. This started me out on an educational approach that did not require the six-gun. They also were instrumental in my obtaining a federal permit in order to collect specimens for the university with my falcon.

One of the interesting flights was at a whitefaced ibis. They are wonderful fliers, large and not often taken by falcons. However, Blackie, an imprinted female peregrine, decided to take one. She broke up the flight formation in a very fine stoop from a high pitch, singling out one ibis and driving it to the ground, binding to its head and long beak. The ibis' curved beak was pointing down to the ground next to its neck. Blackie broke its neck while I was running up to see what had happened. I had seen wild peregrines attack ibises before, but I had never actually seen a falcon take one.

After taking her up, I found out how it had happened. The ibis had had problems with its wing feathers. A significant number of them were missing, leaving it with poor wing lift and little control. Blackie had noticed this immediately, as she did with crows, seagulls and other birds during the next nine years of flying. There were often several thousand crows taking off in a field when she started her attack, but once above them, she regularly singled out one crow and took it in style. In almost every case, I discovered that the crow she had caught had a problem. Lungs, feathers, weak breast muscles or bad wing joints usually had limited the crow's ability to evade her attack.

It is impossible for humans to determine such limitations when over a thousand crows fly at once, but the raptors with their supersight do it in seconds. The inspiring aerial attack of the falcon is a classic example of the basic rule of our planet that we must take to exist.

At the present time with our exploding human population, many in the Western world do not recognize that whatever we eat must first be killed or taken from the soil. Sometimes during my lectures on this subject someone will say to me with great disgust, "You kill birds with those hawks." My question is, "How do you like your chicken?" The answer is usually, "Fried." A very real hypocrisy exists among the majority of people now living in cities who do not realize that someone has to kill or take the food they eat.

The institutionalized slaughter that occurs in packing plants, whether with cattle or chickens, is a far greater problem to the life being taken than it is when a bird or animal is killed by a raptor. When I was working my way through college by yarding bulls in the Armour stockyards, I was amazed by the recognition the bulls and cattle showed when they smelled the blood of the animals being killed. They understood what was happening, and their soft mooing told of their worry about the future. While herding cattle on the ranch, one seldom hears such calling except in the case of a lost calf or some similar death on the range. Even chickens recognize the distress call of their fellows being held by their hock joints upside down before their throats are cut.

Prey taken by falcons is often knocked unconscious in the air and then quickly killed with a bite to the neck which severs the vertebrae. The falcon's powerful beak has a notch in the upper mandible just for this purpose. A similar procedure is involved when a hawk or eagle takes prey in its talons. Nature's way is far more humane than anything yet devised by humanity except a nerve shot.

The comparison may sound silly, but I have been hit by bullets and fragments in war. The shock of either going through any portion of your body causes great gasping and mental disorientation, combined with deep searing pain. Officers carried dope to ease the pain of the men hit in these cases. As an officer, I had already used my dope on several wounded soldiers before being hit. However, it is also true that after the first moments of pain men often can't feel anything as a result of the shock, and this was my case.

Strangely, an eagle sending a needle-sharp talon through your hand or arm is amazingly painless. The first time this happened to me more than forty years ago, it was hard to believe that I saw the point of the talon come out through the bottom of my arm. There was very little pain, and the eagle flew off immediately after showing me that I was doing something wrong. There was no gasping with shock or struggling, just, "I'll be damned, it sure didn't hurt much. Better go back and call the eagle down to the fist." And that is what I did.

One other occasion was a bigger problem but the same lack of pain. We were feeding chicken heads to the eagles, and had one trained to hunt young mountain lions for the Disney film, "Killers of the High Country." We did not have to have the golden eagle actually take a lion, only make a hard run at one. The lion would jump down into a deep crack in the top of the cliff just wide enough to protect it. The training was easy, but I did have to lean the eagle down a bit to be sure she would stoop and attempt to catch one of the little lions.

In doing this, we used a T-perch, held as the Mongols do to this day. It was winter and the slope was covered with ice. The eagle was just above my head on the T-perch. When I slipped I grimaced and stuck my tongue out

photo by Norm Nelson

a little. Seeing what she thought was a chicken neck in my teeth, the eagle reached down with her huge foot and tried to take my tongue. The center toe hit the top of my forehead, the back toe and talon hit under my mouth. She cinched down and the top talon made a slight cut in my forehead. The back talon went up through my tongue from under my jaw. When her foot did not close, she just flew off.

My two sons were with me and were very concerned that I had been seriously hurt. There was very little pain. It was similar to a doctor's needle, but there was a little bleeding. I wiped off the blood and called the eagle down to the T-perch. She flew in, normal in every way, and paid no attention to the bloody streaks I had attempted to wipe off my face.

My family came out of the house and were surprised to see the eagle calmly eating on the T-perch. However, my biggest surprise was how little pain or mental problem I had with my wound. If that had been a fragment from a mortar or artillery shell going through my tongue, I would have been on the ground gasping for air and struggling in agony.

The point is to recognize that a natural death by predation is a far more humane way of going over the great divide than the techniques humanity has devised to take food from the earth by gun or packing plant.

In the last thirty years, the combination of science, motion pictures and television has changed the public's understanding of the true position of predators in our environment. It is a wonderful thing to have lived through a war, just barely, and been a part of this new understanding of life on our planet. It may one day result in no more wars if such considerate thinking continues.

The wisdom of the wild has been shared with me through the peregrine falcon and the golden eagle because they accepted me as falcon and eagle through the process of imprinting.

Imprinting was probably the first step

in the domestication of the dog, horse, cattle, sheep, lion, tiger and most of the wildlife we have tamed in history. Young birds and animals often imprint on the first object they see when they open their eyes. When raised by a human, a young eagle, falcon or lion accepts that individual as one of its own, giving the foster parent the characteristics of its own species. Classic examples of imprinting are the cases of men and women putting their heads in the jaws of lions, tigers, killer whales, or elephants.

Carl Sagan said, "It is audacious of humanity to have only one word, anthropomorphism." I use the examples of imprinting to support our need for words like aguilamorphism, falcomorphism, animorphism and others that would demonstrate our true relationships with other intelligent life on this planet.

My grandfather Steen showed his understanding and concern for horses when he said to me, "Don't put that horse in the pasture alone. He'll get lonesome." It seemed silly sixty years ago, but my imprinted peregrine, Blackie, showed me that such consideration of intelligence was just the beginning. Blackie talked to me as the wild peregrines talk to each other at their eyries, and I understood what she said. But back then, it was beyond my understanding why she took me as her mate.

When Blackie laid eggs in 1950, famous falconers such as Dr. Stabler and Col. Meredith sent me male peregrines to pair with her. She ran them off with great ferocity while I was in the room, yet came to me and asked in peregrine for me to breed and display as wild falcons do. I understood and returned the tiercels to the men who had sent them.

To see how far Blackie would go, I rappelled down a cliff and obtained two young prairie falcons. She raised them as well as any wild peregrine I have ever seen. No other person or bird could enter her eyrie or room without being attacked. It was obvious that falcons could be raised in captivity, but at the time there were enough peregrines in the wild that such effort seemed unnecessary.

In November of 1954, the Journal of the Falconry Club of America published my account entitled "The Peregrine and Her Two Prairie Falcons." The article ended with the following statement which has turned out to be very true. "The whole process did not prove anything although there is no doubt in my mind about the possibility of husbandry with any of the falcons. Certainly the peregrine falcon, and possibly others, could be raised in captivity. The eggs could be taken to hatch in an incubator and the old birds would breed again to lay another set of eggs. Artificial insemination should work too, which would give the falconer chance at a good many fertile eggs."

It was the art of falconry that provided the basis for saving the peregrine in North America. This knowledge applies to all raptors that are endangered throughout the world. The World Center for Birds of Prey perpetuates the hope that humanity will always have these inspirational birds to admire.

In my opinion, the art of falconry has also resulted in the worldwide domestication of raptors. Look at my imprinted golden eagle, Fagan, and my white gyrfalcon, Thor. These two raptors were tamed the same way as our horses then were on the ranch, and still are in parts of the West. The horses would come back to the barn to live, even though they ran wild throughout their territory. The two raptors do the same. They will go into the wild, flying over my mews. They defend the mews as their eyries against people, dogs, or cats. Like the horses, they come home to their eyries and mate, in this case with me. They breed on my hat or my back and consider me one of their kind.

The magnificent golden eagle is so rugged when taken from the wild that it can get in a fight with you and say, "It's either you or me." Yet my imprint, Fagan, has the most gentle ways and thoughts, and considers me an eagle. He brings me sticks to make our nest, brings food, and folds his great talons to walk on my bare back and breed. His powerful eyes overflow with gentleness as he talks to me and helps to build our nest. He is as completely domesticated as my dog or horse and understands the true nature of our life on this planet. It is the result of imprinting, just as with the big cats, but it humbles me to a depth felt no other way. It opens the door to the true understanding of all life.

photo by Ralph Rogers

E6

by Ralph Rogers

I know you wouldn't give a damn, but my blisters are killing me. I should be resting them instead of mumbling to myself while staggering up this hill with a ridiculous gait, putting one foot down on the outside of a heel and the other stiffly on its toe. This doesn't make sense. There is no need for me to climb up here, and even if I do reach my destination, I am either going to find nothing, or you. If you are there, you will do everything in your power to send me away or kill me, just as you have each time we have met.

I understand your attitude. Every experience you have had with mankind has been unpleasant and your first introduction was especially rude. On what could have been an otherwise pleasant day here, you were trapped, held, weighed, and measured by creatures totally alien and frightening to you. Mankind then gave you your "official" name: Greenland, adult, female, peregrine falcon and, as an enduring symbol of that encounter, the blue band on your left leg . . . E6.

No one begrudges your resentment or reactions when mankind invaded your territory again that same summer. The team planned to reclimb your èyrie to band your chicks, apologize to you, and leave, but to their horror, they only found your four unhatched eggs. There were immediate feelings of guilt and some conjecture that perhaps the earlier disturbance had caused the failure, but other peregrines throughout the world had received similar handling with no effect. Only you really know why you failed.

The reports of your failure were on my mind the following summer when I climbed into your eyrie and found, once again, four dead eggs. No one had been there before me: there had been no previous disturbance. Again, why?

I recall cussing you that day while you stooped at me, the air from your wings making a "popping" sound in the ear holes of my climbing helmet. Many times you hit my hands or the stretched climbing rope, adding to the confusion and spraying me with small rocks. Most peregrines quickly give up this aggression; I remember that you didn't. I also remember that there was no tiercel here, leading me to the conclusion that not even another falcon could tolerate such an awful old bitch. And you received your second name — "Bitch."

Supposedly being the more intelligent of the two of us, I should remember the next three years of our relationship, but I can't. It is all reduced to a generic scene where I see myself dangling from a small rope on the face of a cliff above a giant glacial river, and you are screaming, and defending, with all the courage given those of your species, your three or four unhatched eggs. It always seemed to be too much work for nothing.

This year, I was told the cliff had been abandoned, but a single bleached egg had been collected earlier by the advance team. I was relieved that you and I didn't have to spend an afternoon insulting each other again, but I also surprised myself when I realized that the news brought me an unexplained empty feeling. I guess it is curiosity and boredom which bring me up here today. I can't really believe you are gone: you are just too tough to die.

When I finally reach the base of your cliff, I hear the small distant wail of a peregrine, not the vicious attack I have come to expect. Perhaps it isn't you making the noise, or if it is you, you see no threat issuing from a creature moving with such an inhuman gait and walking in circles, like a dog finding a perfect piece of blueberry tundra mat to collapse into. Most likely, if it is you, you don't respond because there isn't anything to defend here this year. Failure came early.

I am tired. My partner and I have worked hard the last four days. We have slept little and hiked long stretches of uneven ground carrying packs heavy with the additional burden of climbing and banding equipment. We have climbed five cliffs such as this one and have banded the chicks from successful mother falcons. There is no amount of money that could get me to work this hard in Montana, yet I feel blessed to be allowed this experience up here.

To me, this part of Greenland is walking trails where only caribou and musk-ox travel, and breathing air purified and cooled by ice 10,000 feet thick. It is drinking water from precipitation millennia old and hearing the deafening silence of wilderness, but most of all, Greenland is peregrines. It is a chance to work with you and your kin, or smell the tundra on the breath of a chick, or sit in an eyrie and see a small part of the world as you see it.

In a few minutes of watching I can tell that even in this land of surplus peregrines, there is only one falcon here. It *is* you, you old bitch, you ran him off again, didn't you?

Confirmation of your survival appears a few moments later when I finally catch a glimpse of the band on your leg, surprisingly colorful after all these years. You are in the midst of at least your eighth summer. The last six years of failures have been documented and occurred in an area where the average peregrine eyrie fledges over three young per year. By occupying this eyrie, and not producing, you have cost the world about twenty young peregrines. All of us on the survey team have spoken menacingly about "what someone ought to do to you," or hoped that you "weren't back in subsequent years." In fact, this year when the advance team rechecked and you weren't here, some, including me, swaggered that it was "about time."

After several hours of watching, neither of us have done very much. I smiled while you gave an insolent young gyrfalcon mild and

photo by Joe Papp

photo by Ralph Rogers

appropriate "instruction" on territoriality and combat flight maneuvers. I saw you wail and "eechup" at a passing tiercel, which flew away as though he knew of your reputation. You have moved very little, and then only to perches which my recollection and your mutes suggest are favorites. This is a melancholy place today caused by the absence of sound from defense encounters, food exchanges with your mate, and chicks begging for food. Goals have escaped us both for the moment.

Through binoculars I can see that since your face isn't all screwed up trying to terrorize me, you appear to have a soft and gentle eye. You aren't one of the black-headed peregrines so coveted by falconers; neither are you one of those classic white-headed tundra falcons. You have that look so familiar to me, just like most peregrines . . . most old wild peregrines, anyway, with a faded blue back and a breast so white it seems to give off light. Funny, I never noticed that before. Perhaps I was too busy practicing my survival skills.

Survival is a big deal for me here. I have all kinds of high tech stuff, some of which is provided at cost by major manufacturers in trade for photographs placed in magazines filled with hairy men and "granola" women. I guess you aren't aware that the weather here can change rapidly and become severe . . . you don't even have Gore-Tex or zippers in your armpits. I have freeze-dried food, ultralight tent, backpack stove and other things to keep me comfortable. Since you are a small animal, little more than a collection of diaphanous air sacks and hollow bones, you must be even more vulnerable, yet you survive simply by lifting a foot if the sun disappears, and moving out of the wind. Physical survival must be something else I have overcomplicated.

My arrival here is a major effort that uses giant airplanes burning thousand of gallons of fuel, following courses set by expensive navigational equipment, radio beams, maps and charts. The last leg needs the help of the U.S. Air Force. Sitting here, I recall the many

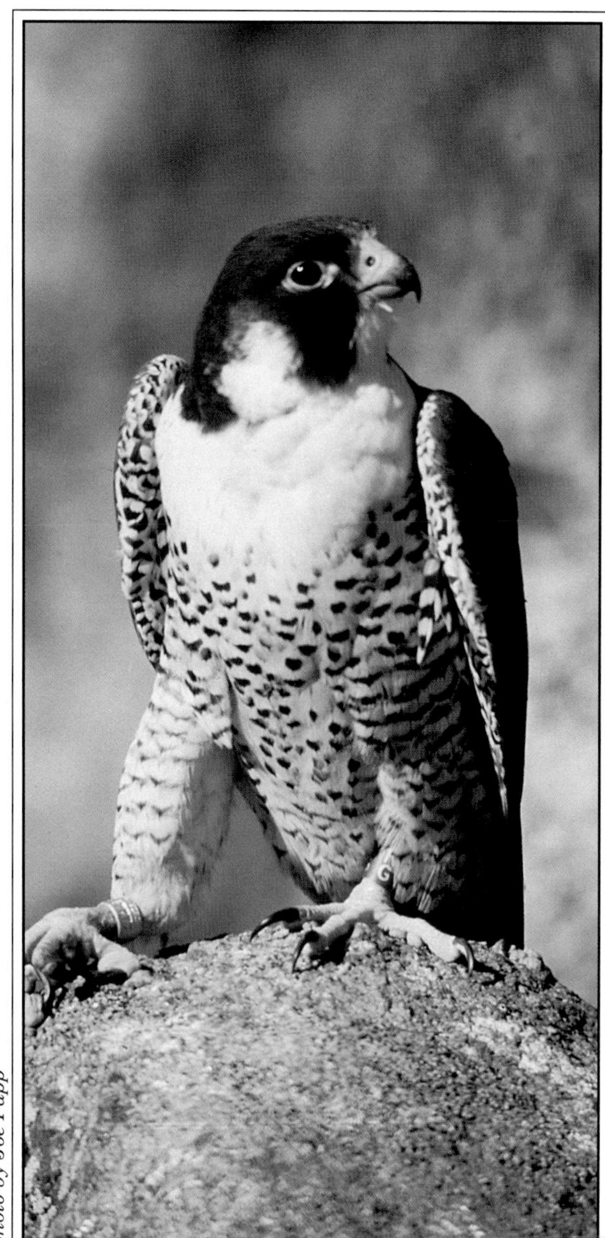
photo by Joe Papp

times I looked out of the window of one of those big jets into the totally monotonous North Atlantic and saw nothing but water, horizon to horizon, hour after hour. It humbles me to think of you sitting there now on your favorite perch, leaving each September to cross that same water, feeding on the wing and resting only briefly until you reach deep into South America. At least sixteen times you have run the gauntlet of natural selection, somehow avoiding starvation, being lost at sea, or getting shot. In recent times you have successfully survived smog, persistent pesticides, Central American wars, and beaches crowded with people, garbage, and medical wastes. I'm sorry. Each year for at least eight, not only have you crossed those oceans and countries swinging to the underside of the globe, but you have returned to this exact spot, sitting on the same lichen-covered rock where you now sit, so relaxed, as if it were nothing.

While shifting my weight from cheek to cheek, comfortably resettling into the mat, I am struck by the warmth of this place. Like all peregrines, you exhibit that uncanny ability to pick a warm cliff, even in the Arctic. Perhaps it is this warmth which has attracted you and other peregrines here for thousands of years. Warmth or calories must be the currency of the Arctic. If you can collect and save enough, you survive; collect even more and you can reproduce; more yet and your babies carry your genetics into the next generation.

The oasis of warmth here obviously attracts small birds, which you eat, extracting more calories and then excreting onto the rocks. Greenland is mostly ice and rock. Nutrients in this form cause a profuse growth of orange lichens. Lichens break down rocks, providing top soil, which increases plant growth, which provides habitat for small birds, which you . . . and so it goes. Falcons are dependent upon small birds who, in a small way, are dependent upon falcons. You

photo by Scott Rogers

take from your environment and nurture it at the same time. I don't know why these relationships are so evident to me in the Arctic and so confusing where man dominates. I do know that the ability to spend time with peregrines, to share part of your simple, uncomplicated, and natural relationships is the most important part of the "warmth" which has always attracted me.

For over thirty years I have been totally captivated by you and your lot. In my younger days I spent every possible moment with you. Our relationship hasn't always been constructive. I have cut class in school, feigned illness at work and done other things which bring me no pride in order to spend time with you. As I became older your existence shaped my life, you "straightened me out." You were the subject of the books I read, the studies I became involved in and the reason I ultimately became a biologist. Spending time with you is one of the reasons I live in Montana, or work hard in Greenland, or volunteer time telling others of your right to exist, or spend money breeding your cousins for release. You were the "cause" for many of the decisions and actions in my life which have led to broader acquisitions of knowledge and growth and a feeling of self-confidence. I am who I am, in large part, because of you.

E6, as an individual peregrine you are enormously flawed, and yet in this moment and place you represent your race well. I apologize for the thoughts I have had in the past; it was the cowboy/arctic explorer/macho persona in me that wished you ill. I really didn't mean it. Looking there at you now, appearing like a single white light on a solid gray cliff, thinking about your life, and mine, I realize that, imperfect as you are, you are one of the most magnificent creatures who ever lived. Thank you for what you have given me. Godspeed, old Bitch.

Perfect Birds

by Marion Niedringhaus

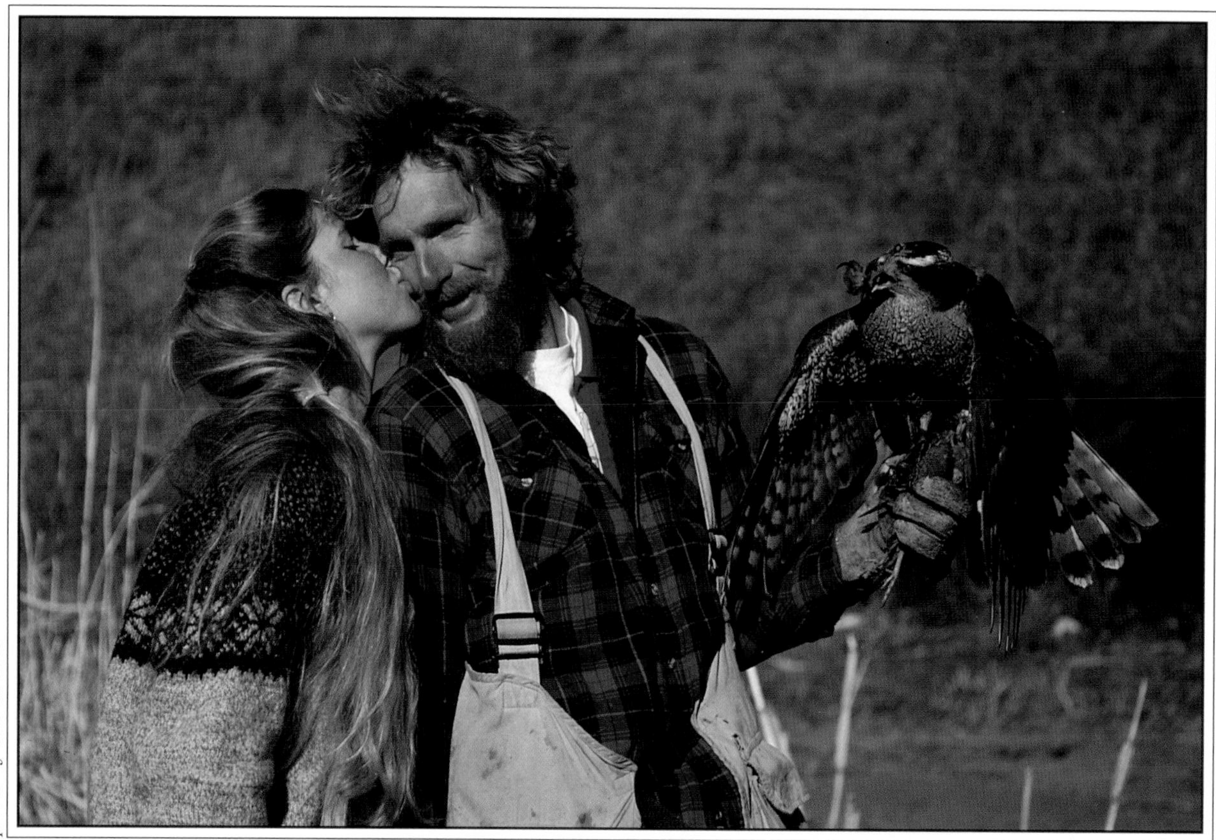
photo by Jill Graves

I grew up around bird lovers. I never was a bird person myself, but found myself pursuing, dating, and befriending falconers, and consequently, spending an awful lot of time wondering what their attraction to birds was, and my attraction, in turn, was for these men.

When I was growing up, many times I would find my father sitting on a deck chair on the dock, reading a war novel and looking up every few pages to watch his birds. A red and tan duck would paddle by.

"Okay, Pointed Head," he'd fire at me, "What's that one? And don't disappoint me."

"Well, let me think—"

"First ask yourself, is it a dabbler or a diver?" The terminology terrified me. I watched for a dabble or a dive and saw neither.

"Don't tell me you don't even know the difference between a diver and a dabbler?"

"Sorry."

"Don't even bother applying to Yale."

"Don't worry," I said.

"It's either a redhead or a canvasback," he said, chewing on a fried pork rind. "Look at the build, the feet. How are they set, far back? How would it fly? How would it eat? What is it, a dabbler or a diver?"

A wrong guess would be worse than not knowing, and I knew I lacked the guts and luck to pull off an enthusiastically correct guess.

"Just tell me what the damned bird is and I'll promise I'll know it next time."

I think he liked knowing more than whomever he was grilling and the fact that he was always more than willing to spout off the bird's Latin and common names gave him a pleasure that overcame his disappointment with me. Rarely did anyone bother questioning him.

We'd sit, my father and I, in the middle of January and often, after a satisfactory bird quiz, watch his trumpeter swan bathe, submerging its entire front half into the frigid water, then bobbing back up again, letting the droplets run down its back. The swan would curl its neck over the white back and, with closed eyes in seeming rapture, methodically preen each feather. My father would slingshot them handfuls of corn he kept in a fifty-gallon barrel, and the swans and geese would all charge to the edge and maneuver their heavy bodies up onto the ice. They craned their necks over the snow banks as their wings beat against the brittle ice along the edge. They'd somehow manage to shake their tails and awkwardly waddle off, hissing at one another and snaking their necks into the powdery snow to retrieve the corn. They'd settle down then, kicking snow from under their bodies, making a nest for the night. In the morning I knew they'd be in the same spot, their backs sometimes covered in light snow, their heads tucked beneath a wing.

My mother, on the other hand, is a parrot person, but just as enchanted with birds as my father.

Her six-inch parrot rides herd on the kitchen, leaping off the edge of the table and glomming onto the nearest passerby's shirt. With cautious planning and few false moves, the parrot can pull himself up the unsuspecting person's shirt a step at a time, like a climber ascending El Capitan, until he reaches a shoulder. He seems quite happy to ride there all day, crapping and pulling on earrings and emitting that musky parrot smell.

My father has never really learned to get on well with the parrots, always popping them a grape and then deftly snatching his fingers back before they could grab him.

"What's wrong with this evil bird? It hates me. I'm not used to animals hating me," he'll say, glaring at an African Grey parrot who narrows its pupils and raises its neck feathers every time he passes by.

"She doesn't hate you. She's fearful. It helps not making eye contact. Just look away and put your hand right up there. Don't act afraid and yank your hand away or you will get bit. She won't do a thing."

"Like hell, I know this evil beast." And my father will tentatively stick his hand out and the parrot will waddle across the top of its cage, beak open, and hackles raised.

On the other hand, my mother has never really taken to my father's swan, who after biting my brother-in-law in the genitals, galloped across the lawn and knocked her down, sending the small terrier she was carrying yelping into the cabin.

"My God, dear. Get rid of that damn swan. See, this is what happens when you try to make a pet out of a wild animal. It's dangerous. And it's unnatural," Mom shouted while picking herself up, the swan standing nearby, wings spread and hissing warm humid fish breath at her. I knew the smell; the same thing had happened to me.

"Now see, there you go, overreacting again. Jesus, dear, he's not after you, he's after the wretched terrier you've got. He's a little confused, you know, an imprint. He's just protecting me."

"Bullshit. Try getting him a mate. Or better, get rid of the sonovabitch before he gelds our son-in-law. Or kills a dog."

But I can't imagine any of them without birds.

I have never completely understood the hold birds have on the select few who make them a lifelong obsession. But I think it's something positive, as opposed to, well, other compulsions like gambling or flashing. Whether I became fascinated by falconers because I had been raised by bird lovers and felt a comforting familiarity or because I recognized some special quality that only bird people share, I don't know. But I found myself as enraptured with falconers as the falconers were themselves enraptured with their falcons.

I met my first falconer on the way to the bus stop one day. A new neighbor, another rancher, drove up beside my father and me while we sat waiting for the bus. Why he drove up just then I don't know, but it doesn't seem to matter now. What did matter was that he had these enormous birds perched on his back seat. Big, dark, hooded things. I watched through the glass as they scratched at their hoods, the bells around their legs ringing off the walls. Brittany spaniels jumped around on the back seat, panting and fogging up the windows with their excited breath. I was ignored like most kids are in adult conversations, but I was happy just to look at the dark birds inside the car. My father, but not I, was invited to go out and "fly" with the falconer that night. I do remember my father saying, after the falconer had driven off:

"There by God, that's the man you should marry. We'll tie up this whole damned valley." I was fourteen years old at the time. I didn't marry him, but some years later my older sister did.

I found my very own falconer on the municipal golf course several years later while I was out riding. On the putting green was an older man hovering over his golf ball, gripping and regripping his putter, shifting his weight and making dry run swings, all those golfing rituals that only golfers fully understand. Just as his club was nearing the high point of his backswing a large grey bird dropped out of nowhere, seemed to hover midair above the golfer for a second, then deftly swooped down, grabbed the ball in its talons and flew off.

From the corner of my eye I saw on the hill a man who was following the bird with his binoculars. It just so happened that I had a pair myself, always carrying them in the saddle bags for just this sort of occasion. I frantically dug them out, wiping the dust and piece of hay off the lenses with my shirt. First I scanned the golfer who flung his putter onto the green, bellowing up at the man on the hill.

"Either you get that goddamned thing outa here or I'm going to shoot the sonovabitch! That's the third ball I've lost." I panned back over to the man, who looked like he was smiling. He cupped his hands around his mouth and yelled back.

"Sorry about that. I'll get him back in a minute." There was a pause. "Did you happen to see which way he flew?" The golfer gave the man the finger and strode off toward his golf cart.

Back on the hill, the man began swinging a rope above his head that had what appeared to be a dead chicken on the end. I fine-tuned the focus. It was, in fact, a dead chicken swinging above the man's head. The man let the chicken fall to the ground in front of him. A second later, again from nowhere, a large bird set its wings and came in for a long slow descent. It landed on the dead chicken and spread its wings over it. It screamed and the man knelt down, picked up the chicken and the bird stepped onto his fist. Seeing that the golfer was gone, I galloped across the green toward the bird and man, leaving a wake of divots behind me.

I had entered a whole new world. His falcon was a gyr named Louise, a large gentle bird who galloped around the living room chasing small stuffed animals tossed across the floor. The walls were covered with falcon art. Falcons, falcons and dogs, falcons and dogs and grouse. Where there weren't paintings there was taxidermy: flying wood ducks, ruffed grouse stepping over miniature logs, and a couple of Hungarian partridge mounts in progress laid out on the kitchen table, wires protruding out the heads and bags of stuffing sitting on a chair. A little plastic bag of glass bird eyes sat next to a half-empty can of beer.

At night Louise slept perched on the beam in the bedroom. In the morning I'd wake to the sounds of falcon shit splattering on newspaper. A Peregrine Fund baseball cap hung on a hook next to the bed. It was the first thing the falconer put on in the morning. Naked, except for the hat and leather glove, the falconer arose and walked out into the morning air, the falcon on his fist.

I was in love for the very first time. Our dates were spent hawking, as he called it, and if we weren't doing that, we sat on his bed and looked at photo albums (one per hunting season) and scrapbooks full of falcon memorabilia, grouse feathers placed strategically next to a photo of the bird and its kill. There were photos of kestrels sitting on backpacks, falcons standing on canvasbacks, beaks bloody and little pieces of down floating down the grain stubble below.

And so I passed quite a few years of my young adulthood this way, ferreting out falconers who frequented my brother-in-law's breeding project.

With spring comes the time for hatching and artificial insemination over at the hawk barns. I sit in the gravel in the hallway while a male peregrine sits atop my brother-in-law's head, happily ejaculating onto an L.L. Bean canvas hat.

"You just can't beat these hats for collecting semen," he says while his bird, a "sexual tyrannosaurus" named Willis, hops around, flapping his wings and clinging to the hat brim. The semen is immediately sucked into a tiny pipette and will be planted in a female who has eyes for only one man.

The falconer enters her chamber and nods approvingly at her scrape.

"She's turned on all right." He chupps to her and she answers, her head down and tail raised provocatively in the air.

In a few weeks, there'll be buyers sitting around the swimming pool sipping rum and cokes, while young, downy-speckled falcons are hacked out on rooftops and circle playfully over cowboys and nervous horses trying to bring in cows below in the hay meadows.

For nine months out of the year, my father spends untold hundreds of dollars feeding the wild turkeys. The turkeys, joined by a half dozen peahens, roost in the ponderosas behind our log house at the base of Big Goose Canyon. The turkeys gather on the lawn each afternoon, scuffling and squabbling among themselves, strutting and scratching at the gravel on the driveway. Then one by one, when the sun begins to slip behind the Big Horns, they methodically strut and pick their way up a brushy, rocky hill just adjacent to our house, where I can see them from my window. Immediately after any loud sudden noise, like a dog barking or a shout to someone across the field, the turkeys will all, in unison, gobble back for a second. The gobbling ends as abruptly as it begins, like the applause at a golf tournament. It's just one more strange thing about turkeys no one understands or worries about. They'll do it only at this time of day. Once they reach about halfway up the hill they can then light off and fly directly into the pines without having to gain so much altitude. It's a testament to turkey intelligence that they've figured this out. They light off in pairs or singly, aiming, I assume, for strategic branches. I watch the creaking limbs dip and sway as each bird lands, then tips back and forth getting its balance and sending snow billowing to the ground below. There's always fighting going on over the best branches, and a turkey will crash down through the trees, snapping twigs all the way down. Watching a turkey fly is a marvelous thing, maybe because it seems so improbable, but seeing two hundred turkeys gliding overhead in the morning, wings set, their huge bodies right over the roof, is an amazing sight; they look like a squadron of B-52's.

I've gotten a lot better at my bird ID's since I've spent so much time with falconers. They expect you to know the birds better than your average Joe, but never as well as and certainly never better than the falconer himself. The only ones that could trip up a falconer would be the LBJ's, Little Brown Jobs. Tweeties. A favorite game is to whip out a Peterson's field guide and cover the bird's name and have them make the identification. "Don't even bother," they'd wave me off smugly, a rum and coke tinkling in their hand. "I know them all." They're rarely wrong and if they were, you'd never know it because they could easily bluff their way out.

Competition among birders running high, my brother-in-law pimps my father from time to time.

"I bet you don't know what that one is," my father challenges from the living room window overlooking his trout pond. My brother-in-law rises to the challenge and takes the binos.

"Careful, careful now. It's a tricky one," Dad says. My brother-in-law crunches on some ice and focuses the binos.

"No problem." He sets the binos down next to a mounted least weasel. "It's a *Dendropicos serindipidus*," he says, telling me later he's completely pulled the name out of thin air. He somehow managed to keep a straight face.

"Very good. That's exactly what it is. I'm surprised you got the genus correct as well. You're becoming a more satisfactory son-in-law all the time," Dad says approvingly.

I ask Dad how he knows all these birds, and from such a distance.

"Because I'm a goddamned naturalist, that's why."

A man I've just met at a wedding reception is a little puzzled about the whole falconry business. After so many toasts to the bride and groom I don't recall how we got on the subject. "How can they keep such a proud bird like that in captivity?" he asks. And it's a sincere question. I fix my gaze on the carnation adorning his tuxedo and try to gather my wits. I find myself, once again, in the awkward position of defending this sport.

I've never flown a falcon, or had the least desire to be a falconer. But I have thought a lot about the sport, and the art, of falconry — usually while trudging over hills, carrying the extra bird on my arm, or sitting patiently in the truck while the falconer braves -30 degree weather to track down his bird with telemetry. And somewhere in my weak defense I am reminded of a conversation I once had with a falconer I admire very much.

In the living room was a framed photograph of a dark grey falcon with a bloody beak sitting on a dead canvasback.

"Who's this?" I had asked.

"A passage gyr I once had."

"What's passage mean?"

"I took her from the wild. Trapped her when she was young."

"And you flew her?" He had nice hands. I remember noticing them while he spoke.

"Yeah. I flew her. At first all I wanted to do was stare at her, all day long. I must have taken a million pictures."

"And she caught game and would come back to you. And you could walk up to her?" I asked.

"Basically, yeah. I mean they aren't like this imprint gyr here who would rather be with people than with other birds. The best you can hope for with a passage bird is that they'll learn to tolerate you. You don't want them to buddy up too much."

"Why not?" I must have sounded like a six-year-old. I should have just surrendered to my childish curiosity and asked, like I used to then, "How come for?"

"Well, so they won't get to liking people so much that they lose all fear. So they don't land on some farmer's barn looking for goodies and then get shot because the farmer thinks it's a chicken hawk out to get his chickens. Happens enough as it is."

"So this bird was born in the wild, knew how to take care of itself, and each time you flew her she could just say, 'to hell with this,' and fly off and be perfectly happy."

"Right."

"And she never did that?" I asked.

"No."

I thought about that for a moment.

"I don't get it."

"Neither do I, sometimes." We were quiet for a minute. "What ever happened to her?"

"I let her go."

"You mean you just turned her back to the wild?"

He nodded. "I fed her up, let her loose and turned and walked away."

"I could never do that. Not with anything I was attached to."

He shrugged and said, "Well, I guess that's the difference between you and me."

I found something very erotic about the whole falconry business. Maybe it was as simple as the smell of leather or being in the fall in the evening light. Maybe it was the grace of a falcon or the eerie sound of the wind rushing over the wings of a peregrine traveling at a hundred and some miles an hour and landing on a man's outstretched fist. I don't know; maybe it was just my hormones acting up. But I do know I have never failed to feel a chill up my spine when I see a falcon pull into a teardrop shape and fall to the earth. It's a sight I don't believe anyone would forget.

The other day I found a falconer sitting at his taxidermy table. He was stitching up the neck of a cock pheasant. I had forgotten how beautiful a bird they are, the feathers with their bronzes, golds, greens and blacks. Truly a spectacular animal. It was only when I stopped to touch the shimmering neck feathers that I realized the bird was still alive. I looked at the falconer, aghast. He shrugged.

"My falcon caught it today. She didn't kill it, and it just had this tear on its neck, so I thought I'd sew it up." He carried the bird to the front door, and smoothed the feathers on its back.

"Pretty little birds, aren't they?" he said. He placed the bird on the lawn and we watched while the pheasant trotted across the grass and disappeared into the timothy of the hay meadow.

"That's what I like about this sport," he said, "you can recycle your game."

Above our porch at the back door is a rotting log that protrudes a foot or more from the rest of the house. The log continues to rot, and according to several who know about this sort of thing, will rot right into the house and cause problems down the road. We have refused to saw it off because, for five years now, my father's peacock roosts there every night. His hens rejected him for the company of the wild turkeys, so he sleeps alone above our heads as we walk through the door. At night on a full moon, after a light snow, I can look out the window and see his blue and green iridescent tail gracefully hanging down and a blanket of powdery snow sticking to his back and tail. Over the years I have tried to imitate the sad, mournful call of the peacock, and from inside the house I call to him. I see his tail shift as he rises, the snow falling away, and he answers. Whether he yearns for his hens who roost with the turkeys or just finds the sound of his own species comforting to him, I don't know.

Momma,

Don't Let Your Babies Grow Up To Be Falconers

by M. Alan Jenkins

Shortly after the two-month period of my life my parents refer to as my Golden Age, I made an announcement about a closely held secret.

"I'm a falconer," I confessed, using the f-word. Silence reigned.

"I thought we were Mormons," was their only coherent reply. In the end, however, they took it bravely.

I am not sure where the itch to attempt falconry began. I do remember having trouble with eagles in grade school, never grasping how two plus two eagles equal four, even though my progressive parents provided me with ornithologically correct dolls. Robert Fulghum may have learned everything he needed to know in kindergarten, but he never had Mrs. Batchelder. I don't recall reading or hearing about falconry, but somehow, genetically perhaps, it seemed an undeniable part of my psyche, a nasty bit of karma. More likely though, the notion crash-landed on my brain during an intense alcoholic fog. My youthful falconry wasn't entirely squandered because I knew if I succeeded, there would be many rewards, and if I disgraced myself, I could emulate the politicians and write a book. However, the decision to embrace the falconer's lifestyle did influence my choice of careers. I became an ornithologist renowned for the ability to name any bird in the world. The red-breasted one I see right now in my garden, pulling on a worm, is named Ralphie.

Now, as a falconer for over thirty years (never mind how many over thirty), I can say with authority that the sport is a venture only begun with trepidation and more judgment than I possess. Were I to be given the chance to recapitulate my life, I would not change that aspect of it. But I would require more money.

In this chapter, I aspire to hint at some of the perils, pitfalls, humiliations and other joys you must endure if, during some suicidal melancholy, you elect to commit to falconry, the noblest of the field arts. I'm certain the authors of other *Celebration* chapters will produce a pollyanna picture of what it's like to be one of our very special (as in special education) fraternity. Read their works, take two, make that four, aspirins and call your psychiatrist in the morning. I, on the other hand, shall pull no punches nor change any names, so as to embarrass the guilty. If you want the fairy tale version, best wait for "Falconry, The Movie," soon to be released on video cassette.

In the days before apprentice falconers were required to be sponsored, our ranks were thinner than my hair. The precept of learning falconry by serving an apprenticeship is founded on Berra's Law: "You can observe a lot just by watching." — Yogi Berra. I endeavored to start my hawking career learning from the few falconers I could locate in my small sphere of influence. The first was an aged French expatriate, who I suspect was a deserter from the Foreign Legion. My fractured French is more destitute than your in-laws, and he spoke "little Englishes." During my pilgrimage to learn at the guru's knee, our conversation (quoted from the translated court records) went thus:

I (smiling): "Bon jour, mon' sewer. Is this day not bulging?"

Deserter (saluting): "You speak francs, what joy, Vive la States Untitled."

I (hesitantly): "Viola!, to matters?"

He: "Proceed using grease."

I (more boldly): "Is not pigeon bashing your subsistence?"

He (red in the face): "Feathers placed where?!"

I (hastily): "I demand you: dear thing, do female owls voyage through your head?"

He (lunging): "A toad to your own bed, or so I am calling your ancestors. En garde! Psalm 50:9 — I will take no bull from thy house."

I (confused retreat): "Alors!, please to send your washing to another school. It is not necessary to wallop my weasel, wet knight."

I gained little practical training from this brief alliance; but I persisted, confident that little is accomplished by reasonable men. I met no other falconers until I reached college. There I learned of a reclusive, almost mythical person in the fourth year of his sophomore class, the president of "The Earth Is Too Flat!" Society. In other words, two pickles short of a Big Mac. "Starsky," as we called him (he called himself "Hutch"), was shaped like a large member of the violin family. He was from the falconry sub-caste referred to as drugstore falconers, all pins and badges, no birds. From him I learned a dialect of falconer's sign language, still seen today in the more remote parts of the Colorado panhandle, wherein hands represent birds and flights take the form of fierce swooping up and down motions. All fighter pilots I know suffer from the same agitated tic. Some denigrate this as "air falconry," a mime, like playing the "air guitar," but Starsky was the best I have seen. He even included authentic sound effects while managing not to spit on his audience. I quit trying to master falconry from Starsky when it came to light that his cardinal training philosophy was based on the premise that if you love something, set it free: if it comes back to you, it's yours; if it doesn't come back, track it down and kill it.

The next few years turned into a painfully long learning experience when I tried to learn falconry from books. My first tome, *Falconry and Other Brain Fevers,* is a little-known classic I still own today. Soon thereafter, I purchased a text I use daily, a dog-eared 1945 edition of the *Falconer's Book of Common Prayers, in 7 Volumes* (Revised Ecumenical Version). I progressed by making mistakes . . . I mean gaining experience. I had to beg for hawks from petkeepers because these were the years before captive avian breeders such as Acme Amalgamated Accipiters. This process soon drove me to drink, for which I am grateful. Even today when in the field, I follow W. C. Field's advice, always keeping a bottle of "stimulant" handy in case I see a snake, which I also keep handy. My therapist cum lawyer advises me against describing more of this tender period of my life, having just recovered from the trauma by the use of therapy of a highly electrical nature. However, since I am not one to heed sound advice, I now divulge for the first time (excluding the defamatory National Enquirer piece) how I came to trap and train my first hawk.

I must digress to explain the social structure of modern American falconry. Most texts about falconry written by non-hunters ("dweebs" in falconry jargon) mention that in medieval times certain raptor species were limited to specific classes of people: an eagle for an emperor, a peregrine falcon for a king and so on down through, and including, elected life forms and ending with the peasant/taxpayer who was granted a mutant zucchini. For some reason, non-hunting authors place importance on this hierarchy, implying that it carries over into today's falconry for egotistical reasons. Such is not the case. Today we practice a truly democratic, unbiased sport from the lowliest flatworm falconer, a member of the legume family, up to the Ayatollah of Falconry.

The birds, however, are ranked according to their various characteristics. In the family of the falcons there are various species that all taste like chicken and need not concern us here. The true bird-hawk tribe has three North American species and several poor relatives in third world countries. The largest of these, the goshawk, is a Freddy Krueger bird with an attitude. The Cooper's hawk is family-sized with a fondness for eyes, and the sharp-shinned hawk can be used as an emergency backup when fully inflated. (You can look this up, it's in the Bible.) After memorizing these facts, I decided I wanted to fly a goshawk (a Latin word from gosh, meaning "that hurts," and awk, "a tender appendage," and from whence came "awkward.")

One day I encountered the man who was to become my true mentor and guide to this crazy sport. I will respect his wish to remain anonymous, but I deny this secrecy has anything to do with blackmail regarding an alleged incident concerning cream pies and a turkey farm. As an alias for this person I'll use John Michael Edward Shorter III, Boyd for short (gotcha John!). John, er, I mean Boyd, was given to spouting off long Latin passages from falconry authors such as Frederick II of Hohenstaufen, Holy Roman Emperor, to whom Boyd referred as "Freddy the Two." Listening to him go on for hours made me know what it would feel like to be forever pregnant. His constant counsel to me was: "No problem." Asked how to remove an angry eagle from my awk he would squint and say, "No problem." Another of his celebrated maxims: "I fear no weevil."

Boyd, with the help of a pound of carpenters and at the cost of a million dollars, helped me build my mews, no problemo. Then the federal exam needed passing and four tries later I was prepared, permit and all, to trap my first goshawk.

Hawk trapping requires bait, and because no animal species of my acquaintance will voluntarily reduce itself to raptor rations, it was necessary to secure some unfortunate piece of life to attract a goshawk to my trap. One dark night my brother (who now refers to me as his former sibling) and I set off to catch some pigeons that roosted in the university's barns. If you think that barnyard dust is the biggest peril one faces in this quest, you have never tried netting pigeons on a moonless night in the Animal Science Department's bull breeding pens. Precautionary donations to a blood bank are advised. Two hours, three landing nets and a Saint Christopher's medal later, I had my pigeon, a sparrow (they taste like chicken) and a measly mouse I reduced to possession by falling on.

Hawks get up with the chickens, so an early morning start for trapping is essential. My diurnal cycle functions on Japanese Standard Time, and it takes several cups of Boyd's coffee to get me to budge from bed. His coffee has some new-to-science, caffeine-adrenalin polymer that causes psychedelic micro-bursts on my retinas. Unfortunately the trunk line to my cognitive skills was, as the British say, engaged, and it was noon before I saw the outskirts of town in my rearview mirror. Our general level of excitement/anxiety rose many magnitudes when we beheld our first goshawk perched confidently on a pine tree a hundred yards from the road's edge. After we dug our way out of the creek I had inattentively driven into, it was still perched there, no problem. The next eleven years of my life were spent trying to force the recalcitrant pigeon into the hawk trap. This pigeon was no fool; even though the leather jacket of the trap protected it from harm, it had no desire to make the hawk's acquaintance. Eventually I triumphed and hurled the trap out the window, barely dodging a logging truck coming downhill (regardless of the truck driver's claim, my father was not a bachelor). The pigeon, whose job was to charm the goshawk by sexily flying around in a mouth-watering way, never opened its wings; a frequent flyer it was not. All this action and several rounds fired by the truck driver scared off my precious prize hawk. I collected the pigeon and trap sadly. It was the first time I ever saw a pigeon grin.

On our way home in disappointment, Boyd spotted another goshawk perched on the forest's edge. We substituted a trap containing the mouse for the hawk-wise pigeon and deftly chucked it under her majesty's hungry, we hoped, beak. The mouse did not want to be grist for a goshawk's mill either, and sat unmoving in a corner of the trap, executing its best imitation of a mound of Milk Duds which have gone through several wash and spin cycles. Not until the last ruby rays of sunset struck her breast did the gos pounce on the trap. The mouse betrayed its presence when it couldn't suppress a sneeze. Amazingly, she was quickly caught on one of my patiently tied nylon nooses, now bronzed and made into a lamp. It was to be a twelve-pack night. NO PROBLEM!

Slight problem: I now must train this sucker. Try lashing a whirlwind with sharp talons to your fist and coaxing it to take food from you while protecting your awks and you'll understand the problem. After a few days of not eating she took some molecular bites of fresh, raw meat while perched on my fist. The next step was to entice her to jump from her perch to my fist for a reward, and then increase the distance she would fly for this reward until she would come instantly at my command from one hundred yards. Who was I kidding here? In any contest of wills between a falconer and a hawk, back the hawk! In the end the simpler mind won out, and she gave in to my inducements of $4/lb. prime sirloin.

Proudly I went out into the hunting field with my trained (?) hawk, "Critter" (as I said, I can name them all). We would start easy by hawking the ubiquitous cottontail rabbit (*Difficultus minimus,* which is Latin for "No, you get the picture"). I took my trustee (meaning recently paroled) dog, "Skeeter," with me. He is part Golden Retriever and part speculation, with a high frequency tail. While Skeeter was off somewhere eavesdropping on mice with his nose, I managed to flush a Q-tipped target animal. Overcome with instinct mixed with surprise, Critter gave chase and spiraled disgracefully to the ground! Rabbits, it seems, keep the locations of obstacles to flying predators well fixed in their twenty-five-kilobyte brains, and never fail to use them to full advantage. This one had ducked under a single-strand, almost invisible, wire fence and Critter, the object of my affliction, had been arrested on encountering the aerial equivalent of a speed bump.

Several other similar incidents caused

me to give up on cottontails and decide that perhaps some immigrant-bashing might be easier. Chinese food sounded good, so off to the corn fields we went in search of those ring-around-the-collar jobs known to scientists as pheasants, or Sally, as I named them. No luck. It is well-known from archeological evidence that Murphy was the first falconer! Well, okay, I knew of a place where I could hawk prairie dogs. Fat as these rodents are, they don't run so much as waddle. However, keep in mind that one of the principles of falconry is that you eat what you catch (crow and muskrat recipes can be found in another chapter; they too can be made to taste like chicken). So this was not my quarry of first choice, but a trophy is a trophy, right? As we sneaked up on a colony of these rodents, a blaze of brown and white exploded under my foot (Skeeter, pursuing a nasal illusion, was long lost) and Critter winged rapidly after it. The bunny swashed when it should have buckled and Critter soon had it. Finally I could call myself a falconer, alert the press!

After many years of hawking following this, I learned plenty more and began to wax philosophical. In the event that you too begin to salivate at the sound of falcon bells, are socially retarded, and decide to take up the sport, here are some rules I have learned from experience and other falconers (both of them) that will assist you:

1. Catechism of Casts: First cast off, first lost.

2. Old Falconers' Lament: All quarry has cholesterol.

3. Long-winger's Law of the Unfordable: The mallards are greener on the other bank.

4. Hybrid Hypothesis: Don't count your eggs until they have been crossed.

5. Fear of Flying Formula: Be thankful that Cooper's hawks aren't venomous.

6. Alan's Advice: Falconers should never throw away leftovers.

As mentioned in the beginning of this already too long chapter, I wanted to alert you, gentle readers, about the difficulties you can expect if you should become infected with this madness called falconry. You still have enough time to change your mind before the decision goes on your permanent record! Instead you may wish to set your eyebrows on fire. I hope I accomplished my task, and I close with the admission that some of what I wrote is even true.

Beyond

by Will Peterson

There were three of us: Charles, the falconer; Tom, who was apprenticing in the art; and I, who knew nothing of it.

"We'll take this road," said Charles. "See if we can show Will some eagles."

"I didn't know there were eagles out here."

"Lots of them. They feed on the carcasses the sheep outfits leave lying around."

This was sheep country, abandoned buildings here and there surrounded by absolutely barren dirt and trash. But gradually, as we headed west, the sagebrush took over, broken only by lava vents. The scarred sides of Big Southern Butte loomed. Approaching the high voltage poles connecting American Falls Dam and the nuclear laboratory, Charles stopped the truck.

"There's one."

Tom handed me the glasses. The glasses brought the eagle up close as she stood airing her wings in the crossbar; she was very powerful and was giving us a scornful, sidelong glance.

"Female," said Charles. "They're bigger than the males. So you can see why I won't fly Jalad around here."

"I thought peregrines were the fastest."

Charles shook his head. "We'll get Jalad up to five hundred feet, maybe a thousand. The eagle's up there five thousand. And the bigger something is the faster it will fly. Last month Pitcher had his falcon in his glasses and she just flew out of sight. After about an hour he picked up her signal and found her a mile away on the ground. Her neck was twisted back, her wings almost torn off, like she'd been broken and thrown away."

Charles drove on, seeming lost in thought. "Falconry is fraught with tragedy. Fraught with tragedy."

"I'd like to get her up to five hundred, anyway," said Tom.

"We'll see," said Charles.

We drove on under the perfect late winter cloudless day, with the scarp of the mountains by Carey curving around the horizon, with snow only at the tops and Big Southern Butte right at our shoulder. There was only sagebrush now, with the occasional rhythmic upthrust of split black rock.

"I talked to a hang-glider once," I said, "who was gliding at ten thousand feet and this golden came out of the sky and grabbed the front of the struts in its talons and screamed at him."

"Yeah," said Tom.

"This is far enough," said Charles.

We got out of the truck and the sweet, cold quiet of the Big Desert covered us. There was a faint breeze, because the wind is never quiet on the plateau of the Snake, made for wind and raptors.

Charles swung the tailgate down and let the dog out of the kennel. She jumped down to the road, quivering with cold and excitement. In the kennel, the male whined piteously.

"You'll get your chance, Mac."

Atop the kennel, the falcon waited, imperturbable on her powerful legs.

Charles picked the dog up by the collar and tail, carried her to the front of the truck and set her on point: head high, tail straight up. Then he slid the palm of his right hand forward along her head, said "Okay, girl. Find those grouse!" and she was gone like Flo Jo, tearing at the road.

We jumped back in the truck and followed as fast as the muddy road would allow.

There were drifts of snow amid the sagebrush. The English pointer, built like a flyweight boxer, was the color of bone, and it

photo by Greg Hachigian

was a beautiful thing to watch her sail through and over the silver grey brush.

"How long can she run?"

"She'll run until she dies if I let her," said Charles. She had returned to the trail now, her paws kicking back chunks of mud. "The road's not too bad today," he went on, as a particularly greasy section made the big truck slide. "Earlier this year there was no way you could keep up with her. But she'll come back. Mac—he never looks back."

"Like Satchel Paige."

"Yeah. After about an hour he'll come looking for you."

We were, after all, in one of the largest wilderness areas in the lower forty-eight: the Big Desert, a sea of lava and sage, but with air so clear and without obstruction the mountains and the buttes offer you the illusion of nearness. We crossed the saddle of a lava vent and turned towards Big Southern Butte. Bonnie was stopped in the road, in semi-point, her tail straight up but wagging.

"Not again!" said Tom.

"We've got to try it," said Charles. "This is the third time this winter."

"Always in the same spot and she's acted the same way. We'll leave Jalad in the truck," said Charles, getting out. "Don't slam the door, Will; and don't give me hell if I make noise." Charles walked slowly up to the dog. Then he turned and waved us in. As he followed Bonnie into the brush, Tom and I walked in a flanking action up the shallow hillside.

There was only snow and mud amid the gnarled trunks of the artemisia; the faint wind was cool, and seeing neither tracks nor spoor, I watched the man and the dog working the little basin below us.

After a while, he waved to us. "All right," he shouted.

We walked back together to the truck. Charles smiled. "Must be the Great Grouse Spirit in there."

I liked the idea.

"They've got to be in there sometime," said Tom.

"I didn't even see any tracks," I said.

"Well," said Charles. "You've got to trust your dog. Out here, if you don't trust your dog, you can't do anything."

So Bonnie took off again, heels flying, and we got back in the truck, traveling due west, with the desert lying silently all around us and the scarp of the Pioneer Mountains beyond.

"We'll let her run to the Ridge."

"What do you call it?"

"The Ridge."

The little dog ran the road, or took off into the brush, leaping deer-like or dodging to the side of us as we drove, and we approached the Ridge, a low, dark shield lying north-south beyond Big Southern Butte.

Charles was quieter now, his forearms over the wheel. Though Bonnie was trying her hardest out ahead of us, the wind was at our backs; we would have our best chance on the way back. I asked him about Jalad.

"Her mother," he said, "was a Scottish peregrine; her father, an arctic gyrfalcon.

"The peregrines are climbers and divers. They exploit great height for the stoop. A peregrine flying level will achieve maybe 55 miles an hour; in the stoop she'll exceed 200.

"Jalad gets her size from the gyrfalcon. And her tenacity. In the Arctic there's sometimes only an hour of light to hunt by. They have to make a kill or they die."

He was silent for a moment. "Pretty selective breeding process."

We were beyond the Big Southern now, had just made a small inroad into the desert, when Charles stopped the truck and whistled Bonnie back. He gave her a pat, put her back into the kennel and let Mac out.

Gnomish, with his squarish head and flyweight muscularity, Mac waited, quivering in anticipation until Charles led him to the front of the truck, set him on point, and set him flying.

"He'll never look back," said Charlie as we got back in the truck and started back east.

"But that's what connects the falconer to the desert. The dog. It's like we need an intermediary. The falcon, she's too wild. The dog is the one that connects us with the vastness, the hiddenness."

We came back through a basin with a low rim of butts and vents blocking the southern view when we saw Mac on point.

"Quiet now."

We crept out of the truck, and as I stood watching Mac motionless at the edge of the road, Charles drew Jalad out of the back of the truck. She waited on his gloved left hand as he removed the hood. Then she flew to the perch atop the cab.

She was a beauty. She was pale white, with powerful shoulders and gold flecks accenting the breast feathers. Her eyes, large, fierce, tranquil, looked beyond.

Charles had put two pigeons in his bag, and as he walked toward the dog he turned back towards her and took one out by its feet. It flapped its wings helplessly. He spoke softly back to Jalad.

"Come on, Jalad. Fly."

And beating her long, scythe-like wings she flew out over his head.

"Climb, sweetheart, climb."

She followed him like a kite, with slow deliberate wing beats, and then turning back into the wind, kited higher.

"As long as she's in the air," said Tom, "the grouse won't fly."

They were out there together: the bird flying out and then setting her wings, sailing against the wind, hanging there and carried up at the same time while you saw her fluttering against the sun and heard in the silence of the wind the faint tinkling of the bells; and the man below, picking his way carefully behind the dog. Then he turned and waved at us, and we walked in from a tangent of seventy yards or so, with the hope that if they flew they would fly back past the falconer.

"This is the kind of sage they like," whispered Charles. "Not too tall, with these tufts of new growth."

So as the falcon flew above us like a kite, we waded through the sagebrush and snow. But no grouse flew; and we met at the rim of the basin.

"I can't understand it," said Charles.

"That's what happens when you bring a neophyte," I said.

"No. They're in here. Well, let's head back."

And we had just started back when a young grouse blew out right at my feet, and after she had cleared the tops of the sagebrush, achieved amazing velocity as she started to swerve away. And there was Jalad after her, flying with those long, deliberate wing beats of her scythe-like wings. Together they disappeared over the next wave of lava, and then we saw the falcon rise up behind it and fall again.

"Looks like she got it," said Charles.

"Maybe not," said Tom.

"No, she got it."

"Angle was wrong," said Tom.

"Everything was wrong."

"We're not going back, are we?" said Tom.

Charles stood for a moment, looking pensively over the brush. "Nah. Will and I will go pick her up. You stay here."

"Well, hopefully she didn't get it."

"Yeah."

"She's getting lazy," said Tom.

We got back in the truck and drove. Charles was angry with himself. "You've got to trust the dog," he said. "They were in there, but I didn't play it right."

"We should have stonewalled her. Made her stay up."

"How do you do that?"

"You just hold the dog. Keep your positions. Make her climb just to stay in the air." He was quiet awhile, then he said, "At least Tom wasn't satisfied. That's a good sign."

"This looks like the place."

He got out and started walking out to the right.

"I thought she went this way," I said.

"Yeah, she got it," he said. And then I too saw her, standing with her back to a ruin of old barbed wire, her white legs spread like pillars over the grouse, her wings out so they covered it. She was pulling the tail-feathers out with her beak and she paused to look up at us with those tranquil, fierce eyes.

I became aware of the faint tinkling of the bells as she stretched out its wings with her talons.

"That's how the old-timers found their birds, before radio transmitters. Yes, sweetheart." He took a grouse wing from his bag and giving it to her, slid the grouse from beneath her talons.

We looked at the grouse. She was a beautiful thing, her eyes closed and quiet, her wings spread out.

"First year female," said Charles. He spread the wing out. "See the new feathers? They grow from the inner wing so the old ones are at the tip. You can tell by the wear and the fading."

He put the grouse in the bag with the pigeons. Then he lifted Jalad to his gloved left fist, securing her there with jesses that also hung from her tarsi, before he took away the grouse wing and slipped the hood over her head. Then he drew the braces snug with his teeth.

And there was Mac, frisking and sniffing around us.

"Mac, goddamn you!"

We walked back to the truck, Charles with that stooped intensity, the falcon on his fist.

"I don't know what to do with him. He's a great dog, he's got a good nose and he works hard, but it's like there's something gone to mush in him.

"What happened to him?"

"Apparently he chased a rabbit when he was a puppy and the Scot who raised him beat him for it."

"He's all right."

"No. He's got to hold. Till hell freezes over if necessary."

He got Mac back in the kennel and

Jalad atop it where she stood, erect, undiminished by the hood.

"That's another problem with false points," said Charles, shutting the tailgate. "The falcon will get bored and she'll start strafing the dogs."

I laughed.

"Laugh!" said Charles. "You spend years training a dog. Years!"

I wanted to explain the basics of comedy to Charles, but thought better of it. "So you hired this guy to train Mac?"

"No. I got him as a pup. I flew over there and got him."

We drove back down the road. Up on the side of the swell, Tom was standing with his hands in his pockets.

"There are birds still in there," said Charles. "We'll use a real dog this time.

Tom walked down through the sagebrush. "I jumped three more."

"Where'd they go?"

He pointed across the road. "Into that hollow."

"Good," said Charles.

Bonnie came flying out of the back of the truck, trembling all over again; and after Charles set her in the point position, she hadn't gone fifty yards before she froze, just where Tom had said.

"All right," said Charles. He brought Jalad out of the back and removed the hood. She flew to perch atop the truck. When Charles took the pigeon from the satchel, she heard the sound of the wings flapping and took off like doom.

The wind seemed stronger now, but it was coming from behind us, from the east, and Jalad flew with it, almost lazily, but when she turned and banked back towards us she soared, her wings full out, her tail-feathers spread.

"She's in the mood," said Charles.

She was flying with the pure love of flight. We stood by the hood of the truck and watched her as she flew farther and farther away, towards the mountains, in the hazy late afternoon light of late winter, riding the edge of the wind.

"We've never let her do this," said Tom.

"Perfect conditions. She's like a leaf on a river. On a calm day you'll see a falcon go looking for air, she'll fly real clumsily, and then you'll see her hook her wings and sail."

She was so far away that when she flew directly away she disappeared, and only when she spread her wings and banked back towards us did she appear again. Then after a few more turns I couldn't see her at all, whether going or coming.

"The worst thing now," said Charles, "would be for her to see something beyond her now and give chase. She could fly out of radio range."

"What makes her come back?"

Charles, looking through the glasses didn't answer. "Well, that's far enough." He handed the glasses to Tom. He slung the bag over his left shoulder and began to walk slowly down the road toward the dog.

"We can't see her," said Tom. "But she sees us."

And when Charles, walking very slowly, had gone twenty yards, I saw the falcon, just a tiny figure, returning in a wide bank. And then she was above him, the sun was semi-high on the left and she hung against it now, the faintest tinkling of the bell, with the sun and the vast desert breathing beneath it. Charles put his hand to the dog and they entered the brush. Then he waved us in.

"This is what you want," Tom whispered. "Jalad high and behind him."

And she was high behind him, hanging like a kite against the sun, and you heard the faint tinkling of a bell, as in a dream. The sun and falcon were at his back as he entered the hollow, the knee-high sagebrush and the dog just ahead of him. And then Tom started running and telling me to run and I'm jumping over sagebrush and catching glimpses of Tom already twenty yards ahead of me and Charles another fifty ahead and I said, hell with this, and stopped, and saw the falcon hovering directly above Charles and at the same time saw the grouse come whirring out in a beeline for freedom and out of the sky Jalad made that funny, wobbling, head-behind-the-back move that divers make and she's diving with wings tucked, a spiraling dive, down into the vortex.

But the grouse was already almost at full speed and plummeting. Jalad missed, short, flaring just above the ground to regain balance, and she was already twenty yards behind when she took off again in pursuit, with those deliberate, long wing-strokes, closing the gap to maybe five as they passed together over the farthest ridge and out of sight.

But the dog remained on point. And as he and Charles worked step by step through the brush, I watched one grouse after another blow out of the hollow until, flying in threes and fours, they swerved across the sky, the distant mountains and disappeared over the next ridge.

We stood transfixed, watching them, the whirring, whistling filling the air and then the silence of the desert returning. We stood by the truck and felt it, the virile silence of it.

"I can't believe they could stay down through all that," I said.

Charles smiled, swinging the tailgate down. "You don't get to be a February grouse by being stupid."

He put the dog back into the kennel and we drove back toward the east.

"She's still not getting high enough," said Tom.

"I know," said Charles. "We've got to stonewall her. Make her climb. You remember I was telling you about Pitcher? He's not even concerned with a kill. It's how high he can get the bird to go."

Then he started a soliloquy, his arms wrapped over the steering wheel. "This is my last grouse hunt this year. She's getting too lazy. There's a new duck season next month and I don't want to take her over there the way she's flying. There's no way she can kill a duck the way she's flying. It would be a disaster."

"There she is," said Tom.

"All right. She didn't get it." Charles smiled. "I didn't want Will to think less of me, taking two birds the same day."

Jalad had perched on a lava vent just off the road. She was showing her profile to perfect advantage. Her bearing was perfect. She was beautiful. Charles got out of the truck and called to her, but in the end he had to climb up through the rocks to her.

A few weeks later Charles came by and told me he had taken Jalad out into the Desert for the last day of the season.

"You know," he said, "I never go out there any more that I don't give thanks to the Great Spirit, just for letting me participate.

"Yesterday we were racing a storm cloud from the west when, just past where we had those false points, Mac went on point.

"No sooner is Jalad in the air than three big cocks blow out of the cover and she's got one. There was a hell of struggle. I ran over to help out, but by the time I got there she'd broken its neck.

"When I reached down to take the grouse away, this is what I found under them."

He opened his hand and showed me the arrowhead of red obsidian, about two inches long before the tip was broken off.

"Wow."

"Yeah," said Charles. "My knees were shaking."

Passagers

by Charles H. Schwartz

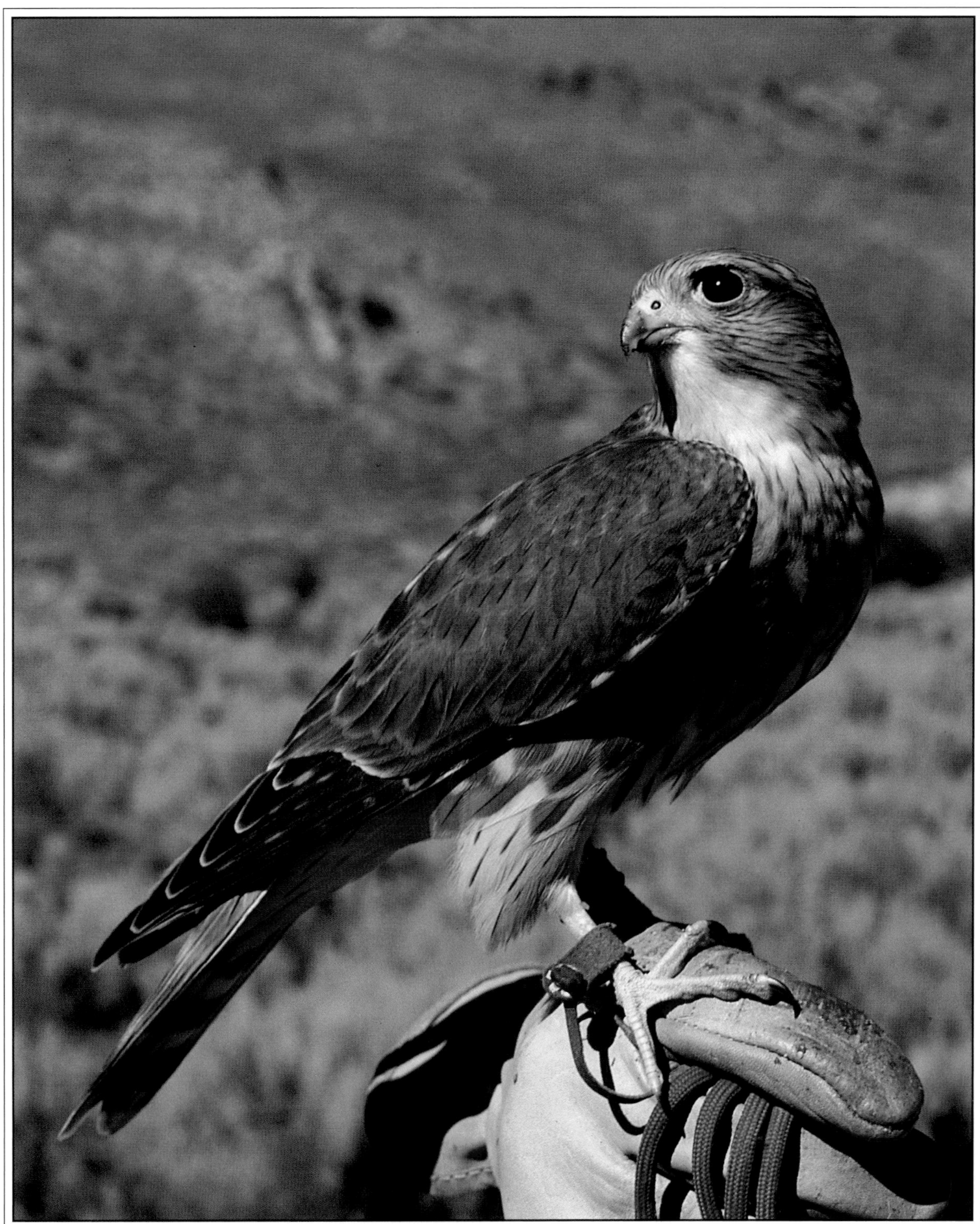

photo by Charles Schwartz

Reese Williams moved quickly, the hissing thud of his pneumatic nailer booming off the plywood floor and rolling out across the sage-covered foothills.

"Hey, Hawkman. Ease up a little!"

The young carpenter laughed as he dropped the tool and slid another sheet of five-eighths across the joists, snapping it in tightly next to its twin. He snatched up the nailer and anchored the ply with four fast shots. Another sheet, another burst and the joists were covered. Reese stood to reload, then crouched like a wrestler, slamming nails along the joist lines, the gun hot in his hand.

The older man shook his head.

"I like your hustle, kid, but cripes you're rough on my gear! What's your rush?"

"I told you, LaMar, I trapped a new hawk yesterday. I want to get out of here so I can start working her."

"Git, then! You're done." LaMar waved his hand. "See you tomorrow."

Reese took the short way home, a twisting gravel road that wound up and over the low mountains that stood between his job site and the river. Once over the top, he let gravity pull him homeward, his truck surging ahead on the steeper grades as he lightly worked the brake to maintain control. *Free-falling through life,* he always thought when he drove this way. He could see the dark squalls drifting north across the vast sagebrush flats on the far side of the river. There would be snow on the desert by morning.

How did he know? Reese wondered. *How did Emmett know about the merlins?*

Emmett Sands had been right about the merlins migrating in front of the first November storm. Reese had learned more about hawk trapping in one weekend with Emmett than he had in his five years as a falconer.

Saturday had dawned fine and clear, the last day of a perfect fall, but on Sunday the barometer had dropped and the wind had shifted to the north. Both days were filled with moving birds, and Emmett had shown Reese how to spot and trap the little falcons.

He smiled as he remembered how Emmett had handled the hissing haggards they had captured in their nets. The old falconer would examine each bird with deliberate care and then hold it to his face, his eyes twinkling. "Ambrosia," he would say, inhaling deeply. "Perfume of the gods!" Then his thick hand would slowly open and the merlin would bolt for the sky.

They were after passagers, the bold, reckless birds-of-the-year, feather perfect and full of promise. They caught six and kept two, a dark, button-eyed male for Emmett and a big, blond Richardson's female for himself.

Reese was pleased. He had his first merlin.

He turned down the narrow lane as the first snowflakes sputtered and whirled in the gathering darkness. A tired and faded house trailer rested inside a grove of leafless Russian olives, its back side hunched against the southwest wind. The windows were dark and the lane was empty.

Shelly must be working late, he thought. He parked in front of the weathered deck that ran the length of the trailer.

Reese glanced through the window as he fumbled with his keys. His new merlin had thrown her hood and bated wildly when she saw him, twisting her tail feathers up in her jesses.

"Damn!"

Reese rushed into the trailer and grabbed his falconer's glove. The falcon bated again, hanging, her wings outstretched, head up, panting. She screamed, "KEK! KEK! KEK! KEK!" as Reese unsnapped the swivel that secured her to the perch. Terrified, the merlin popped up on his glove and rocketed off in another bate. Reese searched for the bird's hood and found it under the sofa. He tried to slip it on, but the falcon stood boldly and bit his finger. Rattled, Reese grabbed the merlin with his free hand and forceably hooded it. Released, the merlin regained the glove, hissing, her head back and beak agape.

His finger bleeding profusely, Reese tried to stifle his overwhelming disappointment as he coldly assessed the damage: one tail feather broken and three others badly bent. A tipped primary in the left wing. The merlin had been feather perfect yesterday.

Shit, he thought, sucking his wound, *maybe Emmett has some feathers and we can fix the tail.* He did not look forward to telling the older man what had happened.

He turned on the television and pulled a beer from the fridge as he carried the falcon on his gloved left hand. The merlin held her wings tight against her body, her head drooping. Reese paced in front of the TV, hoping that his constant movement would calm her, but each time he touched the bird's back, she hissed. He decided not to call Emmett until later, after the evening news.

By seven, he was thoroughly discouraged. None of his efforts to smoothly unhood and rehood the falcon had worked. He stood at the window studying the half-circle of porchlight in front of the trailer. Snowflakes, bigger now, angled in steeply, covering the packed earth with a thin layer of white. The trackless lane stretched off into the darkness.

"Reese! Reese!" Shelly Wilder stamped her feet as she came through the door.

"Where have you been? It's almost eight."

"Bill, I mean Mr. McKuhan, came into the bank just before closing. He said he wanted to discuss my future and invited me up to the Inn. Oh Reese, that man is truly outstanding! Guess what happened?"

"Some rich lawyer takes my woman up to the Holiday Inn for a few hours and you want me to guess what happened?"

"Reese! He's going to run for lieutenant governor! He wants me to be on his campaign staff!"

"The election's not for another year. Besides, you already have a job. When would you find the time?"

"You're not listening!" Her tone changed quickly. "Put that damn hawk up and pay attention to me!" Shelly threw her coat on the floor and strode into the kitchen. She paced back and forth, muttering, then marched back out.

"Okay, Hawkman, what's the problem? Does your little chicken killer have indigestion or what?"

"She messed up her tail pretty bad," Reese said as he turned from the perch to face her. "Now what's this about an election?" Shelly stood squarely in front of him with her legs apart and her hands on her hips. Rugged, yet poised, with long dark hair and flashing eyes.

My God, Reese thought, *she's fine!*

"I have been asked by the next lieutenant governor of Idaho to serve on his election campaign staff." She used the voice she usually reserved for explaining passbook procedures to dry farm widows. "It is an exciting and challenging position that will allow me to use my sociology degree and my God-given talents to assist a highly qualified individual to be elected to office. And McKuhan made it clear there will be continuing opportunities for me once he has that office. The job, incidentally, just might be a hell of a lot more exciting than being a teller at Podunk Savings and Loan!"

"And that means you'll be moving to Boise?" Reese went straight to the heart of it.

"If I accept, yes."

"Huh uh. No way! That slimy shyster just wants to get into your outfit!"

"Reese! Try to see it from my side. This opportunity is perfect. It's exactly the chance I've been looking for. You could find work there. We could go together."

"No! I'm not going anywhere and you're not leaving!"

"You watch, bozo!" Shelly stormed past him into the bedroom, slamming the door behind her.

Reese listened to her crying behind the thin wall and remembered how his prairie

photo by Charles Schwartz

falcon had drifted downwind in a high circling soar, the day he had lost it.

Emmett Sands lived above a bend in the river west of the Indian Reservation. The screened weathering yard attached to the barn confirmed that Reese had found the right place. There were two cars that Reese didn't recognize parked out front. A handsome blond woman dressed in a business suit opened the door. She was barefooted, and her jacket was unbuttoned.

"Hello, Reese," she said. "Come in, come in. I'm Roberta. Em is in the living room."

He shook her hand as he entered the house. She pointed to an oak shelf mounted on the wall by the door.

"Just set your hawk on that and I'll take your coat." She waited as he placed his merlin on the perch and removed his jacket, then smiled as she took it from him. Reese liked her at once. He picked up his merlin and followed her down the short hallway, stopping at the entrance to a large room. A slim, dark woman dressed in old jeans and a bright red shirt smiled at him from the sofa.

Emmett had set his tiny jack merlin on a post-like perch in the corner of the room. The three watched in silence as the short, stocky man stepped back and held out his hand.

"Tyke!" he said sharply. "Tyke!"

The jack bobbed his head and leaned out, straining towards the garnished glove only three feet away.

"Tyke!" he repeated and the bird leaped to his fist, eager to resume feeding on the warm sparrow held in the glove. Emmett greeted Reese with widened eyes and a nod, the jack feeding unconcernedly as he looped the leash neatly into the fingers of his glove.

The dark woman in the red shirt rose to introduce herself and Reese realized that she was part Indian. Deidre took his hand and wouldn't let go, insisting that he sit next to her on the couch. Both women were disarmingly attractive, and the young man was quickly bewildered by their attention and nearness. They quizzed him about his new bird as Emmett stood grinning in the corner, occasionally lifting his hand to rearrange the sparrow.

The women stopped speaking when Emmett picked up a small leather hood. The jack was still feeding, but had begun to pause, looking up frequently. Emmett turned and brought the bird in close to his chest. His right hand came up from beneath and flowed over the jack's head and down his back. The bird stood erect, the hood resting in place. He shook his head once and Emmett eased the braces shut.

"Nice bird," Emmett said, addressing the jack. He ran his hand down the bird's back with satisfaction and then fastened him to the perch.

The women stood to leave. Reese shook their hands again and was left alone as Emmett escorted them to the door.

Waiting, Reese examined the big room. One entire wall was covered with books, some of them worn and cracked with age. A heavy oak desk matched the two solid end tables, and the credenza was cluttered with falcon hoods and leather working tools. Emmett was a finish carpenter and cabinetmaker by trade, and Reese assumed that he had built the furniture himself. There were six framed paintings. Three were of hawks and two featured dogs. Reese liked the portrait of the woman best.

Next to the wide windows in the corner of the room stood a sturdy workbench. It held a massive block of light-colored wood. Among the chips and chisels at its base, Reese uncovered three penciled sketches. It appeared that Emmett was about to carve a life-sized bird dog out of a solid block of curly maple.

"What do you think?" Emmett was watching him.

"I didn't know you sculpted wood. Or is it called carving?"

"I'm not sure myself," Emmett replied. "I've never done it before. Oh, I carved a few duck decoys out of basswood and pine when I was younger, but never anything like this."

"But why?" Reese looked at the block and tried to imagine the effort required.

"I've always admired English pointers. I was down in Georgia once hunting with a friend on a quail plantation. The owner had set a brace of bronze pointers out in front of the mansion. They looked almost real when I saw them from the porch, but when I walked out and touched one, I didn't like its coldness. Ever since, I have wanted to carve one out of wood."

Reese rubbed his hand on the rough maple and thought about the hardheaded setter he had once tried to train. It had been a bitter and disappointing experience.

"I see what you mean," he said, knocking his knuckles where the dog's head would be. "It's probably the most appropriate medium for a bird dog."

They both laughed.

"So show me your merlin. What did you name her?" Emmett asked.

"Shikra. I think it's a Hindu word for an Asian sparrowhawk, but I liked the sound of it."

Emmett nodded and examined Reese's merlin from all sides. He fingered the tipped wing feather and the falcon hissed at his touch.

"And how is she coming along?" Emmett turned away before Reese could answer.

"She threw her hood while I was at work today and was pretty upset when I got home. She messed her tail up bad."

Emmett returned with a faded yellow shoebox.

"Here," he said, opening it, "fish through these. You'll find what you need." The box was filled with molted merlin feathers of every size and color.

Together, they repaired the merlin's

tail, and Emmett demonstrated how to train the merlin to accept the hood. They visited until late in the night, and the old falconer's stories filled the young man's mind with an intense longing for lonely, open places.

Driving home in the snow, Reese felt slightly giddy with his newfound knowledge. What would it be like to float down a winding western river and see two merlins plummet out of a glinting sky, the intensity of their kekking calls leading him straight to their nest? Or to experience the flights on the high desert that Emmett had described, his merlin mounting powerfully without pause, ceaseless and singleminded in pursuit until it was only a speck in the sky?

What would it be like, he wondered, *to live like Emmett Sands?*

Shelly's Toyota crouched in the darkness beneath its blanket of white. Reese's euphoria evaporated as the grimness of his domestic situation clawed its way back into his chest. He entered the trailer quietly and undressed in the dark. He slid into the bed, not wanting to disturb her, but as he settled beneath the sheets her warm hand reached out in the darkness.

"Reese," she whispered. "Oh, Reese."

The young falconer had plenty of time to spend with his hawk that week as Shelly was out each evening. He suspected that she was with McKuhan, but each night she returned about nine. They ate whatever there was, mostly in silence. Shelly was polite but preoccupied. He figured it was over, but then in the night she would pull him close and they would make love with a quiet intensity. On Friday, she held him in her arms until the alarm went off.

A stiff wind blew across the desert that day and LaMar and Reese pushed hard to close in the house. If you worked in the trades, winter had to be taken seriously. Shelter was needed to complete the job in comfort. They finished sheathing in the frame as darkness fell and Reese drove home slowly, wondering what the weekend would bring.

He kicked off his galoshes and entered the trailer, unprepared for what he saw.

"Your hair . . .What did you do?"

"Like it?" Shelly asked. She ran her hand through the short, boyish cut, shook her head and laughed, then slid her hand slowly over her cocked hip to the edge of her very short skirt.

"I don't know. You look . . . so different. Where did you get that dress?" Reese felt panicky.

"We have to talk, Reese." She picked up a glass from the counter. Reese could see that it was half empty.

"I've accepted McKuhan's offer and given the bank my notice. With the vacation I have coming, I can move to Boise this weekend."

"No! I won't let you!"

"Get a grip, Reese. It's my decision, not yours. I'm leaving tomorrow."

"But, but what about us?" Reese heard his voice crack. He thought of himself as another person in the room, watching.

"I don't know about us, Reese. I only know about me. And I know I have to go to Boise." Shelly sipped at her drink. Her eyes never left his face.

Rage jolted visibly through Reese's body like an electric shock. He wanted to strike her, but wheeled away before it could happen. In a moment he was out the door and in his truck, racing down the lane. Shelly stared out the open door. She pulled hard at the whiskey, but the tears came anyway.

Emmett had been working on his carving for most of the week. When Reese stopped by on Saturday morning, he was amazed at the progress the man had made. A dog's head and body leaned out over the solid base, its legs still encased in the wood.

"Where's the tail?" Reese asked. "I thought it was going to be an English pointer."

"It is. I'll carve the tail separately and insert it into a drilled hole later. It's too damn difficult to include the tail in the original. Besides, the block wasn't tall enough."

"You could carve a couple of different tails and try 'em out. See how they look." Reese warmed to the project.

"Yeah! We could have a gracefully arched one for grouse and then one with a kink in it for larks."

"What about rabbits?" Reese was feeling better now.

"Dis dawg don't point no rabbits, suh!" Emmett used his best indignant Georgia drawl.

"Coffee?" Emmett gestured with his empty cup.

"Yeah, sure. Thanks."

Reese circled the carving, caught up in the wonder of it. The wood begged to be touched and he found that he couldn't keep his hands off of it. His caress lingered as he imagined the finished dog standing beneath the roughness. It would be smooth and warm, like . . . .

"Black okay?" Emmett held a mug in each hand.

"Yeah, fine." The two men stood in front of the window overlooking the river, sipping coffee.

"There was a haggard gos in that big cottonwood there on the bend earlier this morning." Emmett nodded upstream, toward the dark leafless giant hanging over the river. Six mallards beat into the wind along the far shore, shot across the water on set wings and slid in below the tree. The two men stared in silence, holding their mugs.

"So tell me about your jack," Reese said at last. He had not noticed the ducks, nor heard about the goshawk in the tree.

"Tyke is ready, but I need a few more days." Emmett turned and set down his cup. The jack stood unhooded on a second post-perch in the far corner. It had been there all along and Reese had not noticed. Emmett picked up his glove and garnished it with several slivers of meat. The bird stepped eagerly onto the glove, snatching the warm morsels one at a time. Emmett unsnapped the swivel and bowed his head as he threaded in the leash. The merlin ignored him and looked down at the glove, as if expecting more tidbits to appear. The man looked directly at the little falcon and the bird stared back, confused but friendly. Emmett picked up the hood, blew into it, and hooded the jack in one fluid motion. He waited for him to rouse and then tipped his head to close the braces with his teeth and his free hand. The jack scratched at the hood and roused again, his plumage relaxed and full.

Reese admired the way Emmett moved around his hawk.

"Consideration." The word just slipped out.

"Yeah, well . . ." Emmett held the jack up, as if all the admiration belonged to the bird. "There's more to it than that."

"What do you mean?"

Reese thought, *Is this man reading my mind?*

"Consequences, too. You can't forget that your actions have consequences when you handle hawks. Offences aren't easily forgiven, at least not early in the game. If you want to be close, of course you must be considerate, but bear in mind that you aren't really needed, not initially. Later, that changes."

"How, Emmett?"

"For me, the challenge is to discover what Tyke wants to hunt," he said as he loosened the braces, "and then help him do it. If I'm successful, we'll both know it."

He placed another tidbit on the glove and removed the hood slowly. The jack looked around, then gobbled the piece of meat. He roused and shook his tail, bobbing his head as he took in the room. There was none of the tight plumage that characterized a fearful hawk.

"Not me, man. I want my merlin to burn down those feedlot starlings like a heat-seeking missile!"

"Well, she's certainly big enough."

Reese sensed he had said something

stupid.

"Why don't you bring her inside? I'd like to see how she's coming along." Emmett set his jack down on the perch next to the carving and snapped the swivel to his jesses. "Wait, I'll come with you," he said, leaving his bird to preen bareheaded in the sunlight.

Shelly's little Toyota was coupled to a U-Haul almost as big, and the front door to the house trailer was propped open with a plastic dog kennel. When he first entered, Reese thought that the room seemed bigger. Then he noticed the things that were missing: the photos, Shelly's chair, the blue glass bottle they had found together up at the old mine. They had both reached for that bottle at the same time, laughed, and said, "Mine!" Reese remembered how easily he had twisted it from her hands and held it behind him, and her dark, laughing eyes as she encircled him with her arms, pretending to want it back.

Shelly walked into the room and he felt her warmth immediately, as if a cloud had passed, revealing the sun.

"I'm ready to leave," she said. "If I've forgotten anything, I'll call."

Reese said nothing, his throat suddenly too swollen to speak.

Shelly looked up at him, waiting. There was only silence, so she kissed him on the cheek.

"Goodbye, Reese." She turned and left.

Emmett ran his thick hands along both sides of the pointer's sleek head and then brushed them slowly down each heavily muscled shoulder. The wood was warmed by the sunlight falling through the big windows. Tyke preened tamely behind Emmett as Reese watched from the couch, his own merlin hooded and jumpy on his glove.

"Is Tyke ready?"

Emmett turned to look at the jack and lifted his left hand slightly. He rubbed his fingers together and whispered, "Tyke! Tyke!" The jack leaned over, straining toward him. He said, "Tyke!" one more time and the bird bated, instantly reversing and regaining his perch. Emmett chuckled.

"Tyke says he's ready."

Reese shook his head with courteous disbelief.

Later, the two men drove into the desert. Emmett cruised the dirt tracks slowly, searching for the right place to fly his bird.

"What are we looking for?" Reese asked.

"An area that is open, free of fences, poles, or trees. I prefer a cheat grass flat where there is hardly any sage, like the old burns where they run sheep in the spring. But it's hard to find a place like that farther out, away from the power lines."

They worked the edges of the desert, a few miles beyond the sprawl of agriculture, until Emmett found what he wanted.

"There!" he said, pointing to the right.

A flock of horned larks dipped and rose in sporadic undulations as if none of them were certain where they were going. The birds crossed the road in front of the truck and dropped suddenly into the grass a hundred yards out. Emmett stopped the truck.

"This is the place. Watch those larks while I get Tyke."

Emmett grunted as he twisted to reach through the rear window into the camper of the truck. Reese was dumbfounded as he watched Emmett strike the braces and remove the jesses.

"Get out of the truck."

Reese eased quietly out of the cab, his binoculars in one hand. He hadn't expected this. This wasn't how the books said it was done.

"Now watch."

Emmett removed the hood and the jack snapped up a tidbit. Then he raised it above his head and the bird bobbed and stared, taking in the huge expanse of desert. Twenty miles away, a giant butte rose solidly from the long expanse of snow-covered lava and sage that stretched endlessly to the north and west.

No telemetry and no bells. What a place to lose a hawk, Reese thought. *This man is nuts!*

The jack left Emmett's glove, flew fifty yards without looking back, then banked when Emmett shouted, "Tyke!" He returned to the truck, circling once before landing on the cab.

"That should pin them. Now let's walk out and see what happens."

The two men moved away from the truck and when they were halfway out, Emmett turned and shouted again. The jack came quickly to his upraised fist and Emmett opened the glove to reveal another small reward.

"Stay right where you are."

Emmett carried the jack to the edge of the grass and when the first lark flushed, the tiny falcon exploded from his fist in a blur of beating wings. The lark mounted up over the desert in pulsing, vertical bursts that the hawk could not match, and the flight transformed into a rising, twisting affair with the jack relentlessly pursuing the lark higher and higher. The two men watched as the jack and the lark grew smaller in the cold blue sky.

"Any second now . . ." Emmett did not take his eyes off the flight. "Get your binocs on them!"

The larger of the two specks surged upward and touched the smaller, which dropped like a stone straight toward the earth. The jack followed, inches behind all the way down, and the two birds seemed to collide with the desert, flying directly into the ground.

"Man, did you see that! He got it! What a stoop! What a flight!"

"Did you see him catch it?" Emmett peered intently at the spot where the birds had fallen, unwilling to move his eyes.

"Yeah. No. Well, he must have caught it, didn't he?" Reese turned toward Emmett, losing his mark.

"Stay here and don't move."

Reese watched through his binoculars. When Emmett reached the spot, he stood still for a few minutes, searching the ground around him. Then he knelt and held out his fist. Suddenly the jack was there, fluttering on his glove. Emmett sat down in the snow to feed his falcon. It took a while.

He returned to the truck a half hour later, the jack gorged and hooded.

"I've never seen anything like that," Reese admitted. "It was like something out of those old British books, only better. You could have lost him at any point!"

"It did go well, didn't it?"

"What happened to the lark?"

"Tyke was staring down a badger hole when I found him. His wings were drooping and he was panting like mad. Boy, that chase opened his lungs! So I showed him a house sparrow and he slammed into the glove like a hungry goshawk. I think we're buddies now." Emmett stroked his bird with affection.

"And now we know what he likes to hunt!"

"Just think," Emmett said, "we get to do it again tomorrow."

"You mean risk it all?"

Emmett grinned. His eyes were very bright.

It was not as easy for Reese to emulate Emmett's technique as he had thought it would be. The big female merlin resisted his attempts at gentleness with resolute ferocity, and he was forced to reduce her weight in order to maintain reasonable control. But Reese was certain it would go well. He had all the bases covered. His merlin wore bells, a radio transmitter, and long, thin jesses for better control in the field. He didn't intend to lose her. He had lost enough already.

A week later, Reese felt that his merlin was ready. Emmett declined to join him, so the young falconer drove out alone, his bird hooded on the seat beside him. He had chosen a cattle feedlot a few miles north of a nearby town. Around three o'clock, groups of starlings began dropping into the corrals from great heights. They came from all directions, but mostly from the town.

He stood outside the truck and loosened the braces as he waited for a passing flock to settle into the corrals. As soon as they landed, another group hove into view and he removed the hood. The big merlin stared at his glove and then at Reese. She did not look at the starlings. He waited as the second flock settled and another appeared in the sky behind it. This flock passed overhead and Reese threw the merlin off, confident that she would give chase with a little encouragement. The falcon fluttered and sailed to a nearby pole where she remained, oblivious of the opportunities passing by.

Disgusted, Reese showed her the lure. The merlin came instantly. He picked up his bird with a piece of meat and quickly hooded her before she could eat too much. This was not what he had envisioned.

He tried a few slips closer in, using his truck to sneak up on the starlings that were milling around the barn. The merlin attacked with desperation, but broke off each time as the flocks mounted strongly into the sky, setting her wings and gliding back to where Reese stood.

He drove straight to Emmett's house by the river. Two cars were again parked near the barn, and it was a long time before Emmett answered the doorbell.

"Hello, Reese. How did it go?" Emmett stood sheepishly in the dim light. A cozy warmth and soft laughter exuded from the dark hallway behind him.

"We have to talk." Reese tried not to whine. "You've got to explain what I am doing wrong!"

"Did you lose her?" Emmett's concern was genuine.

"No, no. Nothing like that. I just can't seem to get the knack of it. She won't fly like Tyke!"

"I see." Emmett seemed to think it over. "Why don't you go get her? Give me a few minutes and then bring her in."

Emmett closed the door and Reese returned to his truck. It dawned on him that his unannounced arrival had caught the older man unawares. He realized that he had never thought of Emmett in any context except as a falconer.

The finished carving stood between two empty wine bottles on the low table in front of the sofa. The smell of roast goose filled the room. Roberta and Deidre greeted him cheerfully but did not get up. The wooden pointer wore an old leather collar with a heavy brass buckle. Three wooden tails lay at the dog's feet. The women giggled and offered Reese some wine. He refused, but Deidre rose and poured him a glass anyway.

His uneasiness slipped away as he accepted the drink and returned her smile.

"Now tell us what happened." Emmett pulled up a chair.

Reese related his bird's failure.

And I've lost my girl as well, he wanted to say.

"So what should I do?"

Emmett got up and refilled their glasses as he considered his response. He picked up Reese's merlin on his bare hand, feeling her breast muscles and then stroking her back quickly.

"Raise her weight a quarter of an ounce or more. And get rid of this junk." He fingered the bells and transmitter with clear distaste. "Then take her back to your spot and allow her to discover herself."

"But I could lose her!"

"If you just want a merlin to carry around, then what's the problem?" Emmett wasn't smiling.

"No, no! I want to see flights like Tyke made that day. I want to see what she can really do!" Reese looked at his merlin as he spoke.

"Then let go, Reese. Ease up on the control. You can't force this merlin to be anything except what she already is."

No one spoke as Emmett handed the

bird back to Reese.

"Hey, this is supposed to be a celebration!" Deidre raised her glass.

"To Woody, the staunchest pointer there ever was!"

"Here! Here!" Roberta giggled.

"To Woody!"

"To Woody."

Reese awoke slowly, aware of someone moving in his kitchen. The smells of coffee and frying bacon reached into the bedroom. Then he remembered that it was Christmas Day and that Shelly had returned. He dressed quickly. It was only eight o'clock.

She turned from the stove when she heard him sit at the table. The furry white ball on her Santa hat fell into his face as she bent to kiss him.

"Good morning, Reese," she whispered. "Merry Christmas."

He smiled and pulled her close, remembering their evening together.

She poured a cup of coffee for him and returned to the stove, humming Christmas tunes as she broke two eggs into the skillet and depressed the lever on the toaster.

"There," she said, sliding the hot plate of food in front of him. "Enjoy!"

She made more toast and then sat down at the table with her cup.

"This is wonderful," Reese said, pretending to be hungry. "You shouldn't have done it."

Shelly smiled, watching him.

"Can we talk?" he asked.

"Of course."

"What's going on?"

"What do you mean, Reese?"

"I mean where are we headed?" He knew as he said it that it wasn't what he meant.

"I don't know about you, but I'm headed for the Lonesome Bull. With luck, I'll walk in the door just as they sit down to dinner. Won't they be surprised?"

"You're going to Montana? Today?"

"Sure! It's Christmas. I want to see my father and brothers. Boise is a lonely place when you live by yourself and don't know anyone. And I wanted to see you, too," she added quickly.

Reese studied the piece of egg on the end of his fork.

"Stay." It was all he could do to say it out loud.

"Reese, we've been through this. I have a career in Boise. It's kind of hard to commute two hundred and fifty miles a day."

He sensed the silence building between them.

"I miss you terribly." He looked across the table at her.

"Why don't you come to Boise? It's warm there. You can find a job."

"And live in an apartment in the middle of a hundred thousand people? No thanks! I'm a falconer, Shelly. I need to live in a place like this. If anything, it's too damn crowded here." He knew he did not understand it any better than she did.

"Bullshit, bucko! You're just afraid."

"Afraid of what?" He fought down the anger, struggling to comprehend what was happening to him.

"Oh, I don't know, Reese." Her voice softened. "Don't you ever think that there could be more to life than pounding nails and playing with hawks? Didn't you ever want something else really bad?"

Her dark eyes reached into his and Reese felt dizzy with wanting her.

Alone again, Reese intensified his efforts with his merlin. An arctic air mass moved in after Christmas, forcing LaMar to extend the holiday. It was too bitter to work outside, or even to fly his bird, so Reese stayed inside the trailer and carried his bird continually, offering her tidbits throughout the day. The merlin seemed to sense the killing cold just outside the door and responded eagerly. On Saturday, it warmed to a windless twenty degrees. It was time to try again.

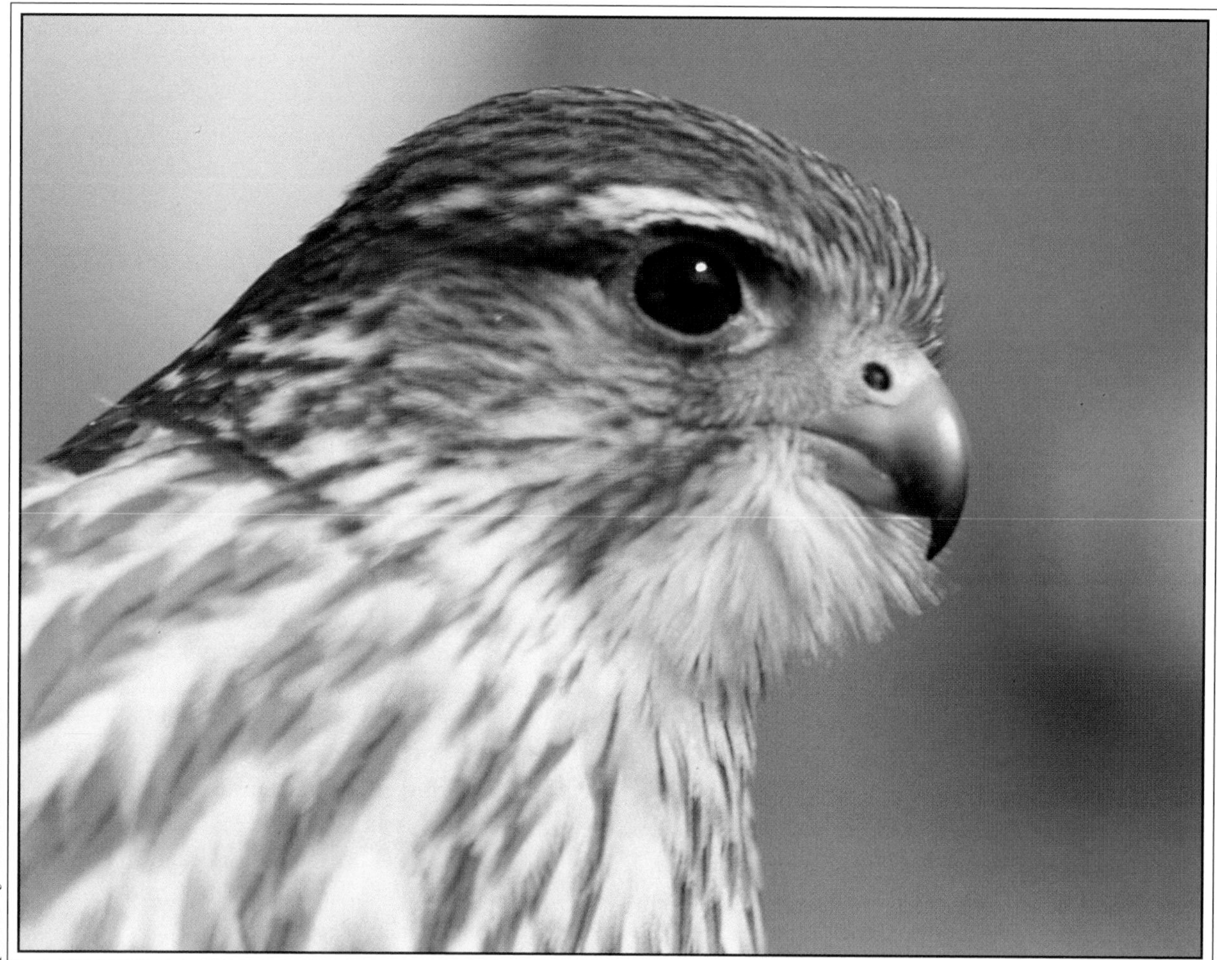

photo by Charles Schwartz

He returned to the open farm land between the town and the feedlot and spent an hour checking power poles. He found a big prairie falcon in the middle of the section, immovable, its deadly presence dominating the entire area. Reese knew it would be foolish to release his merlin as long as the haggard was there, so he parked and waited for something to happen. It didn't take long.

A flatbed truck groaning with haybales crawled slowly down a brushlined drive, flushing three pheasants across an open field. The prairie dropped from the crossarm, and if Reese had not been watching, he never would have seen its white wings flashing inches above the snow. The pheasants set their wings, sailing towards a shelter belt at high speed as the falcon errupted from the earth beneath them with tremendous velocity, throwing itself directly into the last pheasant and riding it into the pines. Reese saw them tumble to the base of the tree, struggling.

The quick and the dead, he thought. *Only the haggards know how to survive this cold.*

For the next hour it would be safe to fly his merlin, unless some other avian shark patrolled these skies. He drove toward the feedlot.

The sun warmed everything that wasn't white. Reese leaned against his truck in the still air, his merlin preening contentedly on his fist. Starlings were beginning to arrive, drawn by the promise of fresh food and a warm place to sleep. He struck the braces and took out her jesses, nervous at the thought of a bate. A small flock flew into view and he removed the hood. The merlin sighted them at once and bobbed her head, pausing only to lean over and rouse. The flock was overhead when she left Reese's fist.

The starlings knew instantly that they were under attack and quickly made for cover, but the merlin flew between them and the ground, forcing the flock into the sky. They recoiled upwards in a tight ball each time the merlin feinted from beneath, like a balloon poked by an invisible finger. The starlings pushed closer to the feedlot, seeking escape beneath the cattle, but each time they started to drop, the merlin forced them back into the air. The fifth time the hawk drove up into the ball, a lone starling separated from the flock and headed straight toward Reese.

He lowered his binoculars to watch it pass fifty feet overhead, his merlin in full pursuit. Up and out they went until he thought surely the black bird had won, but then his merlin began to close, forcing the starling to turn and angle down, the two of them racing toward a pile of junk on a distant rise.

Certain of a kill, Reese jumped into his truck and drove to the dump. He found a rusting combine parked amid piles of lava rock gleaned from the surrounding fields. Two dead cows lay twisted at the end of the lane, their hides shrunken tight against their bones.

Six partridge blew out of the sparse cover, chittering across the snow-covered field, but Reese couldn't find his merlin. He searched under the sagebrush and behind each pile of stones. He looked inside the discarded equipment but could not find a feather or a footprint. A pervasive dread began to settle somewhere above his stomach as the joy of the flight and the certainty of its outcome leaked away, leaving a familiar, aching emptiness behind.

Man, first the prairie, then Shelly, and now this, he thought. *Why do I lose the things that I love?*

"What about us?" he had asked her. The question returned, lurking behind his obsession with the merlin.

"I don't know about us. I only know about me," she had answered.

And the merlin only knows about herself too, he realized. *Is anyone or anything ever really mine?* For a moment, his thoughts fitted together clearly, like something Emmett would say.

He swung his lure, thinking perhaps his falcon had failed to kill and was perched somewhere in the distance, watching, but nothing happened. He stood there, his arms hanging and the lure buried in the snow where it had fallen.

Nothing. Gone.

"You're just afraid!" she had said.

"No!" he shouted. "Not this time!"

Reese stuffed the lure in his pocket and began scanning the fields with his binoculars.

That merlin has made a kill somewhere, he thought, *and I must find her quickly, before she finishes her meal.* He remembered the haggard prairie and glanced at his watch.

Only a few minutes left.

Three quarters of a mile away, two magpies quarreled, their raucous chatter carrying softly across the snow. Reese saw them on the fence posts, then noticed three more flying out from a nearby farm. He peered carefully through the binoculars, but he could not see anything that looked like a merlin.

"Merlins know they are exposed to danger on the snow," Emmett had once told him. *"They will always carry to a safe place to plume and eat their kills."*

Reese ran towards the fenceline.

He found the falcon tucked behind an old cedar fencepost, surrounded by a circle of black feathers. She had gorged herself on the fat starling and was picking at the remains. Reese called her name as he knelt in the snow. The falcon backed away and tried to feak on the ground. Then she scratched the red gore from her beak with one foot.

Reese crawled.

"Shikra!" he whispered. "Ssshikra!"

The merlin looked straight at him and flew away, leaving Reese lying in the snow.

"No!" he shouted. "SHIKRA!"

The merlin turned and sailed back on flattened wings, settling onto the next post. He picked up the remains of the starling, two wings connected by a few threads of sinew, and added them to the piece of meat bulging from his glove.

Reese walked on his knees, not daring to look directly at the bird.

"Shikra!"

Everything hung on the moment. The merlin roused in the sunlight, then picked at her talons as Reese inched closer.

"Shikra! Please." He held out his glove and wiggled the wings with his fingers. The merlin scratched her head and looked away. Reese sensed that if he dared move again, she would be gone.

"Shikra, please," he repeated, softer this time, closing his eyes.

The merlin turned and flew to Reese's fist, bending to pull at the black wings. He offered her warm tidbits and the merlin took them eagerly from his fingers.

It came to him then, as he threaded in the jesses, flooding his heart with a strange mixture of fear and joy. He finished the hookup and coiled the leash, trembling as the emotions raced through him. The merlin feaked and he drew her near, close to his chest. Shikra looked up and Reese hooded her in one seamless movement.

"Tomorrow," he said, knowing what he must do. "Tomorrow."

Pursuit

by Kent L. Christopher

He had always been adventurous, persistent, and enthusiastic about nature.

He was the only one in nursery school able to identify a robin. At thirteen, he had caught and trained a kestrel falcon in preliminary exploration of the art of falconry. His college newspaper published an article titled "Bird Man," which reviewed his studies of nesting ibises, herons, and egrets done for college credit and in collaboration with the state Audubon Society. The interview for this story was conducted while walking a path in the Maine woods, as a trained red-tailed hawk followed through the branches above. The hawk sailed high into the sky when they neared the end of the walk, then folded his wings and shot downward like an arrowhead to land on Bird Man's outstretched fist. This flight foreshadowed many that Bird Man would observe in the future. After college, he moved west, looking for open country where the fastest falcons can really stretch their wings.

Falconry became the glue binding all his major life choices together. From interest to hobby and finally life style, the obstacles inherent in practicing an ancient art in a modern world were overcome. Slowly, an appreciation of the most pure, high energy, and independent life forms on earth evolved.

"Ridiculous," he thought, bumping across a rough section of desert in his truck. Each jolt stressed not only the vehicle, but put his entire nervous system dangerously close to snapping. "I hate this," he knew. "Why the hell am I out here?" he wondered, although there was no doubt about the task at hand.

The day before, Bird Man had lost his falcon. The young bird had been developing well over the past several weeks, flying high, big, and dynamic. Overconfident, the falconer lost his edge. He flew the bird too early in the day. It was too windy, and the falcon had been a half-ounce overweight. "A stupid mistake," he admitted, and mentally kicked himself for making the poor choice. A crazed hunt for a lost falcon was the result of his poor decision. He had searched all afternoon, both from the ground and the air. No "beep, beep, beep" was heard from the telemetry receiver tying him to the small transmitter attached to the errant young falcon. Even from inside the chartered Cessna, thousands of feet in the sky, no signal was raised. Confused, he asked the pilot, "Where can she possibly be?"

"It's your bird," replied the dubious pilot. After their systematic search of several hundreds of square miles, they returned to the airport with no positive results. Bird Man had continued looking from the ground for several hours. After midnight, he returned home. His lovely wife was awake and waiting for him, and there was some solace in that. Her worry had been tempered by the experience of living with a falconer. Expecting the unexpected had become routine. Still, she felt deprived in knowing the young falcon, part of her family, was out in the wilds . . . somewhere.

Competent falconers follow a traditional rule which goes something like this: when looking for a lost hawk, be up and at it by the crack of dawn. Sound reasoning underlies this old practice, but Bird Man was tired, slept in, and was at it not by dawn, but just before noon. Around 1:30 p.m., the sought-after "beep, beep, beep" sounded loud and clear from his receiver. The directional antenna pointed north, and off he chased.

The falcon seemed to be flying, and traveled the air over the rough desert much more easily than Bird Man in his truck. By 4:00 p.m., he was standing on a high knoll, waving his antenna in a northward direction, and listening to a fading beep until the signal was lost. Two possibilities, he concluded: the bird had either landed or was flying and heading

photo by Ronald G. Clarke

away from him. If the former were true, then the falcon should be within five miles. She could be over twenty miles distant if it were the latter. He searched the rest of the day and into the night with no further signal. Evidence was pointing to a bird that had been flying and covering ground, not one that had landed. With a hollow feeling growing in his stomach, Bird Man drove back to his home town.

When he stopped at the local bar for a burger and beer before going home, a man commented as he entered, "Hey Eagle Shits, how's it going? You don't look so good." Bird Man was accustomed to misunderstanding and name-calling. The long, highly respected and honored history of his art was not from the Rocky Mountain West. One old-timer at work liked to refer to his birds as over-sexed canaries! Bird Man politely explained to the local at the bar about his lost falcon and asked if anyone around town had a plane that might take him up in the morning. The country he had to search was far too big to cover adequately from the ground. He got the names of three potential pilots, finished his dinner, and headed home. A morning flight was arranged by phone. He also called his supervisor at work and let him know that he was involved in an important search and might not be around for awhile.

An understanding boss is essential for the falconer who must work for a living. A falconer's wife must be even more supportive, and personality traits commonly associated with saintliness are required of these outstanding ladies. Friends help, but they appear few and far between for the avid falconer, who is often too immersed in his art to see beyond it. Bird Man called his friend, Jake, who was also a falconer and might help him in the search. Other falconers are really more than mere friends, and a mutual interdependency and deep comradeship typically occurs between devotees of the sport. Having no commitments impossible to cancel, Jake quickly agreed to help the next day. He would stay on the ground, ready to take signals from Bird Man up in the plane and, he hoped, retrieve the falcon.

Falconer and pilot took off at 9:00 a.m. the next morning. They flew to the knoll where the signal was last heard. From there, they flew north, covering vast landscapes as they implemented a weaving search pattern. Thirty-four miles north of the knoll, they crossed the Continental Divide at Medicine Lodge Pass. The wide-open sagebrush and grassland were left behind now as they entered the high country with rugged mountains and forests. The small plane flew up a mountain valley, heading northeast. It was elk hunting season, and they spotted several hunters, but no signal was heard from the falcon. In that huge, mountainous expanse, looking for a lost bird seemed much like looking for the metaphorical needle in the haystack. The plane was by now a long way from the knoll where the last signal had been heard. The amount of area to search was becoming overwhelming. Although inspired by the awesome view outside the plane window, Bird Man felt a growing void within as the chances of finding his lost falcon seemed increasingly slim.

The plane continued northeast for twenty miles where the narrow valley opened into a broad north-south plain with a highway running through it. They had planned to turn south and head back, but Bird Man had a hunch. "Let's make a short sweep north," he instructed the pilot. Moments later . . . there it was . . . for sure now . . . the distinct, beeping signal came through the earphones. They made several low passes to approximate the exact location of the falcon, who was apparently standing on or near a rancher's alfalfa field, the greenest thing for miles around.

Throttled up now, they flew south through the broad valley which, forty miles ahead, opened into the expansive Idaho Snake River Plain. Wind, gravity, and full throttle hurled the plane downward, out of the high country and on to the plain, toward a rendezvous with Jake. They circled him, and landed on a nearby airstrip. Quickly, Bird Man gave Jake the telemetry gear with directions to where they had located the bird, and then arranged a meeting place where they would rendezvous again later. Jake drove north and Bird Man flew southeast, back to town to get his truck. Three hours later, he was on the road where the two falconers had planned to meet, but where was Jake?

With no telemetry gear, Bird Man lured for his falcon at several locations along a twenty-mile stretch of highway. It was a long shot at best that the falcon would spot the falconer and respond to his call. He was an insignificant speck in a huge landscape, alone and powerless. Daylight slowly left, and soon it was too dark to lure. Things looked bleak. Perhaps his friend had been more successful. About then, Jake showed up, but he did not have the bird. He told him that when he had arrived in the area hours ago, he had heard a weak signal, but it slowly faded to the northwest and over the mountains. He had tried to catch up, but never heard the signal again. Apparently, the falcon had begun flying and gained considerable altitude, then started to cover ground. Would the falconers ever see her again? Perhaps she was looking for them as hard as they searched for her?

There was an airstrip at the little town of Dell, Montana. A young pilot, the son of a local rancher, agreed to take them up, but only if they flew north and stayed in the valley. "It's too dangerous to fly over the wilderness and mountains at night," he said. The falconers agreed. It was easy to fly safely over the valley. Car lights on the highway, scattered lights from ranches and farms, and clusters of lights from towns marked the way. Everything else was black, except for dark silhouettes of mountains against the starlit sky. They took the plane up high to effectively cover the greatest possible area, but had no luck after two hours of searching. The pilot's father, the rancher, was waiting for the little plane when it taxied back to the hangar. He did not look happy. There was an angry purpose in his every move.

"Where the hell have you been?" he demanded. "Looking for what?! A lost bird?! At night?! In this country?! That's the most stupid thing I've ever heard. Put that plane away and get in the truck. We're going home. Your mother and I have been worried sick, and you're out looking for some bird!" The rancher looked at Jake and Bird Man, saying, "Do you guys work for the Forest Service or Fish and Wildlife or something?" Apparently, he thought that only a government worker could possibly do something that idiotic.

"We're just falconers looking for a lost hawk," said Jake. That was too much for the tried and true Montana rancher.

Explanations stopped. The falconers were courteous and respectful toward the man as they helped put the plane away, then watched father and son drive off in a cloud of dust. They did not even ask if they could try going in the morning.

Jake headed home after that. He had to work the next day and wouldn't be home until after midnight. Bird Man was tired and hungry, and went to the only place open in Dell, Montana at that time, the tavern. While eating frozen pizza fresh out of the microwave and sipping a glass of beer, he got some critical information from the locals about roads and access into the country he planned to check that night. The bird had disappeared to the northwest. That was wild, rugged country with no towns, few ranches, and limited access. Those he talked to had difficulty understanding what could possibly be so important about some bird that a guy would chase it into that country at night. "What would you do," asked Bird Man, "if your young child were kidnaped?" The question communicated his level of determination, but they still wondered why.

He drove all night, stopping every few miles to check for a signal. Standing outside, he waved the antenna through cold night air, especially on high points which extended the reach of his telemetry gear. The truck rolled over two hundred miles of backcountry roads that night, but only twice could he see lights from ranches in the distance. The Bird Man was tired, alone in limitless, wild expanses, and he never heard a signal from his lost falcon. The vacant feeling inside grew strong, but was so dwarfed by the majesty of his surroundings that even the most cold, lonely, inadequate feelings seemed unimportant. He was a part of something much more noble and powerful than that.

Perhaps it was his exhausted state at the time, or the extreme effort he had invested. It might have been the hours of reflecting and remembering the flights he had seen his falcons make at game . . . the stoops from thousands of feet in the air, a living spearpoint throwing herself downward at a flying flock of grouse while he with his pointing dog watched, vicariously experiencing her power. The impact of falcon and grouse, the sky filled with feathers, and after the capture, sitting with his dog next to the successful falcon plucking her prize, somehow this was all of value to him. But was it worth this much?

Is anything worth all you have, and then more? Whatever it was, on that night in the Montana Rockies it had a lasting effect. He was never the same again, and from that moment on he did not just fly hawks, but entered their world wholly. He was as much a part of it all as the hawks, dogs, grouse, sagebrush, hills, and valleys. No longer a mere observer, he was an active participant. His falconry became art, and he lived it fully.

At 6:30 a.m., Bird Man rolled into the Dillon, Montana airport parking lot, and fell asleep in his truck. Two hours later, he arranged to have a local crop duster fly him and his telemetry gear in a last-ditch effort. It was now or never. He had followed the trail too far to call it quits at this point.

Bird Man attached his directional antenna to the strut of the high-winged Cessna using duct tape. The coaxial cable ran from the antenna, down the strut, and into the cockpit through the door. They were ready to go. It was 9:30 a.m. The small plane climbed into the sky, with the telemetry receiver turned on. Bird Man listened intently through the earphones for any hint of that telltale signal. He directed the search through verbal communication with the pilot. Methodically, they covered vast landscapes, making huge sweeps with the radio telemetry.

Mountain ranges, valleys, rivers, and hills stretched out below them in an inspiring display of what remains of the undefined American West. The tiny plane appeared like a gnat flying through a big, beautiful garden, seemingly insignificant, but as much a part of it all as anything else.

The pilot knew the country well. He responded expertly to Bird Man's directions: "Let's make a high run over those hills," or "Let's sweep up the east, then back down the west side of that valley." The pilot was a pro, and his plane seemed like an extension of himself. Bird Man tried to think like his lost hawk. "Where would I be?" he asked himself. All likely areas were checked. Two hours later, after covering thousands of square miles, no signal had been detected.

"Why are you looking so hard for this falcon?" asked the pilot. He and Bird Man somehow seemed close. They worked effectively together. Maybe crop dusters and falconers have something in common by being just a half a bubble out of plumb with the rest of society.

"She's quite a bird with great potential. I've put a lot into her," responded Bird Man. "Ya know, my favorite birds to work with are goshawks and gyrfalcons. Both live in severe conditions and have extraordinary determination. Chase is the name of the game. They pursue with way more intensity than anything else. Ya don't think any of that might have rubbed off on me?" asked the falconer with a sly grin on his face.

"I doubt it," responded the crop duster.

Pointing to a rugged and tall range of mountains, Bird Man asked, "What mountains are those?"

"The Beaverheads. It's the Continental Divide. On the other side is the Birch Creek Valley. We can probably cross over about ten miles south," he said.

"Let's give it a try," replied Bird Man. The plane banked south over rough and wild country. They turned west after flying ten miles, and flew through a narrow mountain pass which opened into a gorgeous seventeen-mile-wide valley. "Let's turn north and fly right down the middle of it," suggested the Bird Man. They covered thirty miles of the valley, and were about to turn east through another mountain pass and head back to the airport. That would be the end of it, failure, a lost falcon. At that instant, when all seemed hopeless . . . beep, beep, beep . . . "There she is! I've got her! We've flown by her now. Let's turn around and make some low passes." The signal was weak, but after three sweeps they had her location pinpointed along a creek.

"It will take me over four hours to fly back to Dillon, get my truck, and drive to this spot," commented Bird Man. "She could be over the next mountain range by then. Can you land this thing right here?"

"Let's take a look," said the pilot. They made some low runs over a nearby road. After checking for fence, other obstructions, and a place to park the plane, the pilot said, "Looks like I can set her down about a mile up from where the bird is at."

"Let's do it," replied Bird Man.

"Watch for cars," said the pilot. They let several pass, saw a break in traffic, and set the small plane down in front of a traveling motorist a half mile behind. They taxied off the road. Bird Man grabbed his telemetry, jumped out, and waved down the motorist as the pilot secured his plane.

"Can you give me a lift about a mile down the road?" he asked the surprised motorist. "We are trying to recover a lost falcon."

"Uh, sure, hop in," said the driver, unsure of just what in the hell was going on. Having grown up out east near New York City, Bird Man appreciated a helping hand from strangers, even if they could not understand why his birds and goals were so important. Just seeing that it mattered was enough for some to give support, something rarely done where he was from. They drove a mile down the road, stopped, and Bird Man jumped out. He ran toward the creek, swinging his lure. Moments later, the white falcon flew in and landed. The falconer clipped her up and let her feed. She had been lost for four days, and she was hungry. The errant falcon had covered hundreds of miles, crossed four mountain ranges and flown over some of the most beautiful landscapes on earth. Indescribable feelings of relief and accomplishment welled up inside the falconer, filling the previous void. A lot of grouse hawking, something to look forward to, was back again.

The pilot came up as the falcon ate her meal. "Looks like you got her back," he said.

"Thanks to you!" said the exuberantly grateful falconer. "You did a great job, and it worked. I'll put a hood on her when she's done eating. She'll ride quietly on the way back to the airport." The pilot and Bird Man walked the mile back to the plane with the hooded falcon standing proudly on the falconer's fist. "Look at that transmitter on her leg," he said, "the antenna wire is almost gone. We're lucky we found her at all."

Money, smiles, and profuse expressions of gratitude were used to pay off the crop duster pilot. He had performed with excellence and was an all-around great guy. Bird Man loaded everything into his truck back at the airport and headed down the road. He stopped for lunch, his first real sit-down meal in over three days. With exhaustion closing in around him, he drove south. On the Continental Divide, the border between Montana and Idaho at Monida Pass, he turned off the road and went to sleep. The drive home would have to be completed later.

Gus

by Victor Hardaswick

On a desolate, late winter afternoon, Gus headed out across the pastures, working the brush, kicking weeds, searching for a cottontail. It would be different now. For the first time in many years, his hound, Old Blue, wasn't along on the hunt.

The goshawk, named Tinkerbell, and Old Blue had worked out a routine. Once the dog had jumped a rabbit, he kept it moving and running in a straight line, setting it up for the pursuing hawk. A working rapport had developed over the years. Each keyed in on the other, making for success. Once the chase was on, Gus would lean back and watch them work, finding satisfaction in their teamwork and watching the intense drama unfold before him.

Dogless now and searching for quarry, Gus gingerly threaded his way through a small briar patch. Suddenly a rabbit bolted. The gos, who was standing on tiptoe on Gus's glove and bobbing her head, shot off in a blinding flash. It was a twisting, turning flight through the brush, under the corral fence, just missing as she crashed on the rabbit near the old hay bales. The gos was up again and on her way as the rabbit broke down the path through the raspberries and headed into a brush pile heaped at the base of the dead ash tree. The determined bird pitched high up into the tree, intently peering with glaring red eyes through the maze of branches beneath her, searching for the slightest movement of bunny fur.

Following the flight as best he could, Gus approached the perched bird, his gaze focused on the eye of the goshawk, orange-red and fierce. In it Gus saw the embodiment of all that she was, the spirit, the intensity, the fire. Someone once said, "The eye is the window of the soul." Nothing could be more true, Gus thought, as he saw the goshawk's piercing eyes discerning her world. At the base of the tree, Gus jumped up and down on the brush pile, hooting and yelling. The rabbit made a break through the weeds, across the pasture and down the slope toward the roadway. Instantaneously, the gos rocketed into full chase, hurtling out of the tree, down the hill and over the frozen landscape after the fleeting brown blur. As they approached the end of the pasture, the gos pitched up, did a wingover, and crashed on the fleeing bunny, who at the last instant reflexively dodged to the right under the fence and safety. The closing bird slammed headlong into the barbed wire.

The loud twang, followed by a penetrating, foreboding vibration, was clearly perceived by Gus, who was still standing near the rabbit's former sanctuary. He quickly covered the hundred-odd yards between them. Kneeling down in the snow, Gus gently lifted his wounded partner in his powerful hands. Cradling her close to his chest, he saw her striking grey and silver plumage highlighted by those magnificent eyes lit by pulsating flashes of bright orange-red. "My God, she is so beautiful . . . ," he thought. Holding her gently, Gus willed her to live. As he knelt there by the edge of the field, Gus felt her heart jump and noticed a tiny drop of blood ooze from her nares. Her body convulsed momentarily, then was still. A whitish membrane slid slowly over her eyes. The goshawk's body remained, but the fire and life were gone from those flashing eyes forever.

Tears welled up in Gus's eyes. For the second time in less than a week, he had lost a dear old friend. Tenderly cradling the lifeless goshawk in his large arms, Gus headed home. A thin cover of crusty snow crunched beneath his boots. Plodding along, he reflected on their life together. Only a few short days ago he had lost his partner Old Blue, and now his remaining hunting companion was also gone.

Old Blue had been a black-blanketed, long-eared, bawl-mouth beagle, descendant of a long line of field champions (Pearson Creek Blue was his given name). He'd been a "walk and talk" hound with lots of mouth.

The twelve-year-old dog had lived free about the place. He could generally be found dozing in the sun, out of the wind on that pile of straw that always seemed to clutter up the yard. Blue could always be depended upon to announce the arrival of the mail or the gas man as they made their rounds. He usually outdid himself howling at the UPS truck as it rattled into the yard before indignantly marking the wheel. Then, jauntily trotting away, Blue was confident he had defended the Holy Grail. He was quite a dog.

When the urge struck Old Blue, often in the evening, he ambled off down the pasture near the old foundation left over from the barn that the tornado took in the wild spring of '62. Finding a rabbit, round and round they'd go, fading off toward the river before circling back near the weed-choked feedlot and then off again.

Gus often used to lie in bed on warm nights, windows wide open, listening to Blue run bunnies by the hour. One night while Gus was listening to the beagle, the heavens beckoned to him. The northern lights lit the sky up with spectacular flashes of light, and the stars were dancing overhead. Gus woke Maggie and pointed out the beauty of the heavens to her. Grumbling about having been awakened, she looked out at the spectacle. Unable to appreciate the intrinsic value of the experience, she wearily shook her head, wondering who in their right mind would come to this godforsaken place. Maggie slumped back into bed, pulled the pillow over her head, and mumbled something about not being able to get any sleep. Trying to repress Gus's rambling and the infernal baying of the dog, she thought Gus had finally lost it. "Gone round the bend," she muttered to herself.

"It sure beats counting sheep," Gus countered, thinking she sure complained a lot these days. He and Maggie had begun, he thought, as one. But as the years passed, they seemed to grow in different directions. "She seems to complain about most everything I love and enjoy," he thought. If it wasn't Old Blue bawling, then it was about the rooster heralding a new day.

Blue hadn't been in his usual spot when Gus got ready to fly Tinker on that warm January day. When Blue didn't respond to Gus's whistles (he didn't hear as well these days), Gus looked for him. Blue's tracks led from the straw pile down the bank near the wild raspberry patch and over toward the river bottom. "Damn dog is never around when it's time to go," muttered Gus, as he stumbled along. The tracks led toward the east pasture fence and then by the overgrown roll of fencing that never did get picked up last spring. Finally, the tracks merged with those of a rabbit. The bounding tracks of hare and hound led over the hill and through the old sunflower patch, straight through the weeds to the edge of the ice and then across the river toward the north bank.

What had happened was clear. Every year during the January thaw, the river would briefly awaken. Little rivulets appeared near the rapids and then disappeared under the ice into the deep mill pool. Intent on the chase, Blue had gotten too close, the thin ice had given way, and he had broken through. His deep scratch marks were evident around the hole. Unable to pull himself out, he'd finally slipped beneath the ice. The aged man read the obvious signs. He knew that his old friend had died while doing something he loved. There was some comfort in that.

Gus also knew from his years in the field that in nature the death of one creature ultimately provided sustenance for another. Somewhere downstream, when the ice receded and the water warmed, new life would spring forth. There was some solace too in the knowledge that the end had come quickly for his old friend, and was not the tormenting demise of some malignancy.

Heading home with the dead goshawk, Gus pondered the intense blow of losing both hunting partners within such a short time. Arriving home, he gently placed the bird on a shelf perch in her mews attached to his home. This room, which she had occupied for nearly twenty years, had been the starting point of countless hours of pleasure in the field. Now its emptiness seemed absolute.

Gus trudged into the darkening house, through the kitchen and into the den. The room was quiet. The memorabilia of a lifetime surrounded him, pictures of his wife and kids, pictures of Tinker and Blue, as well as those of other hawks and dogs long gone. There was the snapshot of his two sons, Cody holding Gus's first goshawk (the one he took during the big invasion year of 1960) and Jeff holding the old basset hound, Jubel, and the rooster pheasant they had caught on that red- letter day in the late fall of '64. That was a long time ago.

Gus had always hoped that his sons would catch the falconry bug, but it didn't work out that way. Oh, they used to go out hunting with him and sure seemed to have fun, but they had never become immersed in the art, as he had. Perhaps it's just as well, he thought. They still enjoyed the outdoors, hunting and fishing as time permitted. Maybe they had learned something, after all.

The boys had attended local schools and graduated from the state university. They were off now in other states, married and living their own lives. One was a welder, the other worked for the phone company. They wanted normal work, "eight hours a day, forty hours a week," they had said, not wanting to be tied to the place scratching in the dirt and chasing critters. They couldn't stand being prisoners of the weather and the banker like the old man. Gus mused at the irony. They wanted to be free, not tied down, yet neither one of them could make it alone. Their wives had to work and send the kids off to day care, yet still they struggled.

It sure hadn't been like that for him. No matter how hard it had been, through the good times and the bad, his kids had been raised at home by a caring mother. Somehow, there was always enough food on the table, bills were paid, time was left to do things together. Gus had raised his family like his father before him. With the Lord's help, they had plowed the earth, coaxed food from the ground, smelled the new-mowed hay and worked the cattle. Those had been simpler times.

Gus had met Maggie when he was twenty and she eighteen. She was pretty, and they had enjoyed one another, fell in love and married. When the young couple moved to their little place near the river, Maggie had looked forward to leaving the city where she had grown up. Together they fixed the old place up – a coat of paint here, a few flowers there. It was tidy and comfortable and it fit their needs then. In the beginning, while Maggie raised the boys and he worked the place, life was satisfying and time-consuming. Their time together seemed good. Gus always managed to bring Maggie a little something on those special days, and she returned a smile and a word of encouragement.

The birds had been there from the beginning, and Maggie supposed that they had always been a part of Gus's life. At first, she was happy he did something he enjoyed so much. "Somehow, Gus finds solace in falconry," Maggie would tell her mother. "He's always around the place, taking an hour here or there to work with his bird." Many gourmet meals of duck and rabbit resulted from his hunting. Game, sautéed in wine with the meadow mushrooms they gathered and served on a bed of wild rice, sure was good. They had dipped fresh-baked bread in the gravy and washed it down with a glass of the plum or elderberry wine that was always aging in the cellar. Those were happy times.

As the boys grew, things gradually began to change between Gus and Maggie. At first, it was little things that seemed to cause the friction — Gus spending too much time with his bird, feathers or fur from butchered quarry left in the sink, or an occasional hawk mute and the ever present mud tracked over the floor. Then Maggie began to verbalize what was really bothering her. "We're in a rut.

We never get out of here; we never have enough money; why don't you get a real job, make enough money so things aren't such a struggle?" She would often say, "If you put all the time and effort into a real job that you put into this place and those damn birds, we would have enough money and free time so we could do things together and live like normal people."

When they were first married and the kids were small, the lack of the usual modern conveniences, the clothes and the other tangibles of the affluent world didn't seem so important to Maggie. Then the relationship cooled and her needs seemed to change. Maggie was no longer happy with just enough to get by. She wondered, "Is this what life is all about? What have I got to show for all these years? I'll be dead in twenty or thirty years and look at me," she thought. In the beginning, she mused, it had seemed wonderful in its own way, the love and the excitement without the stress of city life. Eventually, it felt like being buried alive out in the middle of nowhere. Maggie finally vented her frustration. "I can compete with a barroom, even with another woman, but there is something about those damn birds and the loneliness out here that completely defeats me."

But Gus thought they had everything they needed. "You've got everything right here," he would boast. "There's a sense of liberation living here, it courses through your veins."

"It's too damn barren out here, a moonscape," replied Maggie.

"It's like fine Scotch whiskey, an acquired taste. Anything you can't find here you can do without," Gus countered. He figured she was just going through mid-life crisis — maybe needed some estrogen therapy, he had joked. As far as he was concerned, they had each other, the ground, the sky, the wide-open space, their health and their faith. What else really matters? Maggie never did understand what he was talking about, he supposed. Gus still wondered what Maggie had needed and searched for.

Maggie finally left. That had been over five years ago and it was tough, especially at first. Gus had busied himself with his chores and his bird, and eventually things improved, but he never completely recaptured the old joy of living.

During brief moments of reflection, Gus often thought back to those happier days when, in his dry way, he would respond to friends' questions about how he got his wife to put up with the loneliness way out there, and with his hawking.

Gus had often replied with an owlish grin breaking over his face, "Wives are like an endangered species. If they can't adapt, they become extinct." They would all laugh then. Now, that statement haunted him.

As Gus reflected on his past, feeling the recent loss of his two cherished hunting companions, he gazed out the picture window at the molten-gold sun setting on the harsh winter landscape. His posture slumped with the realization that he was too old and too tired to begin over again. What was left? As he struggled, alone with his feelings, the sudden flicker of a wingbeat in the twilight outside caught his eye. A hunting sharpshin flashed in among a flock of sparrows feeding on seed scattered across the snow beneath the window feeder. As this tiny raptor seized a hapless victim, dragging it beneath the old lilac bush to begin her meal, Gus was reminded of the wisdom of his friend, Joseph Spotted Eagle, the old Cheyenne shaman whom he had met many times over the years out on the high plains. Joseph often spoke of the prairie, "where the wind was full of spirits, the spirits of ancestors who still live out there." Joseph appreciated the power Gus had to "reach into the sky." He counseled Gus to use his power wisely, to live harmoniously within the natural order.

The old shaman had explained the ways of the elite of the Cheyenne who counted coup. To get close enough to touch an enemy and return unharmed was the highest honor one could achieve. The true measure of the brave was the number of feathers on his coup stick, each signifying that touch without the kill.

It was a concept that conformed with Gus's own philosophy of the hunt, which had evolved after many years of partnership with Tinker and Blue. At first, it was the kill that seemed important — the more the better. The impetuosity of the young man, hawk and dog eventually gave way to maturity and the realization of where they all fit into the natural order. Gradually, the kill became less important and whenever possible, the quarry was released unharmed. When life was taken, Gus developed a reverent attitude, showing profound esteem toward the fallen quarry for giving itself to the hunt. He sensed his own mortality, knowing that he too was just a small part of a big world. Gus had his own ways of thanking the Great Spirit for providing the awesome, terrifying but wonderful life experience.

Gus gradually had come to believe that he had grown more into a fully functioning human being by learning the ways of nature. Through hunting, Gus had been witness to unspeakable beauty. He had observed and learned to appreciate the awesome complexity and inspiring power of nature. In the process, he had found some of the pieces of excitement and awe that fit together for him. This process of learning to value the hunt (the coup) more than the end result (the kill) allowed him to discover the esoteric but living thread of continuity that linked him to nature and to his misty origins in the Pleistocene.

As he again focused his attention on the feeding hawk who was busy with her meal, he realized that the crepuscular hunting of this tiny hawk had stirred dormant feelings. From deep within, a belief that maybe, just maybe . . . Gus got up and trudged out to the storeroom where he dug out his old bal chatri, a trap that had caught many hawks over the years. Back inside, he straightened out the crushed nylon nooses. Morning would arrive soon.

photo by S. Kent Carnie

The Pumphouse

by Jim Nelson

"Dan?"

"No."

"What do you mean 'no,' you haven't heard the question yet!"

"I overheard Debra on the phone with Kelly last night. I'm not letting her drive to California, Jen, she's just a kid."

"She's not. She's seventeen years old and has a good head on her shoulders. And they won't be alone, Kelly's aunt and uncle will be with them."

I shifted the truck into fourth gear and shot my wife my best exasperated look. She countered with her best inscrutable stare. I glanced at my watch. If we didn't get to the pumphouse soon, it would be too late to fly the falcons.

"So . . . they'd be traveling with Kelly's aunt and uncle? Sounds good to me."

Squinting at Jen I saw suspicion there.

"By the way," I asked casually, "you meet them yet?"

"Yes."

"So, out of curiosity, how old are Aunty and Unk?"

"Mid-twenties, I guess," she muttered, drumming her fingers on the dash and scowling out the window. Spokane fell behind us as we shot past the downtown exits.

I let it drop. Winners should be gracious, don't you think?

A station wagon of Boy Scouts zoomed past. Suddenly red lights flared, and the back of the wagon swerved, falling back. Soon a half dozen Scouts, noses to window, stared into our truck, mouths forming "o's", and fingers pointing.

"Dan, one of these days some rubbernecker is going to kill us over those birds," said Jennifer, shaking her head.

"Know wattcha mean, babe." I smiled and waved at the Scouts. "Remember the time that El Dorado nearly drove us off the road."

My wife flashed a smile at the memory, then it faded.

"That was when we had Dewey, wasn't it?"

I nodded, sorry to bring up a painful memory. Dewey was Jennifer's first hawk, a beautiful red-tail. He had lost his life landing on a power pole.

I reached for her hand, small, warm, and familiar.

"Hey, no regrets. If you got 'em fly 'em, right? You got to let go of the jesses. If you don't take risks the birds never develop."

"You're right. But I miss him."

Glancing into the rearview mirror I could see the falcons perched in back. They looked fine. I stared up the interstate, my mind on red-tailed hawks and power poles, teenage girls and California.

The next exit brought us to the West Plains. At one end stood Spokane Airport, and facing it across several miles of open wheat fields and uncultivated land, Fairchild Air Force Base.

Besides jets and planes, the skies above were graced with another kind of flying machine, the trained falcon. Local falconers gathered here like ducks to water. An ideal training ground, the great expanse of empty land held good numbers of Hungarian partridges. Skirting the largest section, we strained to spot birds. No luck.

"It's up to Cutter," Jenny commented as we nosed down a narrow dirt lane into the field.

"Let's hope he points a covey fast, or we won't have daylight," I answered.

"There's the pumphouse!" exclaimed Jenny.

The pumphouse, old, weathered and

long abandoned, loomed majestically above this deserted land.

"Hallelujah, Jen! Looks like we got the place to ourselves," I chuckled gleefully, pulling the truck to a halt.

"Thank goodness! Last time we had to take a number to get the birds in the air. But I wish the wind would die down. Bet that's why no one else is here. Should we risk it?"

"Sissies," I sneered, "if the birds get blown downwind we'll grab the telemetry and track 'em down."

"I know. But I worry. Anything can happen in between. While you're trying to get a fix on the signal, the bird could be sitting on a kill near the road just waiting to get hit; or it could land near some hunters and be shot; or you could arrive too late and an owl might catch it out after dark."

She was right. Every time falconers released their feathered friends any of a multitude of things could go wrong. I had my own way of looking at it. To me, not to fly was the greater tragedy. No guts, no glory.

"Jen, if you've got a feeling, don't be swayed by me. You know how hardcore I am. Every falconer has to make his own choice. In the end, that's what you live with. Like being a parent."

My wife gave me a long measured look.

"All right, Dan, you've made your point. On both issues."

Jennifer slid from the cab, strode to the back, reached into the canopy, and eased her tiercel hybrid Athos off the traveling cadge. Next she fished through her game vest and extracted a small baggy, pulling from it a generous quantity of deep red pigeon breast. With practiced ease Jennifer teased the hood braces open and slipped the bird's head gear down and away from its face.

Athos looked about curiously. Jennifer made a small squeaking sound and contracted her fingers inside the leather glove. Athos glanced at his feet, then quickly gobbled at the meal. Within moments the food vanished and a bulge appeared in his crop.

A falcon with a full stomach was not safe to fly, especially in the wind. Jennifer had made her decision.

"Okay, Mr. No Guts No Glory, let's see what Lady De Winter can do today."

Jennifer returned Athos to the cadge and I eased my peregrine falcon, Lady, from her perch. Together we worked to attach the two tracking transmitters to her legs, just in case.

At last I turned to the large airline carrier at the back of the truck bed. Inside, Cutter sensed his time had come and danced with excitement.

Jenny laughed.

"Listen to him, a one-man band, whining, scratching, and thumping all at the same time."

I grinned and readied myself for the coming explosion.

"Whoa, Cutter, whoa!!"

The setter blew out of the kennel and skidded to a halt at the edge of the tailgate. I leased him and braced myself.

"Heel, Cutter! Good boy. Holy criminy, Jenny, walking this mutt is like walking a moose. Help me out."

Jenny took the lead from my hand.

"Good Cutter," she crooned.

Cutter gave a good-natured grin, then resumed lunging ahead.

"Sit, Cutter."

Cutter sat.

"Oh, you're such a good boy," Jennifer praised. The poor dog dropped to his belly and quivered with excitement.

She reached down, unclipped the leash and Cutter froze, ears cocked forward, eyes straight ahead. Her hand crept behind his skull and tapped him between the ears.

"Birds!"

If you've cheered thoroughbreds through the gates, you've seen Cutter on birds. His white form flowed through the field.

We hiked the golden stubble into the

wind until suddenly Cutter froze.

"What do you think?" Jennifer hissed.

"Looks good to me," I whispered back.

Unclipping Lady, I slipped the hood and let her breast the wind. A seasoned hunter, she immediately launched and began a steady spiraling ascent.

You can write about it, talk about it, or videotape it, but only out there can you feel the breeze, smell the loam, and gaze at the marble statue that's your dog, domed head high, plumed tail curving gracefully over a heavily muscled pair of thighs, and ribs peeking coyly from a coat of porcelain white.

And six hundred feet above you is the falcon, wings swept tight and pumping rapidly, pausing only for a quick rouse. Then she's back on task, waiting on.

The moment is yours. Elements in place, they wait your command: the decision to urge dog forward, to send partridges bursting up, to unleash a lightning-bolt downwind plunge from the falcon guaranteed to devastate anything in its path.

Drink it in.

"All right, Cutter! Get 'em out!"

Then . . . unbelievable disaster!

"What's wrong, Dan?"

"I can't believe it! A false point! Cutter, how could you?"

Cutter, a guilty look and nose to the ground, rushed in frantic circles.

Upstairs the falcon, now bored, swept downwind.

"Come on, Cutter, find 'em!," I shouted.

"Get 'em, Cutter! You can do it!" Jenny urged.

"This isn't working, Jen. Cutter blew it."

"Lady's way out of position, Dan. Better bring her in."

I yanked the lure out of my vest and tossed it high. The distant rowing wings never missed a beat.

"No good, Jen. She sees something."

This wasn't good. We sprinted to the truck, stopping only to 'glass' Lady with binoculars. Now a speck in the gathering dusk, she continued to sail downwind. Suddenly, she dropped from sight.

"Lordy! Dan, did you see that stoop?"

"Yeah. Did you mark her down?"

"Behind those trees west of the base."

"That's too close to the main road back to town. Let's get over there, now!"

We piled in and roared off.

"Careful, Dan! It won't do any good to kill us before we get there."

Arriving at the trees, I had to wait for a break in traffic to hop out with the radio gear. Moments before we had been standing in an empty field. Now we faced a major thoroughfare. It seemed unreal.

"You can't help her lying in the morgue in a body bag, honey."

Taking that as my signal to go, I darted between vehicles to reach the far road bank. Rush hour drivers gawked at the lone lunatic holding a small blue box in one hand and frantically waving an aerial over his head with the other. At that moment the little blue box was my only link with Lady De Winter. The box, the aerial, and the faint but steady beep, beep, beep.

A weak signal. If she were down it would be blasting from here.

"Good news, and bad," I announced, lunging back into traffic and swerving across the main highway onto a small northbound two-laner.

"The good news is, she's all right. The bad news is, she missed her kill and she's on the move."

"More good news, and bad, Dan Brown. The good news is we're still alive. The bad news is we won't be for long if you don't keep your eyes on the road!"

"The strongest signal's due north, so she's moving downwind," I explained, ignoring the shot. Soothing transmitter signals flooded the cab.

"I don't know where, Lady, but I know you're there. Wait for papa!"

Jenny gave my hand a squeeze. Suddenly, she raised her arm for silence.

"Listen!"

I concentrated.

"You're right. They're getting louder. She's backtracking!"

We both craned our necks out the window, but no luck.

Slamming on the brakes, I was up the bank and seeking a signal in the time it takes most people to tie their shoes.

Returning, I found Jennifer in the driver's seat. She cautiously eased onto the deserted road.

"She's flying due south into the wind," I reported, reluctantly conceding the helm. "Her signal fluctuates. It keeps getting louder, then fainter, then louder again. She's riding an aerial roller coaster. When she dips behind a rise the signal fades. Then she shoots up into the breeze and the signal gets intense again. She's out there playing games and we're down here tearing our hair out. Could you for-crying-out-loud speed this thing up?"

Please, Lady, I thought fervently, don't go near any hunters . . . or poles . . . or roads.

"Oh, man! The hazards out there. Debra doesn't have a chance!"

My wife, silent, kept her eyes on the road.

We drove on, not talking, hypnotized by the rhythmic chirping of the signals. And then they were gone.

"Damn! We lost it! We've got to get it back! It's getting dark. FOR PETE'S SAKE LET'S GO!!!"

"You're worried about owls," Jenny stated, shifting gears and swinging out to pass cars in front of us. "Don't worry, Dan, we'll find her."

More than reassurance, I appreciated seeing the speedometer needle swinging to the right. Jennifer had seen what owls could do.

"We've got to get to higher ground . . . fast!"

"Where?"

"Let's try that fill mound south of here. With height I should regain the signal."

Jenny eased into the construction site. With the acrid smell of dirt in my nostrils I scrambled up the mound, slipping twice, clawing loose gravel for balance.

On top I scanned the twilight with binoculars. None of the bird silhouettes on the horizon fit the form or wing beat of a peregrine. One had a decidedly owlish look.

There was no time to waste. Holding my breath I began to methodically sweep with the yagi. Aggressive static, no beep.

What's going on? I wondered. The batteries are fresh. Maybe she landed and bit the transmitters. But both at once?

"Come on! Talk to me!" I roared impotently. But the wind and darkness did not answer.

Back in the truck Jenny counseled, "Stop thinking like a ham radio operator. If you were Lady, where would you go?"

"I'd . . . of course! The field!! It's dark; she's tired, hungry and seeking us out. She probably flew straight back to where the flight began."

A short time later we hunched close to the receiver at the field's edge, straining for sound. Nothing.

"So much for falconer instincts."

"I'm sorry. Should we keep cruising until . . . (bleep) . . . Wait!! What's that? Dial up the gain."

(bleep)

Standing on tiptoe and holding the yagi high, I rotated slowly to the right.

"Nothing. Wrong direction."

I swiveled to the left, swinging the boom through the blowing darkness.

(bleep)

"There! Now more to the left."

beep

"Still more."

Beep!

"Again . . ."

BEEP, BEEP, BEEP

"That's it, Dan, coming right from . . ."

"Of course! The pumphouse itself! That old hulk has more missing windows and gaping walls than a tenement slum. Bet she slipped inside for shelter. No wonder we lost the signal."

We raced through the dark to the pumphouse.

The ride home should have been jolly, but on the freeway Jenny grew pensive.

"I'm glad she's back, Dan. I was afraid we'd never see her again."

"Oh heck, Jen, I shouldn't have made such a fuss. I should've known she'd return. The pumphouse is home. She'll always come home."

"Dan?"

"No."

She sighed. "Thought I'd give it one last try."

I hadn't forgotten Debra either, though I'd managed to put it out of mind awhile. Why was I always the heavy?

My daughter didn't make things easier.

"Hi, Mom. Hi, Daddy. No luck, huh? But you got 'em back. Is that why you're late? Did one fly off? Which one? De Winter? Lady, you wicked thing, you'll give Daddy a new crop of grey hair. Here, let me help you with your game vest, Mom. Dad, can I put Cutter in the kennel?"

I rolled my eyes, "Why me?" at Jennifer. She shrugged her shoulders, "Tough taters," in response.

Later, in the brightly lit kitchen, cookies and milk all around:

"Daddy, remember I told you Kelly has an aunt studying to be a vet at U.S.C. Davis?"

(What do you mean "no," you haven't heard the question yet.)

"Well, she and her husband are up for a visit. They're young, but I know you'll like them. They're going back this weekend, and Kelly is going with them. But the really exciting part is they invited me too! Can you believe it? I've always wanted to see the Davis campus! Daddy, I know it's asking a lot, but can I go? I'll be all right, I promise."

(Don't go near any gun hunters . . . or poles . . . or roads!)

My tongue and throat rasped like sandpaper. I hated this. Some day she'd understand; she'd appreciate the tough choice I made. I took a deep swallow of cold whole milk. It tasted like tap water.

"Debbie, honey, I know how much this must mean to you. . ."

(You have to risk, or the birds won't develop.)

". . . and you know Mom and I trust you . . ."

(You've got to let go the jesses.)

Jenny caught my eye.

(If you got 'em, fly 'em!)

". . . so, it's like the old saying, pumpkin . . ."

"I know, 'No guts, no glory,' right? Dad, are you telling me I can go?"

(The pumphouse is home. She'll always come home.)

"Yeah, little girl . . . I guess I am."

There remain things in life as satisfying as a good falcon flight . . . like a tight, warm squeeze from a happy teenage girl.

The Prodigal

By Kenn Filkins

Jon Cullberg always greeted the last day of the hawking season with a mixture of excitement and sorrow. The final day was to be savored like ruffed grouse served with wine sauce. Jon knew that brisk days afield with his goshawk on the fist and grouse in flight would be replaced by muggy months with mosquitos abuzz. Not a pleasant thought.

Jon swept aside the thought of mosquitos with the morning paper, took a drink of his coffee and walked over to the patio door. Outside Diann filled the birdfeeders as the long shadows cast from the tall oaks, aspens and birch stretched across the snow. Jon watched as each of her breaths hung on the still air in front of her face like tiny clouds, then, one by one, disappeared. The snow, hardened from a week of sub-zero cold, crunched under her feet as she approached the door.

Jon Cullberg tucked the sports section under his arm and slid the door open for her. Diann glanced at the paper under his arm but said nothing. They both knew what it said and it too contained a mixture of excitement and sorrow.

STATE WRESTLING
TOURNAMENT HOLDS SURPRISES

Mt. Pleasant, Michigan (AP) — The Clare Pioneers, this season's surprise team, scored another upset victory at Rose Arena. Led by senior Kevin Cullberg, Clare is poised to win its first state championship today.

Cullberg, ranked second in the state at 189 pounds, pinned Troy Stein of Three Rivers in 3 minutes and 3 seconds.

Tonight Cullberg will wrestle number one ranked William Jefferson of Flint. Whatever the outcome, Cullberg's climb to the top has been staggering in this, his first year of competitive wrestling.

"Kevin (Cullberg) may be the best natural wrestler coming out of Michigan this year," said a scout from the University of Iowa . . . .

"Bitter out there again today." Jon spoke first. He had tried to sound casual but his words fell out like silverware.

"I'm worried about my snow-birds and chickadees," Diann responded in flat tones.

"It's a wonder anything can survive in this weather," Jon said, forcing away the silence that had become too common lately.

"Didn't you tell me that horned owls are nesting now?" Diann asked, sounding more natural and walking over near Jon.

"Yes," Jon answered without turning from the glass door. "They're the only thing more deadly than winter."

"Can we hang the wind chime Aunt Janet gave us last Christmas?" Diann asked slipping her hand under Jon's arm. "She's coming tomorrow for Sunday dinner. . . ."

"Why do we need a wind chime when we have bells?" Jon asked. "Falconry bells. . ."

"Wait, I know this one," she insisted, raising her hand and continuing in a voice that sounded like the public address announcer at K-mart. "Falconry bells — small acorn-shaped spheres of hollow metal that create a piercing shrill. For centuries, these bells have signaled the predatory union of man and bird. And if you will go to the flashing blue light in aisle number . . ."

"Enough, I get the idea," Jon said. "But I can sit here and tell you what the hawk is doing just by the ring of his bells — like Morse code from the bird. A hard rattle means the hawk's struggling to fly after a squirrel that ran into view. The hawk will be at the end of the leash, flapping wildly. An erratic tinkling — like a baby hitting a pan with a spoon — means the hawk is tinkering with the pine cones off our spruce. A ring like a telephone means he's calmly scratching his beak. . . . A short, faint ring means a rouse."

"You act like I've never heard that before," Diann began, then quoted him. " 'During the hunt, bells sustain a life-line between a man and hawk.' "

Jon smiled at her. Diann's cheek, still red from the cold, reminded Jon of the winter day when he'd first seen her on campus.

She paused and pointed toward the glass. Jon turned toward the patio doors.

"There's that black squirrel again," Diann said. "This cold must have forced him out of the forest."

The squirrel scampered across the crust for an easy meal.

"Who else puts out wheat bread and peanut butter?" Jon teased her.

Diann paused, turning her ear towards the glass. "I cannot hear the bells from here!"

Jon too strained to listen. He heard nothing. He slid the door aside and stuck his head out. Cold air pained his lungs and he sneezed from the bright glare off the snow.

The slate-gray hawk stretched his neck, then flew hard from his perch. The leash held him back. The whistle of his wings was the only noise. The last bell was broken and silent. The hawk bounced back to the perch and then bolted again, but the leash held. Sitting, the squirrel held the bread, completely unconcerned.

"Close the door, Jon. . . ."

"Prodigal's last bell broke," he answered, rolling the name over in his mind.

Prodigal means "lavish," and in its extreme, "wasteful." He was both. His fanatical pursuit of quarry could easily be called lavish, but his volatile nature created wasteful fits and sulking moods.

One day Prodigal would pursue pheasants with the determination of a shark in bloody water. The next, he would fly to a tree and sulk for an hour like a spoiled kid. Thinking back, Jon felt like the father of the biblical prodigal son — angered that Prodigal was so wasteful and wandering, yet rejoicing when he returned.

Prodigal tugged at his leash. It was time to hunt. Jon closed the door.

The squirrel scampered back toward a birch tree at the edge of the wood lot. As it climbed the tree, Prodigal stared after it.

"Want me to run to K-mart and see if they have any on special?"

"Very funny," Jon replied. "Did the mail come yet?"

"Yes, but your bell order wasn't in it. You know it takes forever to get bells from Asborno."

"I've used his bells since I was a teenager," Jon answered. Asborno was a man worthy of Jon's patience.

Jon had ordered bells a month before when Prodigal's other leg bell had broken. Jon's first bells — still in perfect working order — were pushed so far back in his mind that he did not remember them.

Kevin entered the room carrying his green and white Pioneer bag and sat in the oak rocking chair. With his sandy hair and blue eyes, Kevin looked much like his dad, twenty-five years ago. They both had powerful legs and broad shoulders. "The perfect wrestler's build," the sports writers had said of them. Jon and Kevin had been close, spending days deer hunting the cedar swamp, fly-fishing for bass, or drifting a river for steelhead. But Jon had avoided all of Kevin's wrestling matches. Jon

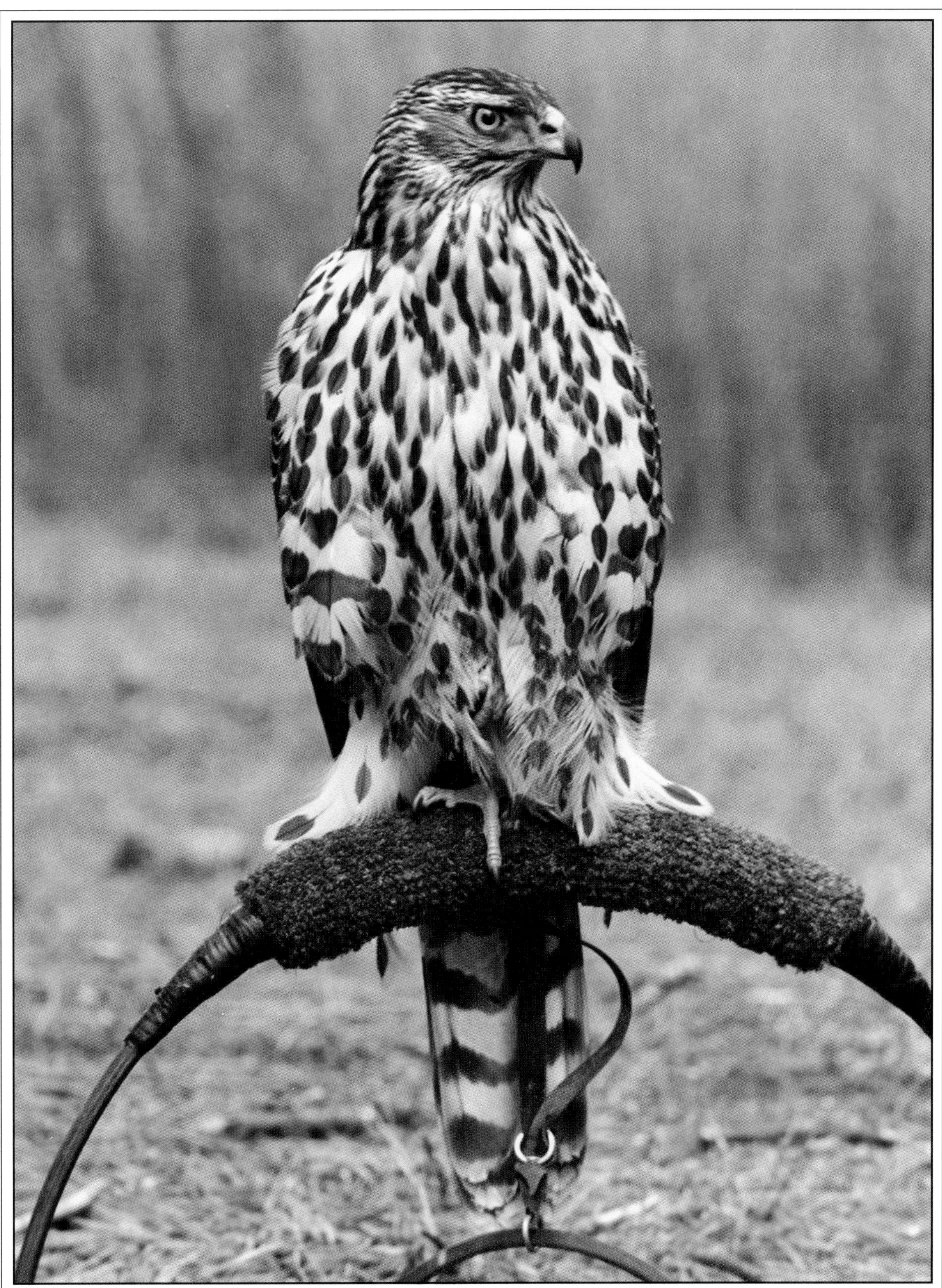

photo by Gary M. Cargile

had tried to convince Diann that he was just unusually busy.

Today would end the hawking season and was also Kevin's final wrestling match. Jon wanted to watch Kev, but he could not. It wasn't the hawking that would keep him away. He knew they thought differently.

"The *Morning Sun* said you overmatched your last opponent in the tournament," Jon said.

"Yeah," Kevin said quietly, barely glancing up.

"You could have seen him yourself," Diann said, moving closer to Kevin.

"I called you," Jon said, still facing the glass door. "You know I had to finish that bid for Dow Chemical."

Diann had heard those words before.

"Every match you've found some excuse," she insisted, raising her voice. "The first match, it was the GM bid. The second, for Saginaw Gears. Then on and on . . ."

Jon glanced over his shoulder at Kevin but said nothing.

"Are you going to the championship today?" she asked Jon bluntly. Diann was one to speak her mind.

"You know I fly Prodigal in the afternoon. And this is the last day of the season." Jon felt trapped.

"I don't care about your damn hawk. . . ." Diann yelled.

Kevin's grip tightened on his gym bag.

Silence rattled through the house. Jon caught Diann's green eyes, then looked away. Diann never swore.

"Kev is wrestling for the state championship," she retorted. "And you tell me, you're going hawking? This is the biggest night of his life and all you can think about is that damn bird. What kind of father are you?"

Not as good as my father was, Jon thought as he stared outside.

"You can't fly without bells anyway. You always say it's like a pilot flying at night without instruments," she continued, taking the edge off her voice. "Jon, it's so important to him . . . ."

Silence hung in the room. Jon was in a no-win situation. The oak chair moaned as Kevin shifted his weight.

"Come with us, Jon," Diann asked.

More silence.

"Why don't you use those old bells from that red box in the attic?" Kevin suggested, exploding from the chair like a wrestler from the mat.

The secret slipped out almost by reflex.

"Put those bells on Prodigal, and get going," Kevin yelled, pointing his finger at his dad. "I don't want you there anyway. You're afraid I'll win the championship. When you ran from the challenge."

Jon spun around, stunned by the words. He knew that even Diann didn't know that about him.

Kevin thundered down the hall, his heavy gym bag flapping behind him like a paper bag.

Jon's mind rattled with images of Iowa, farming, high school, his father and bells. . . . He tried to push them back. He tried to sweep them aside like thoughts of mosquitos but he could not.

Kevin's revelation puzzled Diann. But her anger outweighed her curiosity, so she stood, hands on her hips, glaring at Jon.

Jon felt her eyes on him as he watched Prodigal bounce back to his perch. Jon needed bells. He walked past Diann and started toward the attic.

Diann pressed her fingers to her eyes to hold back the tears. Jon knew he should explain it all to her, but he kept climbing.

Diann knew little of Jon's past. When they had met at Central Michigan University, he rarely spoke of his family. The years had not changed that. Jon had told her that he was an only child and that his parents had died in a farming accident.

She had seen the red box in the attic and had assumed that the Gorly widow left it. During the move, Kevin also had seen the

Redwing shoe box bound in cotton string, and had opened it. Its contents had sparked his interest in wrestling.

Today when Jon pulled the cotton string, a knot tied in his stomach. Inside, Jon saw again his own wrestling ribbons and medals, Iowa newspaper clippings and a pair of falconry bells, linked with a leather tab. Jon picked up the bells while trying to ignore the rest. He could not.

The clippings were yellow and brittle from age. Most were neatly trimmed. As Jon read the one on top he wondered how many Kevin had read.

IOWA'S ALL-STATER WRESTLES BY THE BELL

Des Moines, Iowa (AP) — In last night's Regional Tournament, Tama's star wrestler Jon Cullberg pinned his opponent in the first round. Amidst the yells and cheers one sound rang clear — bells. Falconry bells. Jon's father, Curt Cullberg, rings a pair of falconry bells during Jon's matches.

"When Jon hears the bells he knows I'm pulling for him," Curt said. "When he was in junior high, Jon had potential, but he would forget to go for the legs. So I took a pair of bells off his hawk. I rung them during his match when he needed to be aggressive."

Now a seasoned competitor, Jon needs no reminder, but his dad still rings the bells. And when the "piercing shrill" hits his ears, Jon knows his dad is pulling for him.

Jon Cullberg has signed a letter of intent to wrestle for the Iowa Hawkeyes . . . .

Jon began to piece together why Kevin had such a sudden interest in wrestling. Last winter Jon took a pay cut so they could move north. For Diann and Jon the sacrifice had been worth it. She wanted to be near her ailing mother. Jon wanted away from factory grind.

Jon knew that adjustments had been hardest for Kevin, who had been uprooted in the middle of his junior year. After Kevin found this box, he began attending wrestling practice and advanced quickly. Wrestling had helped Kevin fit in. Jon had allowed it to drive a wedge between them, and he knew that this must change. He must change it. But how?

When Jon moved he knocked over the Nike shoe box next to it. Out of it fell a collection of Kevin's medals, clippings, and trophies. But Kevin had no bell.

Jon's truck coasted to a stop on the crunching snow on the shoulder of a dirt road. He sat looking into the cedar swamp. The heavy snow dropped by the last Alberta Clipper draped all the pine, spruce and cedar trees. The bare oak, birch and aspen trees that towered on the rolling hills looked unburdened by the snow and seemed cheerful. The forest usually was a great source of calm for Jon, but today it was not. It was the bells. Haunting. Reminding . . .

The snow crackled beneath Jon's boots as he walked down the frozen stream. The sound echoed off the icy snow and was swallowed by the cedars that lined the bank. He heard nothing but his own steps. The shadows stretching across the stream reminded Jon that time was short. Prodigal sensed it too and stood taut on the fist.

Jon hiked the frozen stream as his roadway through the forest. Thick brush reached out over the stream. At one bend Jon recognized the pool where Kevin had caught his first brook trout on a fly rod. No matter where he went, he couldn't escape the memories. There was no place to run.

His feet kept walking.

The thin dust of snow which had fallen the night before created a new page upon which the forest critters wrote. Tracks crisscrossed the stream. Near the bank a white form dashed out from under a bush. Prodigal

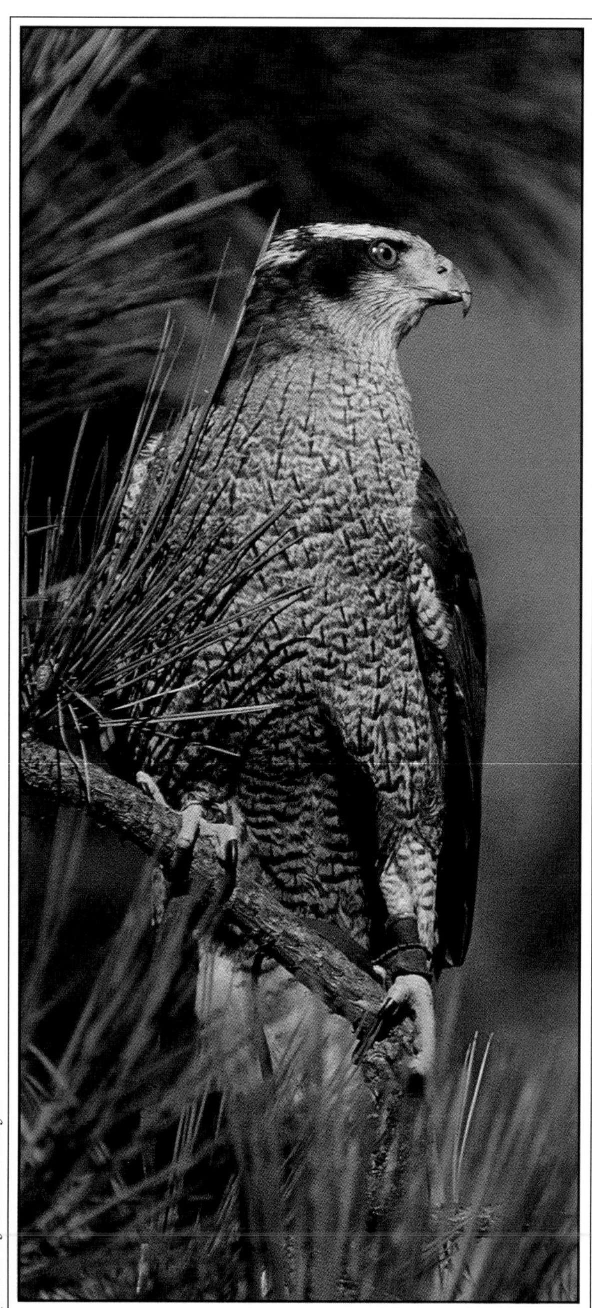
photo by Alison Meyer

flinched, gripping Jon's glove. Jon paused.

The snowshoe hare lumbered around the bend in the creek and disappeared into the bramble. Prodigal refused the hare — he had wrestled with its kind before. With its brawn and powerful feet, the seven-pound hare had thumped the twenty-four-ounce goshawk. Prodigal's quickness had caught the hare a second time. But it kicked him off again, sending chest feathers flying and knocking him on his tail. It left him with two broken tail feathers and a bruised ego. Prodigal had refused every hare since, even the small yearlings.

The wind did not whisper as Prodigal sat restlessly on the glove. Standing still, Jon heard a squirrel chattering, a woodpecker's rhythmic knock, and a car with a loud muffler rumbling down a distant road. The ring of Prodigal's bell pierced the silence like a rifle shot at dawn. A dry chill swept over Jon.

He felt he was being watched.

Jon left the easy walking of the stream and began weaving his way through the brush to an area thinned by loggers. As Jon walked a deer trail, small branches brittle from the cold snapped as he brushed against them. At the edge of the logging area, Jon found a fresh kill. A dusting of snow covered the dead rabbit, and fur tufts circled it. Wing primaries of a large owl drew lines in the fresh snow like a child's spread fingers in white sand. Frozen blood stained the snow, but there was no sign of a struggle. The hare had died quickly.

Jon mused about the power of a great horned owl. Owls always smell of skunks they eat. Even a tough, well-armed skunk was no match for this silent night-stalker. Jon knew that their hearing is uncanny and that they can tell in complete darkness what direction and distance a noise comes from. Jon wondered if they were nesting nearby. Now was their nesting season in which they allow no intrusion, especially from a competitor.

As Jon thought about the owls, Prodigal bolted from the glove. He looked up to see what Prodigal had seen. A pine squirrel was scampering up a birch at the far side of the clearing. Prodigal flew low, and pitched up into the tree above the squirrel. Prodigal searched the branches, but the squirrel kept the tree between them. When Jon ran up to the tree, the squirrel vaulted to a cedar. Prodigal darted down, but missed as the squirrel escaped among the cedar's thick branches.

When Jon rattled the cedar, it sprang

back onto the birch. Prodigal missed on his next pass, but forced the squirrel down the tree. Prodigal jabbed at the squirrel, while it kept every branch between them. Twigs snapped and bark flew as the squirrel scooted around the trunk and began to climb again. Prodigal stalled his descent by swinging out from the tree. Their frosted breath hung in the air. Both squirrel and hawk panted. Prodigal, far from discouraged, was in frenzied pursuit.

"Lavish," Jon mumbled, shaking his head.

As Prodigal powered up near the squirrel, Jon finally saw the hole. An instant later the russet tail disappeared. It was over.

But Prodigal kept up the vain pursuit. He bounced off a limb, grabbing at the hole. He sprang up fitfully time and again, to no avail.

Jon drew the whistle from his jacket and blew it. Prodigal did not look down. He glared at the hole, then over his shoulder to the western horizon. Jon knew the look. Raising his glove, Jon whistled again, then paused.

They both heard another noise.

Jon thought the sound was the wind howling through a hollow tree, deep and long. But no breeze stirred.

Prodigal gazed over his shoulder.

"A great horned owl," Jon said aloud, warning Prodigal.

It fell on deaf ears, as darkness began descending like a blanket over the forest.

Jon heard the owl again, closer this time.

"Or is it a second owl?" Jon asked himself. "It may be its mate."

Double trouble.

Owls and hawks are competitors, Jon thought. Rivals. More like gladiators than wrestlers, their match is to the death. Jon pushed the thought away. But it came back. A torn newspaper from the red box kept emerging. Memories followed him everywhere.

FARMING ACCIDENT
CLAIMS COUPLE

Tama, Iowa (AP) — Today all Tama mourns the loss of Curt and Judy Cullberg, lifelong dairy farmers of Tama area. Their deaths raised the total due to farming accidents to five in Iowa this year.

Last Monday, Curt was pulling a manure spreader with a three-wheeled tractor along their farm pond when the bank crumbled. The tractor and trailer flipped into the pond, breaking through the ice.

Details are sketchy, but the Tama County Sheriff believes that Curt was knocked unconscious and pinned in the water. Curt was found by his wife Judy, who in panic swam fully clothed into the frigid water. She drowned trying to save her husband.

Their son, Jon Cullberg, Tama's Senior All-State wrestler, found them. Following the funeral, at the overflowing Tama Church of Christ, Jon was asked if he would still wrestle in the state championship next week.

"That is what Dad would have wanted. He was my biggest fan," Jon said. "I'm going to win this one for him."

Prodigal bolted from the tree. The rattle of his bells startled Jon, like hearing a ghost. Jon ran through the brush trying to follow Prodigal. Frozen branches snapped and popped as he thrashed through the forest. Limbs raked his cold face. He listened for bells but heard none. The sound of his boots breaking brittle snow dominated the forest. He stopped, heart pounding, took a deep breath and listened.

Silence. Then Jon heard bells toward the stream. Jon's arrival startled Prodigal, who flew to a tree on the opposite bank. As

Jon walked onto the stream bed, two grouse flushed from the near side. Prodigal exploded from the tree. All three climbed quickly. They flew straight up and over the cedars that lined the bank, then disappeared into the twilight.

Jon charged into the dense brush for a hundred yards and then stopped to listen. He heard nothing.

As Jon stared for any sign of movement, every color melted into shades of black and white. The moon shone through the trees, as the snow radiated with light. The forest seemed alive.

The green cedars became transformed into black silhouettes. Jon felt dead.

Then two sounds came as one: faint bells up on the ridge and a long hoot. The bells were a liability.

"A no-win situation," Jon thought. The bell would alert the owls to Prodigal's position. They'd find him first.

Jon grabbed at the saplings and pulled himself up the ridge. But he knew that running was not the solution. He stopped to listen. He wanted to run. It was always his way to deal with no-win situations. He had been running for years, but the memories always followed.

> IOWA'S BRIGHTEST WRESTLING STAR WITHDRAWS
>
> Iowa City, Iowa (AP) — Tama's wrestling program was dealt its second blow this week in the state championships. Today Tama's All-American wrestler, Jon Cullberg, withdrew from the team.
>
> "We are still in shock," said Tama's wrestling coach, Paul Seltz. "We asked him to stay, but Jon is doing what he thinks best. I have no further comment."
>
> Tamas' chances to repeat for the state title are further weakened by the loss of Jon Cullberg. Last week, Tama lost Sam Wagner to an injury. Sam remains paralyzed from the waist down.
>
> The withdrawal of the heavily favored Jon Cullberg still remains a mystery.

It was no mystery to Jon. After his parents died, Jon had driven himself to win the championship. In his zeal, he had injured his teammate in a practice. Paralyzed from the waist down, Sam never recovered. Jon had never meant to hurt anyone. He did not know what to do. A no-win situation. So Jon ran. First from the championships, then from Iowa, now from Kevin. Now like Prodigal, the more he ran the worse it became.

One owl hooted from the south, another answered from the west. Prodigal's bells rang between them.

"His bells will betray him," Jon whispered.

Jon knew what he must do.

The bells echoed again through the forest. Jon pulled up the neck warmer and clawed his way up the ridge.

An excited crowd filled Rose Arena with chatter and chants as the bleachers swayed to the rhythm of the frantic families and friends. Everyone searched for victory as Kevin and Diann looked for Jon. Diann held a slim hope that he would come. Kevin did not. Whenever Kevin glanced up at her she crossed her fingers. But he saw her disappointment, even through her smile. Finally Kevin's match arrived. The coach paced back and forth in front of the Clare squad. Everyone knew Kevin's match would decide the team state championship.

The coach stopped in front of Kevin and began his pre-match counsel. "Kev. Be aggressive, watch for Jefferson's single-leg grab and use your legs. . . ."

Kevin heard the sounds but not the words. He glanced up at Diann, who smiled again. Kevin's shoulders drooped.

"It's up to you, Kev. Go get 'em," the

coach cheered, slapping him on the back.

Kevin ran to the center of the mat, but he looked sluggish. No fire gleamed in his eyes. Jefferson scored two takedowns within the first minute.

Score: four to zero.

By the end of the second round, Kevin had fallen behind seven to one.

Kevin's only hope in the last round was a pin. But Jefferson had not been pinned since junior high. Kevin tried a risky leg grab to gain a pin. Jefferson countered, escaped and spun Kevin for a takedown. The score grew worse: ten to one. They were at the edge of the mat and the referee called for a restart. Kevin then managed an escape, but victory was far from his reach.

Score: ten to two.

Kevin's coach wiped his face with a towel. Diann held her face as if to hold back the tears. Some Flint fans raised a banner, "POUND THE PIONEERS!"

The wrestlers circled facing each other head to head, grappling for an advantage. Jefferson held Kevin at bay. Less than a minute remained. Jefferson could cruise to victory. The crowd rose, screaming. The wrestlers waited for the final buzzer. Kevin's coach hung his head. The noise was deafening. Defeat was near.

Cutting through the noise came a piercing, challenging shrill. Kevin's heart leaped. He knew what that sound was without looking. Kevin's revival caught Jefferson by surprise. And Kevin used it to his advantage, charging under him, grabbing his legs and spinning Jefferson onto his back. Diann screamed. . . . The referee fell to his knees, watching Jefferson's shoulders and slamming his own hand to the mat. The bells rattled again. It was a pin!

The prodigal was home. 

The Car

by Mike Person

The man was dying.

At least he guessed that the term would be technically appropriate, since he calculated his current life expectancy to be in the neighborhood of a quarter hour.

The fifteen minutes coincided with their estimated time of arrival. Of course, that ETA was based on the assumption that the car would not be delayed as a result of being struck by a falling asteroid. The likelihood of a catastrophic event of this nature could certainly not be ruled out in light of the preceding events of the day.

Taking his eyes momentarily off the road, the man glanced to his right at the lightly freckled face of the young adolescent seated next to him. The boy, lost in his own thoughts, stared vacantly forward through the windshield and out into the deepening twilight.

Looking at his son, the man was overwhelmed with a sudden flood of paternal emotion. "Lord! How I love this kid!" he thought.

It wasn't as if he didn't love his other children every bit as much. He did. It was just that between this one and himself there was something different, something special. This time there was the fire of a shared passion. In it, their relationship had been welded, forged, and tempered until it far exceeded the dimensions generally reserved for fathers and their sons.

The hooded falcon on the boy's gloved left hand raised a foot to scratch its jaw and then roused. The sound of its bell drew the man's thoughts back in time, to earlier that same afternoon . . . .

Actually, the day really hadn't started out all that badly. In fact, the first inkling of any problems wasn't until after work, when he went to the repair shop to pick up the van and learned that, despite any promises made just that morning, the vehicle was not going to be roadworthy for another twenty-four hours.

There was no sense in making a fuss about it. Nobody would understand how important it was to the man and the boy to keep that hawking van running. People would think it was crazy that they spent each day anxiously awaiting the arrival of mid-afternoon, when they could race home from office and school, load falcons and setter into the van and go hunting. Now the whole day had been ruined by a stupid axle that broke for no good reason, right out in the middle of a plowed field.

At least he'd been lucky enough to catch a ride home with a neighbor whose company he enjoyed. However, that hadn't done much to improve his mood, which got even gloomier when he arrived late to find the boy had already taken up the three peregrines and had them weighed, hooded and ready to travel.

"Maybe Mom would let us use her car," the boy said, after hearing the bad news and considering the options.

"Do you mean her brand new car, the first new car she's ever had; the car she has washed and polished eleven times in the five days since it arrived; the one she wants to park in our bedroom every night? Is that the car you mean?" queried the man.

"We could promise never to ask for it again," countered the boy, skillfully avoiding a direct answer.

"Son, I'm even afraid to ask," said the man with a visible shiver. Mentally he gave such an endeavor's chance of success a more optimistic rating, somewhere between zero and nonexistent.

"Aw, please, Dad," pleaded the boy. "We should get some great flights today. The weather is perfect, and besides, they're forecasting a big storm, so for sure we won't be able to fly tomorrow and maybe not even the next day."

"You want to what?" she asked, eyebrows raising in disbelief, and then proceeded to answer her first question with her second.

"You want to go hawking in my brand-new car?" The voice was now racing the eyebrows for altitude.

"Are you out of your everloving mind?" she added more as a statement than a question.

Realizing that he was already facing defeat in an argument which so far had been a monologue, and feeling that there was little to lose by taking the offensive, the man leapt boldly into the breach with a mumbled, "But we'll be really careful with it, dear, and we'll never ask for it again."

"You must be kidding," she said, adding, "there isn't even enough room in it for your hawks," in a tone that implied the matter had now been settled by this irrefutable physical fact.

"We'll only take one bird with us and the boy can carry it hooded on his fist," he said in a spirit of compromise.

"And I suppose now you're going to tell me that this particular bird is housebroken?"

"No, but we'll put a piece of newspaper on the floor and make sure the bird is always over it."

"Well, at least you weren't planning on taking the dog," was squeezed out between her clenched jaws with a look that dared a rebuttal.

"Sweetheart, now you know we need to have the dog with us, but she'll lay quietly on the floor and we won't let her get dirty or run near any water or mud," he said in a calm, reasoning tone, sensing victory within his grasp.

"No, you can't use my car and that's all there is to it," she replied, with an emphatic negative shake of her head.

Having exhausted reason, she had

been forced in desperation to resort to the ultimate weapon, matriarchal tyranny.

It was definitely time, the man figured, to call up the reserve.

"Pleeeease, Mom. I'll vacuum it just as soon as we get home and I'll wash and wax it for you every Saturday for a month," interjected the boy. As if on cue, the light glistened off barely suppressed tears of disappointment in the innocent, young, brown eyes.

"Boy, a new car sure does smell nice inside, doesn't it?" the boy observed, as they pulled out of the driveway. His head was turned to the right and his eyes were already scanning the passing countryside for the sight of an unwary game bird.

"Yeah, it really does," replied the man. "And if your mother has anything to say about it, it will be the only car in the world that still has this smell when it's five years old." Then, with the dire parting admonitions of his wife still echoing in his ears, he cautioned, "Watch that you keep your hawk over that paper. We sure as heck can't afford to make even a hint of a mess in here."

Fifty minutes later the car pulled over and parked on the edge of a large, familiar pasture. This particular area, overgrown with native weeds and patches of buck brush, was known to be frequented by sharp-tailed grouse.

The man called the white and orange English setter out of the car, "whoaed" her, set her up with a pet and a pat and then whistled her into the field. The boy, carrying the falcon, crawled through the loose wires of the dilapidated fence and waited for his father to catch up.

Between them, they managed to attach the radio transmitter to the falcon's leg. Then the man checked its function with the receiver. Throughout the procedure, both kept watch on the dog as it quartered in the distance of the field.

"Perfect day for it," said the man as they walked out into the field.

"Clear, cool and breezy, and the wind is from behind us," agreed the boy. "She ought to go right up out of sight."

"Point!" was exclaimed in unison as the setter, working toward them, crested a small knoll and slammed from an all-out fluid run into rock solid, head and tail high, rigidity.

The next couple of minutes passed with agonizing slowness while the pair waited to see if the dog would move, flag, or in any other way lessen intensity and cast doubt on the precise location of the bird.

Even after it became obvious that the dog was not going to relocate, neither of them made a move to continue their advance. The silhouetted beauty of the pointing setter in its classic pose had combined with the colors and scents of fall and the crystalline beauty of the day to cast a magic spell which neither wanted to break.

"Isn't that a sight?" murmured the man, finally.

"Yep, she sure is pretty," sighed the boy as he stroked the back of the falcon. "And I suppose you left the camera in the car again."

"Since when is it only me that forgets the camera? I didn't notice that you had broken arms."

"Well, it is your camera," said the boy.

"We-elll, it ii-is your bird," mimicked the man.

"And," said the boy, "who owns the dog, might I ask?"

"And who, young fellow, might I ask, is the Apprentice Falconer around here?"

"It seems to me that the so-called Master Falconer should be setting a better example for the Apprentice to follow."

"Well then, you just turn that worthless bird of yours loose and the old Master Falconer will give you a lesson on how one properly flushes the quarry."

During the four or five minutes that it took them to walk forward to honor the dog's point, the falcon had rung up to a very respectable altitude and set its wings to wait for the prey below to show itself.

Slowly and carefully, crooning soft words of praise, the man approached the dog. Finally, the only thing separating him from the quivering dog that faced him was a twenty-foot diameter patch of waist high scrub willow.

As he gave a final glance skyward to verify the position of the falcon waiting-on high above, the man felt the familiar rush as his pulse and respiration quickened in anticipation. His mind's eye was already witnessing that brief moment when all time would stand still as the tiny, shortened T-shape transformed itself into a slate blue thunderbolt, and descended from heaven in a heart-stopping vertical stoop.

"Ho! . . . Ho! . . . Ho! . . .Ho! . . . ," he shouted. At the same time he ran forward, arms flailing and legs kicking at the brush that now surrounded him.

Centered in the willow patch he caught a fleeting glimpse of black and white movement near the ground ahead of him. Still advancing, he barely had time to wonder what a magpie was doing there and then to wonder what rare meteorological phenomenon was responsible for the mist with the full colored rainbow that had materialized right in front of his eyes, when he ran head-on into an impenetrable wall of stench.

With eyes burning, olfactory nerves nuked into oblivion and his chest heaving for air, he had some difficulty focusing on the boy's panic-stricken warning cries of "Skunk! Skunk, Dad! She pointed a skunk!"

"Catch her! Don't let her go after it!" the man managed to gasp between violent, uncontrolled fits of retching, wheezing and coughing.

He needn't have worried about the setter. Getting closer to that critter was the furthest thing in the world from her mind. She was already at flank speed and in the process of avoiding the danger of fallout by rapidly distancing herself upwind from ground zero.

The boy first reassured himself that neither the dog nor his father were in dire need of his immediate attention. Then he took out the lure and busied himself with the task of recovering the falcon.

By the time the hawk was hooded and back on the gauntlet, the man had pretty well recovered from the primary effects of the incident and concluded that if skunk juice could be bottled, the manufacturers of Mace would be put out of business.

"You okay now, Dad?"

"Yeah, I think I'm probably going to survive."

"Well, I guess we might as well head back. It doesn't look like there are any birds around here today," said the boy.

The man nodded an unspoken assent, and they began walking in the direction of the parked car.

"Have you noticed how skunk smells a whole lot worse when you're really close to it?" said the boy.

"Yeah, I noticed."

"It looks like the pup noticed it too," said the boy, referring to the setter who was walking at heel, but with twenty feet of separation.

They walked on for a few moments in silence.

"That sure was funny," said the boy.

"Oh, you think so, huh?"

"Uh-huh. I can hardly wait until the field meet next week so I can tell everybody how the great Master Falconer showed the lowly apprentice how to properly flush a skunk."

"Son, has anybody ever told you that nobody likes a smart-ass kid?"

As they arrived at the car the man finally vocalized the unspoken question that had been on both minds, "What are we going to do about your mom's car?"

"How about if I drive and you ride on

the hood with the bird?" asked the boy, who was still two years away from the legal age for a learner's permit.

"How about if we just open all the windows and let the air blow through?" said the father, and then added hopefully, "Maybe all the smell will evaporate."

They traveled for ten minutes in relative silence. Neither had made any further reference to the incident in the field.

"Dad?"

"Uh-huh?"

"You know that new car smell we were talking about?"

"What about it?"

"Well, we sure cured that problem, didn't we?" said the boy with deadpan voice, attention focused straight ahead.

"Partner, I'd say that was the understatement of the century," said the man, equally deadpan.

Each caught the other's furtive, sidelong glance and simultaneously they broke into snickers which rapidly grew into crescendos of laughter.

"You should have seen the expression on your face when . . . ," the boy started, and then surrendered again to the laughter.

"I can imagine," said the man, finishing the thought and struggling for self-control. "Have you seen the way the pup keeps looking at me?"

"She figures you must have that skunk hidden in your pocket," the boy gasped breathlessly, and both dissolved into new waves of merriment.

"I bet she never points another skunk," said the man.

"Me, too," said the boy, "especially since she knows the punishment is having to ride in the same car with the Master Skunk Flusher."

It was some time before a semblance of order was restored as each voiced humorous new insights into the experience.

"Ducks!" exclaimed the man as he took his foot off the accelerator.

"Where?" said the boy, his head swiving left to search out of the windows on the driver's side.

"On the far side of that slough," answered the man, indicating its location in the field with his chin.

"I see 'em," said the boy as he spotted the three mallards on the water.

Seen in detail, the slough qualified more as a large shallow puddle. Roughly fifty yards in diameter, it was the last of some runoff water that had collected in a slight depression in the pasture. Its shallow depth was proven by the numerous clumps of grass and weeds which protruded from its surface. That it was temporary, and rapidly shrinking in size, was indicated by the fact that it was surrounded by a twenty-yard band that was still wet. Its use as the primary watering hole for the thirty-odd head of cattle grouped at the far end of the field was attested to by the fact that their comings and goings had churned the entire wet area into a muddy mess. It looked like a war zone, stippled with craters and innumerable water-filled pockmarks of indeterminate depth.

"Let's see if we can get permission to hunt it," said the man, looking ahead a mile to the nearest buildings.

The car turned off the road into the farm lane and continued on to park next to the porch of the two-storied, white frame farmhouse.

The man opened his door and stepped out to stand by the car, as a large, overweight blond woman interrupted her sweeping of the porch and stepped down from it to approach the car.

Still carrying the broom, she got within ten feet of the vehicle and stopped.

That she had just reached the outer limit of the odor zone was obvious. Her facial expression transformed, with astonishing speed, from one of smiling welcome into another of nose-wrinkled disgust.

"It's awful, isn't it?" said the man and then offered by way of explanation, "There was a dead skunk spread all over the road back there and I ended up running over it. I sure hope it wears off the tires soon."

Without waiting for any comment, the man continued to speak. "We're sorry to bother you. We just wanted to ask if we could hunt some ducks that are sitting on the water in the pasture."

"Well, I don't know," she said. "We have cattle in there and my husband isn't home right now."

"We won't bother the cattle and we don't use guns. We want to hunt them with the falcon."

The boy, still in the car, raised the peregrine where it could be easily viewed through the open window.

The woman made no attempt to get any closer, but she did bend down and squint nearsightedly into the car.

"It won't attack the cattle, will it?" she asked.

"No, ma'am," came the reponse. "She only hunts birds, and they get away from her more often than not."

"What about my ducks?" asked the woman, looking over her shoulder toward the middle of the big yard where half a dozen large, white domestic ducks paddled sedately around a decorative pond.

"Oh, don't worry about that," answered the man. "This bird has lots of experience and only goes after ducks when they are flying. She won't bother them on the water like that."

"Well, I guess it would be all right then," the lady said as she backed uncomfortably away from the source of the of the terrible odor.

"Thanks very much, ma'am. We really appreciate it," said the man, and without delay he reentered the car, turned it around and drove back down the lane.

"Look at that, Dad! I told you we'd get a great flight today."

Both necks were craned, faces turned skyward, eyes straining to catch sight of the falcon high above as she faded in and out of view, circling on the very edge of the maximum range of visibility.

"She sure does love to fly," agreed the man.

"This is going to be a classic," declared the boy with confident enthusiasm.

"Whenever you're ready," said the man.

"Let's do it!" called the boy, already starting to run.

Hollering, throwing stones and waving their arms, both figures charged headlong out into the muddy zone surrounding the water.

Ten steps into the attack, the man realized that solid footing was fast receding into the depths of foul-smelling, sticky, gumbo goo. Two leaps later he stumbled as his left foot suddenly pulled free of its knee-length rubber boot. Momentum carried him lurching forward. In the desperate attempt to regain his balance, he scarcely noticed it as the second boot departed in a similar fashion. Teetering to an upright, if precarious, halt, he failed to see the boy ahead of him, diving headfirst through the air.

Arms stretched forward in a futile attempt to break the fall, the boy had lost it completely. He landed full length, face down in the muck. The impact was accompanied by a visible splash and an audible "splurp!"

Oblivious to the boy's dilemma, the man had just realized that he was up to his knees in it, sans boots.

"God bless it! Of all the bloody, rotten . . . . " The string of expletives was temporarily interrupted when he suddenly teetered one last time and sat down hard.

"Shit! . . . Shit! . . . Shit! . . . . "

This profound, if somewhat monotonous, train of thought was interrupted for a second time by a persistent call.

"Uh, Dad? . . . Dad!"

"WHAT?" he snarled, not in the most genial of moods.

"I need some help here, Dad."

"YOU need some help? Hell, I'm flat on my ass and I lost both my boots in this gunk. Come on over here and help me find them."

"I can't, Dad."

"What do you mean, you can't?"

"I mean I'm stuck and I can't get up and I'm about to drown."

In falling, the boy had driven his stiffened arms straight down into the mud up to his armpits. With the full weight of his upper body directly above these anatomical anchors he was totally helpless. The slightest struggle drove him deeper into the muck. Only by holding his head back and twisted to the side was he able to keep his face out of the water.

Detecting a note of panic in the explanation, the man struggled hurriedly to his feet.

"Hang on, Son! I'm coming!"

In the short time it took him to flounder across the distance separating them, the man had time to notice that a considerable portion of the muck they were wallowing in was not soil.

It appeared that the cattle had not been overly concerned about the ecological considerations of a polluted water supply. In fact, judging by the number of droppings per square foot, the old water hole did double duty as the old latrine.

Having arrived in the vicinity of the boy, the immediate challenge became how to effect the rescue. Several fumbling attempts at gentle extrication failed. Finally, the man moved to stand facing the youth, astraddle his head. Bending down, he reached forward with both arms and grasped deep handfuls of the shoulders of the boy's clothing. Tensing every muscle in his body and grunting with the exertion, he heaved violently upward on the slight young form. In a single motion, the huge effort tore the boy loose from the powerful suction trap, lifted him free of the surface and set him on his feet, facing his father.

The two of them just stood there staring at each other for a long moment as they caught their breaths.

"Thanks, Dad. I wasn't sure how much longer I could last."

"That's okay, Son," panted the man. "You really were stuck in there."

"Did she get a duck?" asked the boy.

"I don't think so. I don't really know. I never saw them flush. Did you?"

"No."

Both turned toward the water. The mallards were still moving, seemingly unconcerned, in and around the clumps of grass.

"The ducks are still there," said the boy. "Where's the hawk?"

"I don't see her right now but she's probably still up high, waiting," said the man, and added, "It's a shame but I think we've had it with these ducks. We can't get close enough to flush them with the hawk in the air."

"Yeah, I guess so," the boy reluctantly agreed. "I'll wade out to dry ground and call her down while you find your boots."

"Okay, Son. It's a shame, but that's the way it goes sometimes."

A short time later the man waded out of the mud, carrying his boots. He called out to the boy where he stood, swinging the lure.

"Any sign of her?"

"Not yet. You better get the telemetry out."

Within moments, the antenna was assembled and the receiver was emitting loud intermittent beeps.

"She can't be far away," said the man as he pivoted the antenna slowly through 360 degrees.

No sooner had the antenna oscillated and come to a stop pointing in the direction of the farm house than, from the same direction, came the very faint sound of distant human shouts.

Realization dawned simultaneously on them both.

"The duck pond! Let's go! Hurry!"

Unencumbered by age, paunch and bare feet, the younger of the pair handily won the race to where the setter awaited them in the car. He was waiting at the passenger's door, poised with right hand on the handle when the winded elder arrived at the driver's side.

"What are you waiting for?" gasped the man, who then froze in a mirrored position as the unspoken reason surfaced in his mind.

They might have been there still, caught on the horns of the proverbial dilemma, if the breeze hadn't freshened and brought renewed sounds of distress from afar.

"Oh, hell! Quick, get in before they shoot her."

Waves of relief washed over them as they careened into the farm lane and saw, in a glance, that their worst imaginings had not come to pass.

Skidding to a stop in thick clouds of dust, they jumped out of the car and surveyed the scene before them.

The duck pond was a beehive of activity. On its bank was the big blonde woman with the broom. She was jumping excitedly up and down, waving the broom around and screaming at the top of her ample lungs, "Go away! Get away from here! Leave them alone!" Every few seconds she would run part way around the pond and the whole process would be repeated. In the middle of the pond, the big white ducks were doing a lot of quacking. This was periodically interspersed with a lot of splashing and diving as the main player in this mini-drama approached. The center of all this activity was the AWOL falcon, which was playing dive bomber, and appeared to be the only living creature on the property that was actually enjoying itself. Oblivious to the activities of the woman, the falcon was performing acrobatic "lazy 8's" as it dived on the ducks, cast steeply up, winged over to reverse direction and repeated the maneuver.

"You call your hawk down and I'll calm the lady down," said the man to his son as they double-timed across the yard.

"It's okay, ma'am," called the man. "We're here. We'll catch the hawk. We'll get her away from your ducks."

Turning at the sound of the voice, the woman took an involuntary step backward, shaken at the sight of the two figures that were bearing relentlessly down on her.

The smaller of the two looked exactly like the Creature from the Lost Lagoon. Except for its eyes, it was covered from head to toe with a mixture of mud and what looked suspiciously like cow dung. On top of that, it was swinging some object around on a rope and making unintelligible noises that sounded like "Ho . . . Ho . . . Ho . . . ."

The larger of the two had a face and voice like the man who had earlier been in to ask permission to hunt. Except now he was barefooted, and all four of his limbs were covered with the same disgusting goo that was on the smaller one.

As they approached her, reason won out over panic and she decided that this was indeed the man she had talked to a short while ago, which meant that the shorter one had to be his son. Following this reasoning to its logical conclusion meant that the hawk they were talking about getting away from her ducks was the same one that she had been promised would not bother her ducks.

Taking a deep breath, for the purpose of giving these terrible people a piece of her mind, she let herself in for another surprise. That awful stink that she had smelled during their first meeting was definitely not coming from the tires of the man's car.

All of this was more than the poor woman could handle. These people were obviously lunatics. What's more, they were probably dangerous, and she had unwittingly let them know that she was here alone.

Panic reasserted itself. Eyes wide with fear, she dropped her broom, backed rapidly away from the madman who stood between her and her home, and then turned to run for the nearest haven of safety. This happened to be an old farm truck that was parked on the far side of the yard.

Once there, she scrambled into the cab and slammed the door shut. After locking both doors and checking that the windows were rolled up, she picked up a tire iron from the floorboards. Armed now, she watched and waited fearfully for the expected assault.

Stunned by the obvious effect he had had on her, but not denying the gravity of its nature, the man's thoughts immediately turned to self-preservation.

"Better hurry and get her hooded and let's get the heck out of here," the man said to his son and added, to himself, under his breath, "before her husband gets home or she calls the Mounties."

His son, who was just picking the falcon up on the lure, merely nodded and started walking toward the car.

Looking past the boy at the car, the man was reassured to see that the distance was too far for the woman to be able to read their license plate.

He picked up the broom, carried it to the house and placed it on the porch. Then he walked to the car. Just before he joined the boy in the front seat, he turned to smile and wave at the pale face pressed to the window of the old red truck.

The car's departure speed equaled that of its second arrival.

Twenty minutes and forty miles later, the sound of laughter, punctuated with snatches of conversation, could again be heard emanating from the open windows of the car.

"Did you see her face when she saw you coming across the yard at her?" roared the man with tears in his eyes.

"Well, that was nothing compared to what happened when she smelled you," was the breathless retort. "Do you think she's still holed up in that truck?"

"I sure hope so. Otherwise the posse

will be out after us by now." Momentarily sobered by the thought, the man glanced furtively in the rearview mirror.

"Do me a favor, Dad. If you see any of my friends, warn me so I can duck down. I wouldn't want anybody to know I was related to anybody that smells as bad as you do."

"Is that so, Mr. Wise Guy? Well, I have some big news for you. You look exactly like I smell, and you don't smell so good either."

"At least somebody can get close enough to me to recognize me without getting sick."

"Who's going to recognize you anyway? You look like you've been snorkeling in a septic tank."

The only attempt to inject a bit of seriousness into the hilarity of the moment failed with its statement.

"It's sure a good thing we didn't let the dog out of the car to get all muddy and dirty."

. . . **'Y**es,' mused the man as he dimmed his headlights for an oncoming vehicle. "It has definitely been one hell of a day — and the worst is yet to come. They say that there are times when death can be a merciful relief, and in a few minutes I will be facing the ultimate ordeal. Well, when they bury me, my epitaph can read, 'Here lies an innocent victim of Murphy's Law.' "

His reverie was interrupted.

"Dad?"

"Hummm?"

"Instead of going home right now, couldn't we just go on into the city for a few days?"

"Oh, I don't think so, partner. Why would you ask a question like that?"

"Well, I was thinking," the boy continued, "if we don't go home for few days, Mom will get really lonesome and worried about us. Then, when we finally do go home, she'll be so happy to see us that she won't even care about what happened to her new car."

Then in a very somber and worried voice, "Dad, if we go home right now, Mom is going to kill you."

The "Falcontry" Expedition

by Ken Felix

Hunting and fishing should have come as naturally to me as they did to nearly every other Pennsylvania farm boy. But back then, it seemed that the most productive hours of game and fish procurement were blanketed under the cover of darkness. Just the thought of setting out for the backwoods turkey hunting in the pre-dawn din could send a gush of tepid liquid cascading into my socks. I'm not certain of the exact cause of my intense fear of the dark, but it must have had something to do with Donald. Donald was a typical little brother, eager to please and dumber than four hundred sheep. These were characteristics which would later prove valuable to me when I needed assistance with my falconry endeavors.

At any rate, I began to search for an outdoor activity I could enjoy in the light of day, a sport that would put game on the table and, most importantly, one that Dad would allow. I should mention that dangerous paraphernalia were considered contraband in our household. Guns were absolutely out of the question. After enormous effort on the part of Donald, Mom and myself, Dad did allow each of us boys to possess one "store-bought" fish hook. The aforementioned turkey-hunting expeditions also involved the employment of a homemade sling shot (also contraband) as an instrument of the hunt. You know, the kind made from a forked stick, a slice of old inner tube and bailing twine to anchor the rubber to the wood. I always had a swollen right thumb from where the rock hit while trying to fire the apparatus, and a red left wrist from the many times the bailing twine failed. I remember that Donald was always trying to figure out a way to utilize his fish hook as a projectile in the sling shot.

Sometime during my pre-pubescent period, a neighbor kid named Rodney told me about "falcontry." Rodney was one of those kids who was able to construct anything, a sort of juvenile structural engineer. He once assembled some scraps of wood, a wrinkled piece of tin roofing and various bits of discarded farm implements into the world's first satellite. He never received public acknowledgement for his accomplishment, however, because the reentry trajectory of his satellite put it on a collision course with his father's chicken coop and Widow Lindenberger's outhouse. His fuel formula is to this day a closely held secret, but as I recall it was a concoction of cow manure, creosote and a mysterious purplish ooze Rodney called "Crescendo."

"Ken," Rodney explained, "I seen pictures of this falcontry sport in my cousin's encyclopedia. You just go out and get one of these pea-green falcons and you can catch all the pheasants you want." It sounded fantastic to me, and better yet, it fit all my requirements for a suitable outdoor activity to a T.

The first obstacle seemed to be the acquisition of a bird of prey. In those days, raptors were considered vermin, not protected by any state or federal law, and available through mail order catalogs from wildlife dealers in the South. The problem was that I didn't have enough money for a postage stamp, let alone the $20 Trail's End Zoo wanted for "a perfect for falconry" roadside hawk. I would have to procure my hawk from the wild.

Rodney generously offered to assist me by constructing a capture device. Since I held his mechanical prowess in high regard, I accepted his offer. To the best of my recollection, the device he created bore some resemblance to a bow net, but was much more intricate and sophisticated. Rodney never did believe in simplicity of design. I am certain, however, that it somehow utilized the Power Take-Off (or "PTO") from our Ford 8N tractor. Ever since the satellite incident and the subsequent banning of "Crescendo," Rodney had been forced to resort to the PTO to supply the energy for his contraptions.

One sweltering July afternoon, Donald, Rodney and I set out to capture my hunting hawk. Situated in the uppermost crotch of the huge sycamore tree in the swamp behind our cow pasture was the nest of the local "chicken hawk." Years of intense study of the natural history of birds of prey since that time have convinced me that the buzzards were, in fact, red-shouldered hawks.

There were three babies already in the late brancher stage jumping about in the canopy of the enormous tree. They screamed incessantly. Our noisy approach on the tractor didn't appear to alarm the juvenile birds in the least. Throughout the time that Rodney was assembling his capture device at the base of the tree, the fledglings observed his activity with the cocked heads so typical of inquisitive eyasses.

While Rodney set about the arduous task of setting up the trap, Donald was in search of bait for the device. We decided that "miniature kangaroos" (woodland jumping mice) would serve the purpose best, as they were inclined to bounce about frantically when their tails were tied to the board inside the jaws of the trap. My job was to sit atop the tractor seat and warn the other members of the expedition should the parent birds return to pick our eyes out. Rumor had it that Old Lady Lindenberger became Widow Lindenberger when her unsuspecting spouse ventured too near the nest of this very same pair of chicken hawks.

After what seemed an eternity in the intense heat, Rodney's final adjustments were completed. Shortly thereafter, Donald arrived at the sycamore with two miniature kangaroos entrapped in a vented mayonnaise jar. "Donald, you got sauerkraut for brains or what? I told you to punch the air holes in the lid from the bottom side up. You did it backwards and just look how bad those kangaroos have cut up their heads!" I reprimanded. "No time to get more, we'll just have to use these."

The three of us, completely enthralled with this exciting and dangerous undertaking, were totally oblivious to the fact that the tractor's radiator was boiling over. We left the motor running to keep the PTO in a state of readiness in the event that one of the fledglings would fall victim to our trap, and of course, in case the return of the parent birds necessitated a hasty retreat. We hid among the cattails and waited to claim our prize.

As one would expect, Murphy's Law prevailed and the mother buzzard returned. I was the first to spot her soaring overhead. For an instant, I considered warning my compatriots of the impending danger, but self-preservation dominated compassion and I clamored frantically for the tractor. Apparently my rapid departure was warning enough, as the other members of the party quickly followed my lead. We three preteens covered the sixty yards between our place of concealment and the tractor in a time that would have made the Olympic Committee mandate a steroid test. In our haste, we still failed to notice the great cloud of white steam emanating from under the hood of the old 8N.

As I slammed the transmission into third gear and popped the clutch, the red-hot engine sputtered one last agonal cough, and died. Simultaneously, we all peered skyward to behold the huge raptor of local folklore screaming downwards upon us. The creature appeared more awesome than any war-eagle as she plummeted out of the heavens.

Rodney was petrified, Donald had a pair of Oshkoshes full of odorous intestinal garbage, and for the first time in broad daylight I had warm wet socks. We had no recourse but to react in the most appropriate manner. We buried our heads between our knees and quivered. The rush of the wind as the great bird sliced the thick July air just inches above our trembling bodies nearly tossed all three of us from the tractor seat.

Miraculously, not one of us was even scratched, and all six eyes were intact. It was Donald, no longer able to remain with his head in such close proximity to his smelly trap door, who first lifted his eyes and came to the realization that mama hawk's intended victims were not us but the miniature kangaroos within the trap. "Wowee!" exclaimed Donald, "Let's catch her and have a real hunting hawk!" Rodney was already beginning to activate the manual override on the capture device. (The satellite incident also taught Rodney to incorporate redundant control systems into all of his subsequent contraptions.) All three of us gave a mighty heave-ho on the trip cable and the device swallowed up our hawk exactly as Rodney had planned.

While entrapped, she appeared even more awesome than during her stoop. Beak agape and hackles raised, she rolled over on her back, spread her wings and cocked her formidable talons into a position of readiness for battle. Immediately I thought of Donald's best attributes: eagerness and stupidity. "Better grab her, Donald," I ordered, "before she escapes."

Rodney, being a bit less sadistic than I, made a meager attempt at limiting Donald's impending agony by offering him a pair of Playtex Living Gloves. "They look just like the falcontry gauntlets I seen in the encyclopedia," he declared.

Donald hastily dawned the flimsy rubber gloves and dove into the task in his usual eager and stupid manner.

"AAAHHHHHH!!!" he screamed, as

mama hawk drove her talon through the gloves and deep into his hands.

It was difficult, with Donald hollering and flailing about, to slide the burlap sack over the hawk. But after thirty or so minutes, we were finally able to secure the bird in the bag. That still left the problem of getting her claws out of Donald. Even with all our combined strength, we were unable to pry apart the great bird's feet. Rodney had a brainstorm, but since the tractor had died, the use of the PTO was impossible.

It was nearly nightfall by then, and Donald's hands were numb enough that he only occasionally let out a pitiful whimper. We were desperate, especially Donald. We even tried to make the hawk release her grip by removing the bag and allowing her to escape. She held relentlessly. I'm convinced she enjoyed the ordeal somewhat because every once in a while she was given to convulsive clutching with her feet. This action would start Donald flailing again.

Just when it all seemed hopeless, I had a brilliant thought. "Kill or be killed!" I screamed. Rodney and I hustled Donald and the hawk to the swamp and plunged the bird and Donald's arms under the murky green water. Within seconds, the hawk released her grip, stroked to the surface and flew off heavily into the setting sun.

The trials and tribulations of the day had ended. We crawled home to lick our wounds. (Figuratively, of course; just the sight of Donald's ungloved hands made me puke.) That afternoon we had learned many valuable lessons, the most important of which was that Rodney's capture device really did work.

Tomorrow we would try for one of the babies.

Two Boys and a Turkey

by Keith Thompson

photo by Keith Thompson

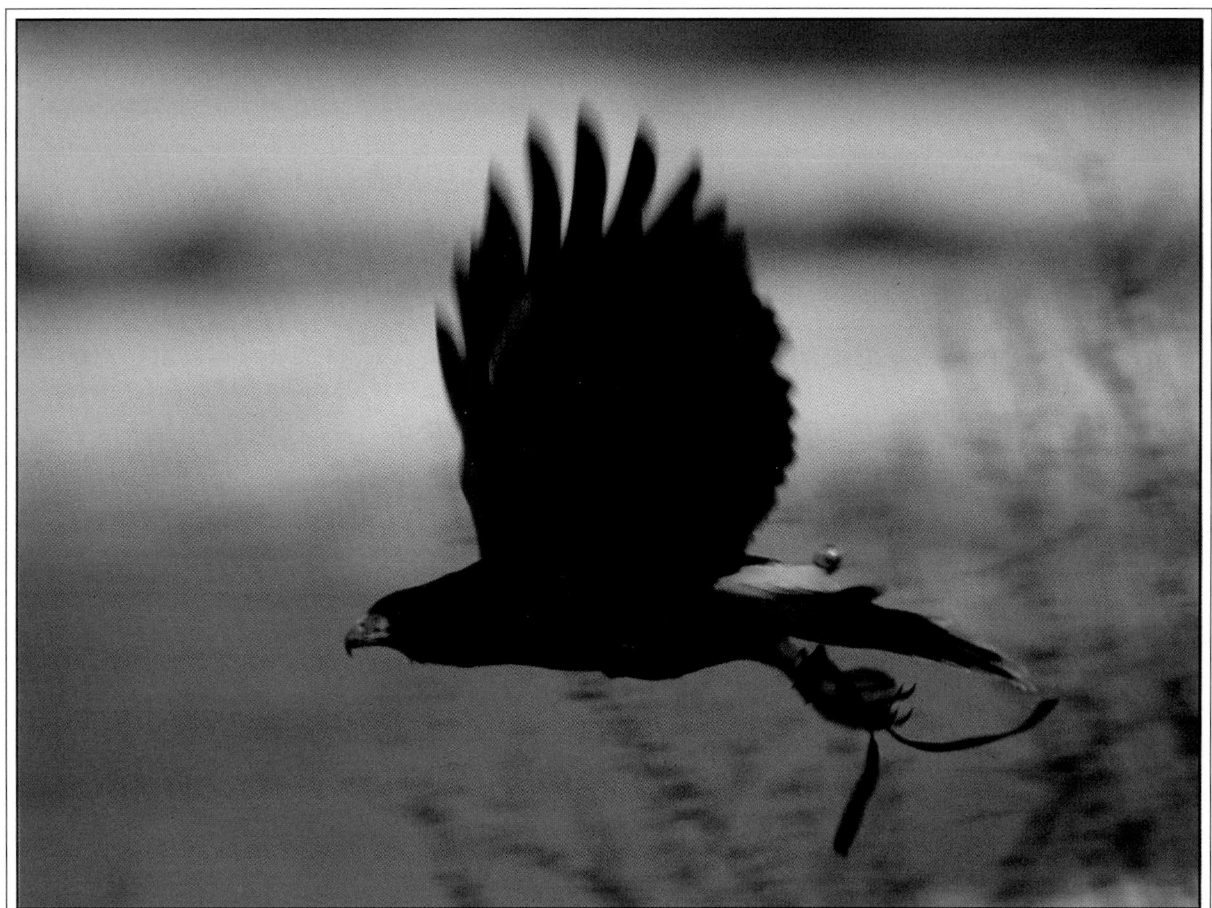

photo by Keith Thompson

The land lay barren from the cold of winter. The sycamores towering over the house had long since been stripped clean by icy winds. The fields stretching out in the river valley looked brown, stark and naked. I wondered where the covey of quail was and how they were faring. Would there be any left to reproduce in the spring? My two Harris' hawks were keen to fly. The cold crisp nights sharpened their hunger. They needed to satisfy the innate craving of a predator to hunt and kill, to preserve life.

Today I would leave the valley in search of more fertile hunting fields. I had driven forty miles in about an hour when at last my pickup rolled to a stop along a string of overgrown fields. There were a few scattered woodlots, but mostly weeds. The place was surrounded on every side by the city. It was feral ground, owned by industrial complexes. It stood out as an eyesore to the folks around, but to me it was a place much more interesting than the drab concrete world surrounding it. There were piles of twisted and tortured oaks dozing in great heaps to remind me that corporate America was planning more "progress" to come. It was late winter and game had long since become scarce. The harshness of winter had effectively culled all but the strongest and fastest creatures.

I'm certain it would seem odd to most, why I had came here at all. My home sits deep in farming country. The green and fertile fields of corn and soybean surrounding the house had been harvested, leaving only huge expanses of plowed and sterile ground. I live in a small house with my wife and daughter, along the bank of a river. The landscape of the place is dominated by my towering breeding barn that houses two pairs of Harris' hawks and a pair of peregrine falcons. There are two Harris' hawks and a goshawk that live in small chambers in the yard that I use for hunting. Pigeons constantly circle the house from my loft, and there is a building given over to the raising of coturnix quail, to provide food for all of the birds. There is precious little time to spare around here, but on the weekends when I do get some extra time, I load up the birds and set out in search of better hawking fields and more abundant game than the valley holds. I live in the country, but increasingly find myself traveling to the city to hunt. To the untrained eye, the place from where I came must appear like a much better place to hunt than the place to which I am traveling. But in farming country, unfortunately, the land is farmed to maximize production. No land is wasted; there's precious little left over for the small game that I seek.

When I stopped, the two female Harris' hawks in the back knew immediately that we were at our destination and became fidgety. Their bells ran out loudly in the metal camper as I stepped out. I opened the doors to the crates that held the birds and they impatiently hopped out onto the tailgate, viewed their surroundings for suitable perches, and flew out to some trees.

As the birds flew I noticed two small boys, perhaps ten years of age, staring in my direction. They had a look of utter amazement on their faces. I try to be discreet about my activities because critics have declared open season on hunters and anti-hunting sentiments are running at an all-time high. I'm not ashamed of what I do, quite the contrary, but by being secretive I avoid confrontations in the first place. Years ago it was reported in a local paper that a falconer was hunting a certain area, "killing hundreds of rabbits with hawks." The city council convened a town meeting, and the consensus was that this mystery falconer be caught and stopped immediately. A plainclothes policeman was dispatched to handle the job. I continued to hunt there the rest of the season anyway, always being careful not to be seen. After all, it was a great spot. The rabbits were grossly overpopulated, denuding every living plant as high as they could reach, and the area held large populations of quail. Next season I went back to find the whole thing covered in concrete by a huge shopping center, exactly like the one two blocks away. I often wondered where all the concerned citizens had been.

If I had noticed the boys, I would have waited until they had passed to let out the birds. I went about my business, slipping on my game vest, shouldering my falconry bag, grabbing my flushing stick and checking to see that my equipment was all in order, pretending to pay no attention to them. But closer they came, more slowly now. I couldn't help but notice how they seemed fearful of approaching, and yet at the same time overcome with curiosity. The city had taught them the dangers of approaching strangers, but the natural curiosity of two ten-year-old boys soon overshadowed their fears. They timidly walked up and began to ask questions.

"Hey mister, what are those?"

"Hawks," I answered as I continued to go about my business.

"What kind?"

"Harris' hawks."

"What are you doing with them?"

"Hunting."

"What are you hunting?"

"Oh, mostly rabbits today."

"Do they bring 'em back?"

"No, afraid not."

"Where'd you get 'em?"

"These two were hatched out of an incubator."

"What's their names?"

"Nellie and Bianca."

"How old are they?"

"Nellie is eleven and Bianca is thirteen."

"How come they don't fly away?"

"Because they're trained."

"Do you come here often?"

"How come we haven't seen you here before?"

"How do you get the rabbit away from them if they catch one?"

They had obviously decided that I was harmless. As soon as I would get an answer out to one, the other would shoot out a question. My answers were short, like my patience, but with every answer came replies such as "neat," or "wow," or "really?" The two birds gazed down as if to say, "Come on, let's get with it!"

They were fast becoming bored with this turn of events. I slowly walked away, continuing to answer questions as I left but attempting to walk out of the conversation. Then I stopped, turned around and said, "Why don't you two guys walk along with me and see if we can scare up some game?" Their mouths dropped open as they turned to each other in disbelief, and then they hurriedly jumped in beside me.

As we walked out into the field, I scanned the horizons for any signs of danger. The world can be a pretty hazardous place for two birds that have come to unquestionably trust humans, even ones with guns, and there's also the ever-present danger of electrocution when hunting in city fields. I tried to foresee anything that could cause us harm. These birds have been my constant hunting companions for over ten years now, and we have grown close, intimately so. Each often knows what the other will do before he does it. These birds have traveled all over this country on hunting trips with me. We have hunted and flown in every type of terrain, against many kinds of quarry. I have often found myself dreading that awful, inevitable day, when our trio would be forever broken by the death of one of us.

As the two boys and I walked on, I began to focus on the task at hand, finding some game. I probed my flushing stick into hidden holes in weed patches and thorn bushes in an attempt to kick up a rabbit. The two boys had their attention focused on the birds as they flew past, their wingtips sometimes just brushing our shoulders as they swooped past. The hawks would wait until we caught up before flying out ahead of us again. They knew that out in front they would be in the best position to intercept quarry.

Game was scarce, and the few rabbits we jumped found close and easy refuge in the large tangles of trees stacked around in the field. I was used to more action than we were getting, but the two boys were so fascinated by the whole show that I found myself focussing more attention toward them than toward the birds. We plowed through thorns that tore and ripped at our legs and I slowed the pace somewhat so the boys could keep up. They thought that I must be pretty tough the way I always crashed through the heaviest cover, undaunted by the thorns, until one finally asked, "Hey, how come these thorns don't bother you?" I pointed down at my heavy brush slacks with the nylon, briar-proof fronts.

We kept moving but the two birds seemed to get nothing but bad breaks and what few rabbits we did see, escaped. Twice we jumped rabbits that scrambled to cover only seconds before the birds caught up to them. Nellie and Bianca were trying hard to score, and I could sense their frustration. I knew that the first rabbit up that was a little off the mark, or a little too far from the sanctuary of the log piles, would be quickly taken by the hawks. I was becoming frustrated, too. On a good day we might have taken a limit of rabbits by now. I sensed that shooting for quotas meant nothing to these boys. They appeared not to notice that we hadn't caught anything. For them, the magic of watching the birds work was wonder enough. The boys were amazed that these wild creatures could be working with us so closely, so perfectly obedient. The hawks needed no signals, no rewards, no enticing. They knew their job, and they went at it with all of their being.

If the birds lagged behind a little, the

kids would walk backwards so as not to miss a wingbeat. “Hey, did you see that?” one would yell out with excitement. They noticed small things, like the way a bird would pull its wings in tightly against its body as it shot between two saplings, the way a bird would be momentarily flying upside down as it tucked into a dive, or the way one would ruffle, shake and readjust her feathers after a headlong crash through the briars. These were city kids who had grown up without the space and the unlimited freedom available to a country boy like myself. They had had little opportunity to explore and learn about the natural world around them. Every new move the birds made seemed to provide the boys with something to wonder at and ponder. What kept the birds from hurting themselves as they hurled themselves recklessly into the ground? How does a bird really fly? What keeps their feathers from breaking? They could see firsthand, and understand, why a rabbit wore a camouflaged coat of hair, and that running and jumping were not just things rabbits did to be cute. Every form, every adaptation, every seemingly insignificant detail had a real purpose.

A rabbit shot out from under a creek bank, but before the two birds could close the distance, it slipped like liquid into a log jam. The birds pitched up on top of the pile, and looked at me as if to ask if I could re-flush it for them. But the rabbit was safe. Normally, by now I might have been thinking about packing it in and looking for a fresh spot, but the boys were enjoying themselves so much that I found it hard to be anything but entertained by their antics.

Wilderness to these boys was the little patches of weeds and woods we were now exploring. There was little of the mystery here that I knew as a young boy, the feeling that I could hike all day, driven on by the wonder of what lay over the next hill, the possibility of getting lost, the deep blackness of an unexplored cave, the dizzying height of a river bluff, the swirling fury of the rapids. The number of species of animals that I could observe seemed endless. The plants and animals that I found as a child were my teachers, the whole world a classroom. How it differed from the one these two kids had! This was their turf, and they were eager to guide me around.

With much difficulty we crossed a stream to a spot they said would hold more rabbits. I was glad to get away from those accursed log piles. We were walking through dense woods and tangled underbrush now, again not the kind of terrain conducive to taking lots of game. I couldn't see the birds, but I heard their bells as they followed above. There was no need to watch them. They are the kind of birds that always keep up, like shadows. Only birds that worked like these could be trusted in a place like this. The sounds of their bells told me not only where they were, but what they were doing.

Both birds suddenly shot out ahead of us with the wingbeat and demeanor that told me they were not simply changing perches, but were kicking into pursuit. The three of us crashed through the underbrush, trying hard to keep up with the flight. I saw both birds make shallow dips towards the ground. Years of flying at game and observing the various types of flights gave me a sense that something was out of the ordinary. It's nothing I know how to describe, but I know it when I see it. Perhaps they were hounding a dog, cat, fox, or even a coyote. If a bird bound to one of these it could be injured or even killed. I raced ahead, leaving the boys behind. Through the trees I made out what had excited the birds, a wild turkey, a mature gobbler, crouched nervously and slinking along the ground so that his beard dragged in front of him. This wasn't the first turkey these two birds had come up against, and like the ones before, this turkey was too terrified to fly, choosing instead to take its chances in the dense cover of the underbrush. A Harris' hawk, or even two, is no match for a mature gobbler. This turkey could have easily weighed twenty pounds or

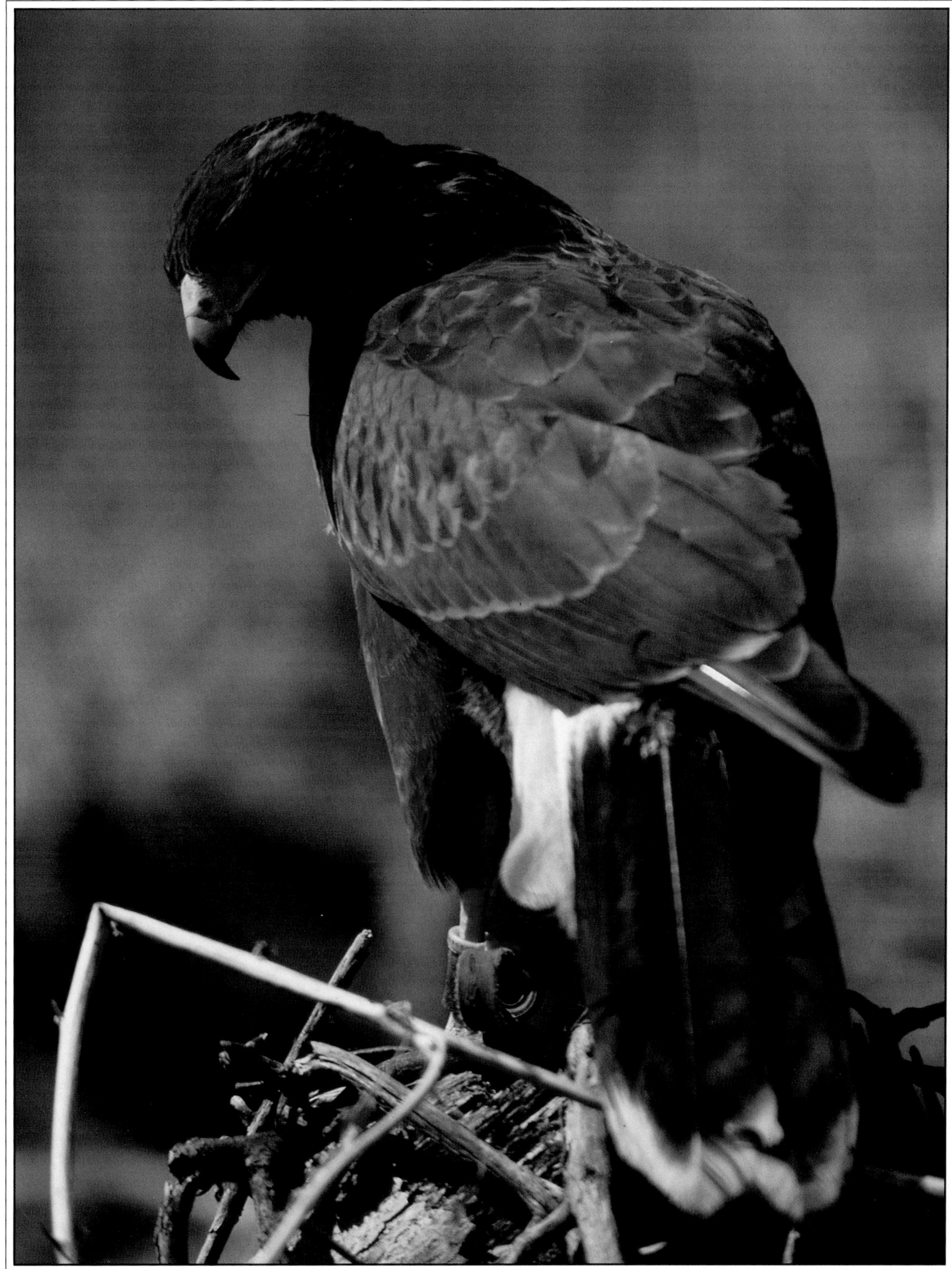

photo by Keith Thompson

more, in contrast to the hawks, which were only two pounds each. But what Harris' hawks lack in size they make up in pure spunk. I lost sight of the turkey, but could tell by watching the hawks that it was just ahead. If it flew, I would know at once by the great whooshing sounds of its huge wings. The boys caught up and we stalked slowly ahead to find out where the turkey was hiding. The hawks knew exactly where he was, but were waiting for the right moment to launch their attack. To fly down a turkey required no special feat, but to hold it down and kill it would require a heroic effort. The birds needed to draw on every bit of their strength, instinct and knowledge of the hunt. It would also require a team effort, and all five of us made up that team.

As we approached a large toppled tree, the turkey suddenly exploded from under our feet. Anyone who has ever stepped on an exploding covey of bobwhite knows the feeling of the sudden shock surging through your body. The only difference is that the turkey is much larger, and therefore even louder. It was the first time these boys had ever felt that sensation. It's the kind of feeling that comes on like a heart attack, and ends up feeling good. From somewhere directly overhead Nellie slammed into the turkey as it rose off the forest floor, half flying, half running. The turkey quickly broke free. No sooner had it struggled free from the clutches of the first hawk than Bianca crashed into it. The strong, thrusting wings of the turkey sent dried leaves flying outwards in a circle as the hawk held on for all she was worth. Just as the first hawk regained its composure and tried to assist the other, the turkey again broke free. It scrambled on into the woods ahead of us, with both hawks in close pursuit. The hawks were close behind and pumping hard, their adrenaline rushing. Quickly, all three birds disappeared into the foliage ahead. Running as fast as we could, we found two huge piles of turkey feathers where each of the hawks had once again caught up to the gobbler, but had once again been thrown off. Then there was quiet. No hawks or turkey in sight. No sounds of hawk bells. Just silence.

We walked over to where the three birds had first struggled, and amid piles of turkey feathers we found seven perfect tail feathers. The boys were jumping up and down, screaming to each other, "There really is a turkey here!" It was indeed an odd place for a wild turkey. The boys had caught a fleeting glimpse of him early one morning out the fogged-over window of a school bus. When they related their find to the other kids at school, they were ridiculed and taunted. Their parents had explained to them that wild turkeys don't live in the city. The kids themselves had begun to doubt their own eyes, and rarely spoke of the sighting again except between themselves. But they had wanted desperately to believe that their little woods really did hold something wild, something mysterious. Now they knew, and held tangible evidence as they crammed their pockets with handfuls of turkey feathers as proof of the events of the day with the two hawks. "Do you think they'll believe us?" asked one. "Probably not," said the other. But now *they* knew. I thought of how it was probably best that the turkey hadn't been killed. The boys still had something special in "their" woods. Somewhere out there was one nervous ragged turkey.

I hurried the boys along, anxious to relocate Nellie and Bianca. Fifteen minutes later there was still no sign of the two hawks. While flying falcons and accipiters, it is fairly common to lose track of your bird, but fifteen minutes of separation from these two was rare. Even the boys looked worried. We spread out and searched the woodlot, and eventually heard the faint tinkle of bells. After some time we determined the direction of the sound, and finally located the birds. After losing the turkey, the birds had spotted a rabbit, and were searching it out in the thick underbrush.

I motioned the birds in our direction, and we headed toward the truck, the hawks following. We trudged back another route and happened upon an old garden. One of us surprised a rabbit and the birds were quickly in pursuit.

The weeds were thinner here, and there was no ready-made refuge for the rabbit to skip into. There was space for the birds to maneuver, and they closed the distance quickly. Nellie caught up first and slammed in, but missed. Bianca caught up next, with the rabbit barely outmaneuvering her. Nellie made a final stoop and crashed into some waist high weeds. I heard the faint squeal that signaled the rabbit had been caught. We moved in quickly to reassure ourselves that we had finally taken something. To me it was little more than another mark in my game book, but the kids had just witnessed something very special. Bianca sat on a low limb nearby, behaving like the perfect lady she was. Her reward would come shortly. "That was the most beautiful thing I've ever seen!" said one of the boys. I wondered how often he had used language like that before. "This is the best day in my whole life!" exclaimed the other. They were both beaming with excitement and pride in the fact that together we had done it, we had caught a rabbit.

We sat around the bird as it fed, and talked about the flight. There is joy in success, but there should also be a reflection over the death of the animal, a moment to be serious. Death demands respect.

The boys were still beaming over the kill. I was struck with the fact that something I had grown to take for granted was so important to these young boys. There was a time, over twenty years ago, when I was about their age and had taken my first female red-tailed hawk. I had watched it leave my gloved fist to fly down a half-grown rabbit along the edge of a dirt road. I remembered having felt then the same excitement and sense of accomplishment that these boys feel now. But repetition and time had dulled my senses.

We walked back, and as the truck came into view, the two Harris' hawks flew on ahead and perched on the top rack to wait for us to catch up. We cut the rabbit in two, and divided it between the birds. As we stood there watching the hawks feed, one of the boys asked one final question, one that touched me with conflicting emotions.

"Why aren't you mean to us like all the rest of them?"

"Like all the rest of who?" I asked.

"Like older and bigger people."

I guess life in the city can be tough on a kid. "There's plenty of good folks out there," I answered. "If you two treat others nice, you'll find them."

I hope that I convinced them that not all men were bad, and that there would be lots of good people out there that they could befriend. And I hoped that after the developers had finished cutting up their woods, there would still be enough room left for a turkey and two small boys to roam.

As we parted, they said they would keep a look-out for my truck parked along the deserted field, but I never saw them again. We had not even exchanged names. I wondered if their parents believed their story about hunting with the two hawks, and about the turkey. I'm certain those boys will not forget that day anytime soon, but then, I haven't either.

Who Was That Guy?

by Richard Holmstrom

It was either 1964 or 1965 when I met my first falconer. I was around twelve years old. That summer and the summer before, a couple of friends and I had been trying our best to kill rabbits with a sling and rock. The southern California town that I lived in at the time, Seal Beach, had a place that we used to call "Bullet Hill." The name came from the fact that the military had, in the past, used the area for a target range, and as a result, there were literally thousands of spent (and sometimes live) cartridges lying about. It was probably not the safest place to be hunting rabbits, but for us it was about the only place. This hillside area lay out onto a flat basin dotted with oil wells. In the past it had been all orange groves, but that was long before I arrived on the scene. It was home to many creatures such as king and gopher snakes, alligator lizards, blue-bellied swifts, horned toads, opossums, and at times, more rabbits than you've ever seen. It also had a healthy population of raptors, mostly red-tails, kestrels and a few burrowing owls . . . all the things that make a place irresistible to twelve-year-old kids.

This was the place where I caught my first gopher snake. I found a trap door spider, which I caught and brought home, then lost in my bedroom (I didn't sleep too well for a week or so). I remember that this was also the place where I was bitten by an opossum while trying to extract it from a culvert. Having heard that they sometimes carried rabies, I of course hid the bite from my parents for weeks. I did not want to go through the series of shots that they had told me so much about. I later figured out why all parents tell their children so much about those awful shots in the belly that people must undergo if stricken with rabies: to stop kids like me from dragging home every critter that they manage to catch. It never worked, of course. I just kept the bite to myself and every morning when I woke, it was a dash to the bathroom to check the mirror to see if I was foaming yet, then to turn on the water to see if it frightened me. That went on for the longest time.

I remember these things as if it were only yesterday, rather than almost thirty years ago. I also remember how very hot it could become on summer days.

It was on one of these hot, humid summer days that found me out in the flats, dog-tired, and convinced I was dying of thirst. One of the drawbacks to this place was that there wasn't any water anywhere and you could build up a powerful thirst in a very short time, especially if you had been chasing rabbits for most of the day. I was on my weary way back home when I spotted an old car parked along one of the many roads that connected the oil wells of the area. A quick look inside revealed that this was the type of car equipped with a push-button starter. My older brother had a car of this type, and I knew that even without the keys, this car would move down the road if you placed it in gear and simply pushed the button. I knew what I was about to do was wrong, but I was dying of thirst. I jumped in, put her in gear and pushed the button.

I was sailing along about five miles an hour when I noticed a man running from the trees that surrounded Bullet Hill. He was running my way. I watched in sheer terror as he proceeded to catch right up to me (and his car) and yank the door open. He grabbed me and threw me to the ground. I think we were both glad that, after his long exhausting run, he lacked the strength to do anything but fling me to the ground and place his knees on my chest. It gave him time to see that I was just a kid and probably also time to get over his anger long enough to not want to beat me half to death. After making me push his car to get it going again (I had drained the battery), he made me get in, telling me he was bringing me home to my parents. My father was a policeman and I knew that this was the biggest trouble I had ever been in, and I also knew that I was in for a good licking. I wasn't, in all probability, going to see Bullet Hill for a while either. I explained all this to the man on the way home, but I don't think he was listening.

It was about at this point that I noticed the strange equipment the man had on the dash, and my curiosity got the better of me. I asked him what that stuff was. I really don't think I expected much of an answer, but I was wrong. He told me, in surprising detail, what the hood, jesses, leashes, and a swivel were. He was a "falconer." He explained he was in the area looking for red-tails. He also told me what he intended to do with the bird once he caught it: he was going to hunt rabbits with it. Click! Up to this point, I had no idea that falconry even existed. Not the foggiest notion that you could do anything with these critters other than stick them in a cage and look at them. Of course that hadn't stopped me, the summer before, from taking a burrowing owl from a nest. I had brought the young owl home, and fed the poor thing something like bread and milk, or hamburger, until it died. I got to thinking of that owl and asked the man some questions on feeding and housing and whatnot. His detailed answers were a revelation to me. Beefheart, mice, even store-bought chicken were better than hamburger.

As I think back on it now, I am sure that my questions about keeping a hawk in good health and proper food saved me from a licking from my father. For, as we arrived at my home, he simply said, "Beat it." I jumped out of that car and he drove off. I never saw the man again.

It may be painfully obvious that I am no writer. However, over the years I have become a somewhat competent falconer. I have graduated from starving young burrowing owls to catching winged quarry with gyrfalcons and goshawks. I have, luckily, never had a raptor die from bad health. The man whose car I tried to steal that hot summer day so long ago has more to do with that than he could possibly know. I would dearly like to tell him that. I hope he is still with us. If not, God rest his soul. He would also be glad to know that I never stole another car. And thirty years later, I am a practicing falconer forevermore.

George and Harry

by Floyd Presley

George and Harry were typical red-tailers. George was one of the better red-tail hawk trappers in Maryland. He had devised many innovations of bal chatri traps, pigeon harnesses, and bow nets. George also discovered several good ridge sites for trapping in the Maryland mountains. Hawk trapping was critical to red-tail hawkers of these times because most believed the only red-tails worth hunting were fifty-plus-ounce hawks. The problem was that fifty-ouncers probably only occurred at a ratio of one in sixty; therefore, in order to get one of these large hawks, a trapper had to catch a lot of birds. Consequently, the red-tailers of this generation were very skilled and very cocksure about their abilities to trap these hawks.

Harry's expertise with red-tail hawks was irrefutable; moreover, he was one of the dedicated mainstay members of the squirrel hunting society and a pioneer in squirrel hawking techniques. Harry's artistic skills and workmanship allowed him to fashion some excellent hawk equipment: he built one of the first spring-loaded bow nets. These qualities, combined with George's skills, naturally forged George and Harry into a team. However, in most ways they were contrary.

Together, they resembled Mutt and Jeff. George was lean and slight in stature with dark hair, dark eyes, dark complexion, and a clean-shaven face, whereas Harry had almost the completely opposite appearance. He was heavily built, six foot two inches tall, with red hair, light-colored eyes, fair complexion and a red handlebar mustache. George was outspoken and dogmatic in his views, almost to the point of violence. Harry was quiet with a laid-back nature. He could see humor in everything and liked to tease people.

Although George and Harry were very different, their love of falconry and especially their fondness for red-tail hawks forged a strong bond of friendship between them. They trapped and hawked together and challenged others to match their attainments. Needless to say, the competition between red-tail hawkers extended not only to wild quarry taken, but also to trapping achievements, such as most red-tails caught in a day, most red-tails caught in one season, and most red-tails trapped from a vehicle. The red-tail hawkers of this era had tough goals to strive for in order to distinguish themselves. This peer pressure caused many rivalries between individuals and groups. Falconry meets and gatherings developed into an atmosphere of "Can you top this?"

Being a product of this environment prodded George to new endeavors. On his daily trips to work along the backroads of the Beltsville farming community, George had noticed a large immature red-tail in her winter territory. Every morning soon after daylight, he spotted this hawk perched on a dead snag in a fence line between two large fields. Finally, George decided to capture this hawk by hand. What a challenge, he reasoned: no one had ever caught a red-tail using this method. George had heard of Al Nye buried in the sand of Assateague Island grabbing peregrine falcons by hand, and some guy in Canada who had caught goshawks by hand from a pup tent, but George was positive no one had ever grabbed a red-tail hawk by hand. He also was confident this feat couldn't be duplicated for some time because, after all, everyone knows red-tail hawks are smarter and harder to catch than peregrines or goshawks.

On Friday night George called Harry and disclosed his plan. Harry immediately agreed to help and even suggested some new ideas. Harry offered to wait by the road as a spotter with binoculars and a walkie-talkie. This way George wouldn't have to continuously

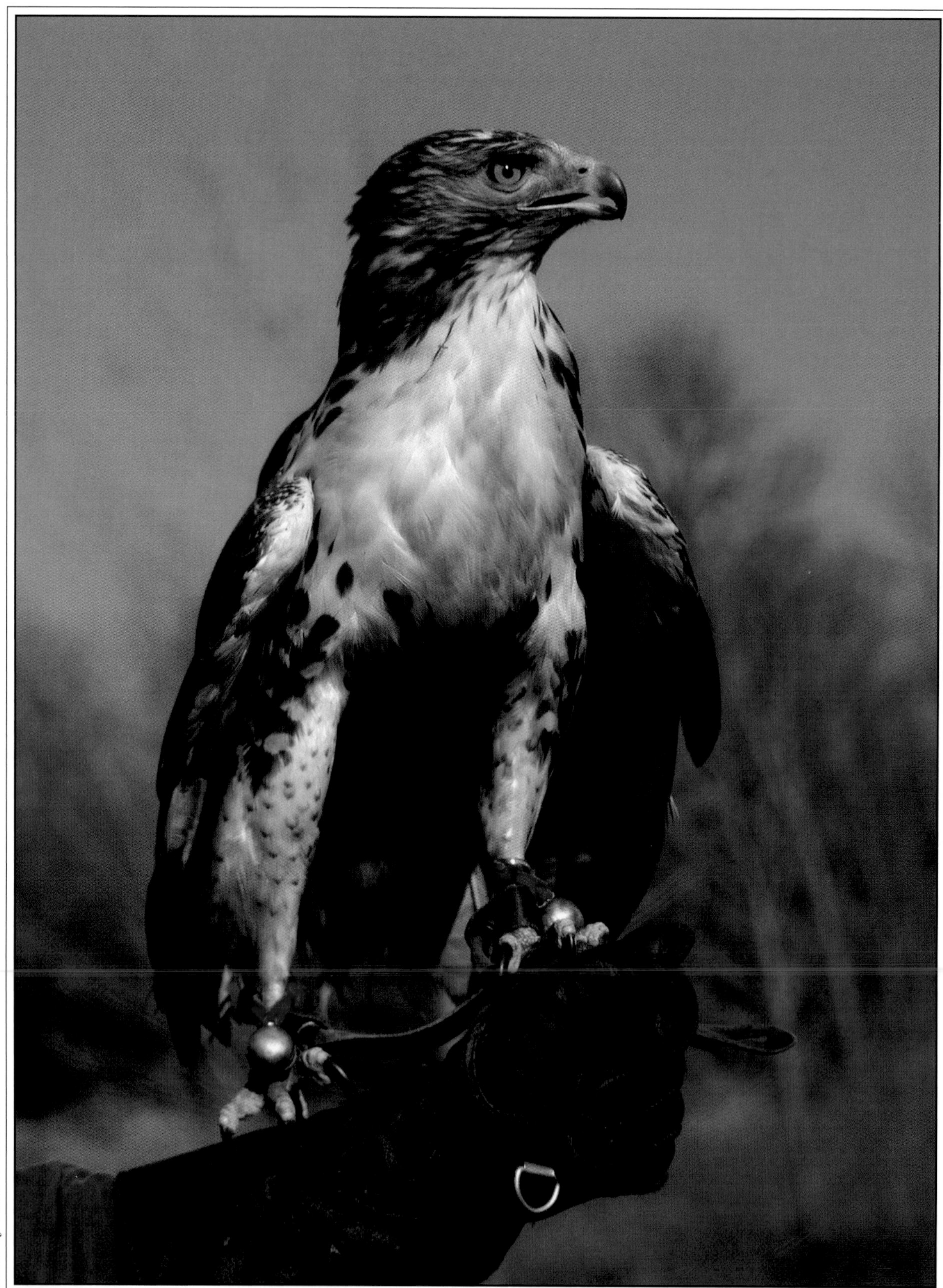

photo by Paul T. Schnell

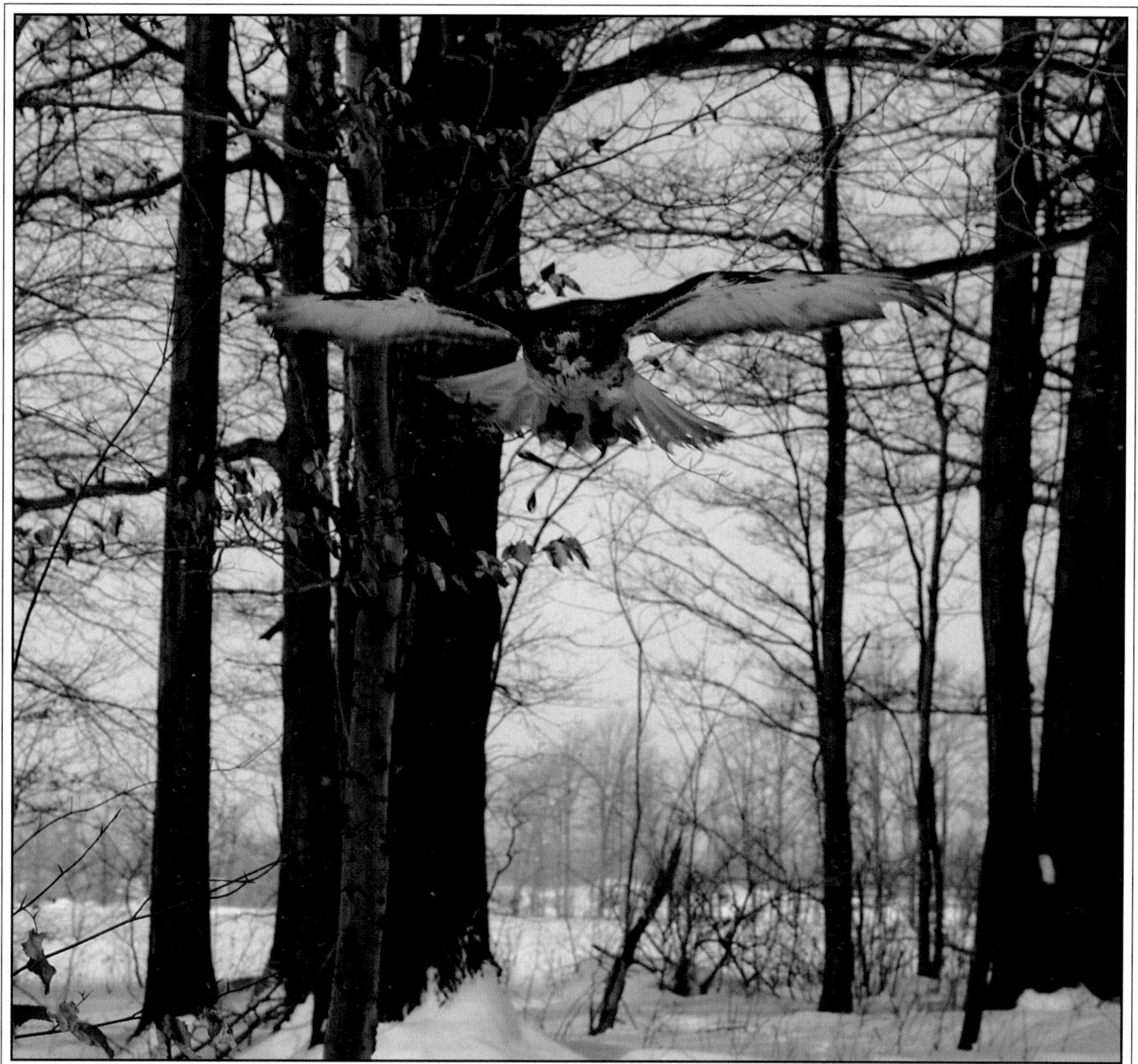

photo by Paul T. Schnell

lure with the handheld pigeon. Constant luring might make the red-tail suspicious, Harry reasoned. George agreed. The excitement and anticipation of hand-catching a red-tail ruined their sleep that night.

At 4:30 a.m. Saturday morning, Harry went to get George. Harry had borrowed a pair of children's walkie-talkies. He also had the binoculars and two shovels. George was more than ready, he was hyper. George was wearing dark clothing and his face was charcoaled. He was carrying three rolled Army blankets, a half-sheet of plywood, and a pigeon in a leather harness. His black-dyed goatskin gloves were the final touch. On seeing George in this outfit, Harry started laughing and said, "You look like something out of a horror story." George replied, "We'll see who laughs last when I grab that red-tail."

As George and Harry mused over a possible trapsite in the darkness, the semi-frozen ground posed a problem. Since a proper pit couldn't be dug, a compromise was made to scoop out a shallow trench in a natural low spot between two cut cornrows. As the first rays of the morning sun broke on the horizon, steam arose from under the collars of the panicky diggers. A hasty decision was made to go with the inadequate depth. Army blankets were substituted for the piece of plywood and the headset. George was forced to lie on his stomach on one blanket and fashion another blanket around his head with one small eye hole. In this position, George had to keep his left arm extended in front of him so he could pull the pigeon across his left palm and grasp the red-tail's legs on contact. George also had to operate the walkie-talkie with his right hand. This juggling act was tricky. After a radio check, Harry began to carefully cover the edges of the blanket with dirt clods to hold it in place. Then Harry sprinkled the top of the blankets with weeds and pieces of corn stalks to make it blend with the surrounding area. From a few yards away, Harry took one last look in the pre-dawn light at their hide. The camouflage looked perfect. Then Harry hustled his walkie-talkie, the plywood, and the remaining tools back to the car.

It was a clear, cool day, without a breath of wind. The conditions for trapping were perfect. "George, can you hear me? Over." "Yes, I hear you loud and clear. Can you see anything yet? Over." "No, but it's not fully light yet. What time do you drive past here every morning? Over." "Around 8:00. Over." "Well, we got about an hour to wait. Over." "Roger over and out." The time passed very slowly for George. He was in an uncomfortable position and he was freezing. His teeth were chattering and occasionally his body shook spasmodically.

A little later, "Harry, what time is it? Over." "7:20. Over." "Do you see anything? Over." "No. What's wrong with your voice? Over." "Nothing, except I'm freezing my ass off." Pause. "Oh, that's too bad, it's nice and warm here in the car with the heater running," chuckle, chuckle. A long static click, then, "You son of a bitch. I appreciate your concern." Pause. "Sorry George, just kidding." Silence, fifteen long minutes and still no red-tail.

By this time George was so cold he began to think he was hallucinating. As his body shivered, it seemed the ground shook too. George peeked through the peephole and scanned the area, but nothing had changed However, George's field of vision was limited to 180 degrees directly in front of him. Then George thought he heard a rumbling noise. "What's that noise? Over." No answer. "Harry, what's going on? Over." No reply. Meanwhile, Harry, still in the car, searched the trees on the far side of the field with binoculars. When Harry lowered the binoculars, he couldn't believe his eyes. A huge tractor with a gang plow attached was heading directly at George. "George, there's a tractor plowing toward you. Over." No answer. "George, get out of there!" No answer. "George, I'm not shitting you; there's a tractor heading directly for you!" No answer. Bolting from the car, Harry ran to the fence and screamed, "George! George! George, run!" But apparently George couldn't hear Harry's warning over the tractor sound. Right at this point, George peeled the blanket off his head and looked behind him. Much to his horror, the tractor was only five yards away and closing fast. George sprang like a frightened rabbit from his form and stumbling, ran headlong for the car. The astonished farmer slammed his brakes and stopped. He watched a man dressed in black with a blackened face run the hundred and fifty yards to the road with a pigeon dangling and flapping from his wrist. When this man reached the fence, he vaulted over it, bird flapping and all, and sped away in a car.

As soon as George caught his breath, he started on Harry. "Why in the hell didn't you warn me?" "I tried," yelled Harry, "but the batteries in the walkie-talkie must have gone dead in the cold." George still wasn't satisfied. He was mad. Then Harry started laughing. "What in the hell are you laughing at? I could have been wiped out!" Harry, still grinning, said, "Think of that farmer. What do you think he thought when a black-faced man came out of the ground in front of his tractor and ran out of the field dragging a pigeon tied to his wrist?" And they both started laughing.

Scars

by Ronald G. Clarke

Falconry is highly unusual behavior in modern times. Devotees dress in odd clothing, raise small creatures to feed the rapacious feathered dragons they harbor right in their homes, decorate the walls with bizarre icons, construct intricate leather devices, and regularly gather with fellow practitioners in remote locations where they can perform their unusual deeds away from the prying eyes of the uninitiated.

Some falconers become totally addicted and literally live the sport. Others devote less of themselves, leaving room for gainful employment and even family life. Between the two extremes are a thousand variations, and at least that many differing opinions. One of the few common fibers through this disparate community is made of collagen. Scar tissue.

All falconers collect scars, but they're like lawsuits: nobody really wants them, but once survived, they become badges of experience, proof of pain endured. And all falconers occasionally point to them with a certain amount of pride.

A simply error in judgment can earn a falconer a new tattoo. See the little white spot in the middle of my fingertip? A gyrfalcon did that. Not on purpose, mind you. I had handed him a piece of fresh chicken, and my blood-smeared fingers looked like that much more food. He simply wrapped his foot around the whole works and started tearing and swallowing.

But human skin is surprisingly tough stuff, and he just couldn't carve off a piece. He buried the tip of his beak in the pad of my finger and bit down. The hard little scar that distorts my fingerprint reminds me how it felt. That memory also makes me considerably more judicious about how I offer food to my birds.

Some scars reflect a bird's inexperience rather than the falconer's. My young peregrine wanted the morsel of quail meat I held in my gloved fist, but she was nervous about flying across the great distance involved — all of twelve feet. In her three months outside the egg, she'd never traveled that far without touching the ground. She shifted from foot to foot and stared at anything but me. A moth flying by was clearly the most fascinating thing she'd ever seen in her short life. Look — a cloud! Amazing.

Finally, she looked directly at the glove and bobbed her head several times. She leaned forward, spread her wings, gave a couple of quick, shallow flaps, and stayed put.

I squatted. She thinks humans are less intimidating when they're curled up at ground level. She zeroed in on the glove and launched herself.

She missed. The falcon flew right past the glove, veered toward my face and landed on my shoulder. Okay, we can deal with that. Here, bird, here's the glove with the meat again. See? You could just step from my shoulder to the glove. Looks easy, doesn't it? Go ahead, you can do it.

I held the glove so she'd have to step onto it instead of just snatching the meat with her beak. She gripped my shoulder and leeeeaaaaaned toward the glove. As she leaned, she hung on tighter. Aside from looking ridiculous, this was beginning to get uncomfortable.

In graduate school, my major professor used to tell wannabe falconers to consider taking up a less demanding hobby. Something less expensive, easier on home life, and less damaging to body and soul. Something like heroin addiction. I should have listened.

I rolled my head sideways and looked up at her. She responded by punching through

photo by Ronald G. Clarke

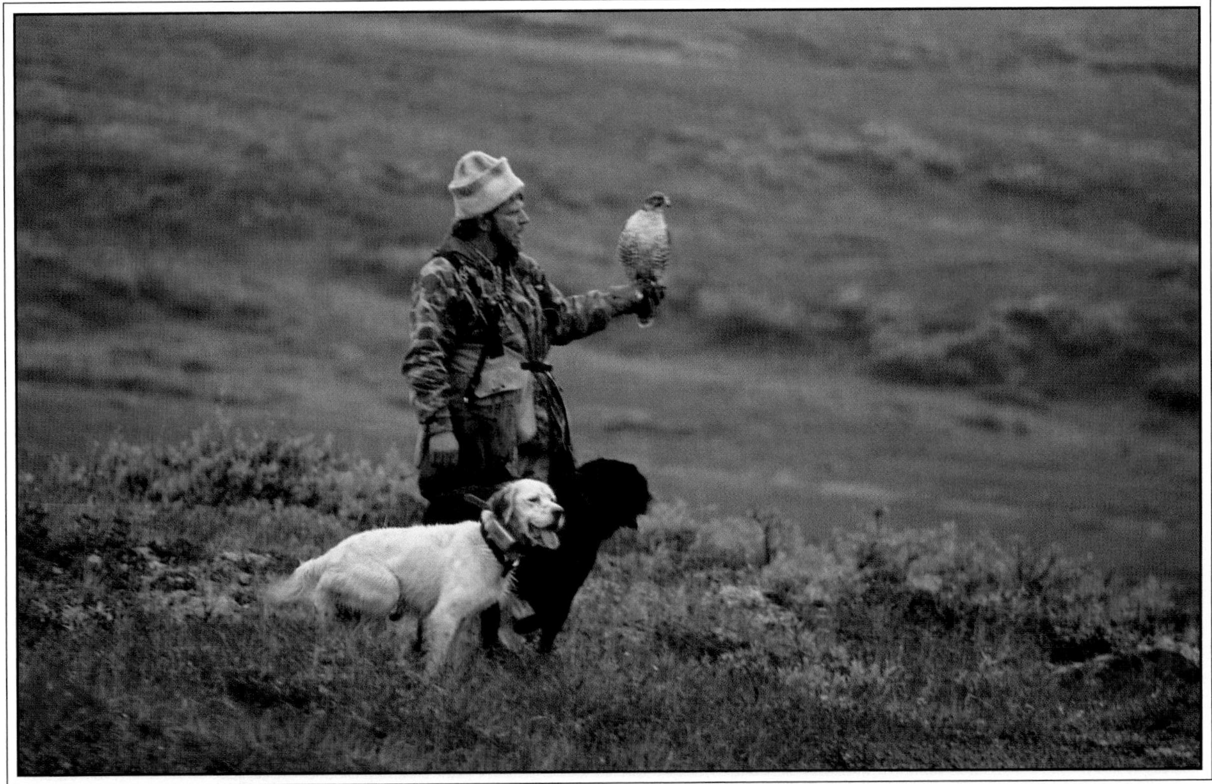

photo by Ronald G. Clarke

my earlobe with one quick stab of her beak. I could feel blood trickling down my neck. Red means food to a raptor; she grabbed my ear and tried to tear it off.

So here's a grown man squatting in a field with a large predatory bird clinging to his shoulder, devouring his head piece by small piece. Falconry isn't a sport. It's utter madness.

If this were mere sport, falconers could hang up the equipment at the end of the season. Oil the glove, clean the cleats, lean the bat in the corner. But baseball shoes don't produce mounds of guano if they perch in one place for a while, and one can't store a falcon in a locker through the winter. Birds require careful attention every day. Falconry is a year-round way of life, whether actively hunting with a bird or just passing time until duck season.

Scar tissue chronicles each falconer's life with birds as surely as any collection of photographs. Who needs slides? Here, let me roll up my pant leg. See this scrape on my shin? That's from a duck hunt two years ago. I was walking out across some jumbled blocks of overflow ice left stranded at low tide, hoping to flush three buffleheads for my gyr. The edge of one block gave way, and I plunged downward about three feet. Not only did an adjoining block grind the skin off my shin, but I twisted my ankle when I hit the frozen mud beneath. But there was a falcon waiting on overhead, and I dutifully hobbled out under the waiting gyrkin and jumped the ducks. He easily snagged a little female and fluttered to the edge of the creek with it. The flight is as fresh in my mind as yesterday's attempt at a mallard at the same spot.

Even the dogs get scars. My gyrkin had knocked a big eastern Washington rooster pheasant to the ground. Out of the falcon's domain and onto the gallinaceous bird's turf, the pheasant proceeded to kick some sense into the mighty hunter. The rooster left the gyr sprawled in the dirt and cackled as he flew away. Dr. Mondo picked himself up, roused, and leapt into the air. Flying back toward me, I could see he was displeased and looking for revenge. And there, about 200 feet below, was Emmy Lou, my German wirehaired pointer, romping through the winter wheat with nary a clue of impending peril. The gyr folded up, dropped from the sky and struck her solidly on the rump with both feet. It sounded like a tennis player whacking a rug slung over a clothesline. Lou flattened and froze. Mondo mounted for another assault. When it was finally over, the dog was so emotionally battered that she thereafter refused to get out of the car until the falcon had flown and was rehooded.

On the other hand, Fletcher, the world's most laid-back springer spaniel, took everything in stride, even goshawks. When they're hungry, the big accipiters don't fly so much as react. Chase. Catch. Eat. Their minds aren't awash with complex thoughts that retard reactions. Chase. Catch. Eat. The tiniest flash of movement in the brush trips the handful of synapses in their hard-wired little brains, and they're off before they even know what they're chasing. Chase. Catch. Eat.

Sometimes Miss Sluggo, the female goshawk, would fall from my fist to grab Fletcher's stubby little tail. Hey, it wagged — it could have been prey. Anything's fair game to a gos, especially if it's red and resembles meat. Look —a panting springer spaniel's tongue! Chase. Catch. Eat. Fletcher just scrunched up his face and waited patiently for Sluggo to realize that what she had grabbed was not worth hanging onto. Eventually, she'd extract herself and Fletch would bound happily on his way. Scarred, perhaps, but terminally mellow.

The goshawk's fetish for anything red caught up with me, too. I should have paid attention to the jingling of her bells as she bounced from perch to perch in her mews, eager to fly. I should have noticed the fire in her eyes that would have told me she was hungry and ready to hunt. Instead, I ventured sleepily into her domain, and was set upon instantly. She'd spotted the small twist of red elastic binding my hair in a pony tail, and cracked me viciously on the back of the head.

At least nobody saw that, and the scar is hidden by my hair. A friend's female Harlan's red-tail didn't afford him the opportunity to suffer his indignity in solitude. She was in a tree, waiting for him to produce the lure. As he hauled it out, it caught on the edge of his pocket, but the hawk didn't care. She fell out of the tree, spread her wings and glided toward him. The harder he pulled, the tighter the lure stuck. She was ten feet away and closing fast when he realized the lure was not coming out in time. He bent over to hide the lure, figuring she'd go past and give him another chance to get the lure out.

Now, this was a no-nonsense bird. She didn't step lightly to the glove, she punished it with a hard-hitting, tightly-clutching assault. She especially enjoyed pounding the lure, in the air or on the ground. The big red-tail wanted the lure — she knew he had it somewhere — and simply swatted that part of him that stuck out when he bent over. If he has a scar from that episode, I doubt that he'd show it to you. I, for one, wouldn't care to see it. We tried hard not to laugh. Really, we did.

There's a mountain behind Vanderbilt Creek, but on a typical Juneau day, it's hard to tell. The peak is obscured by clouds and fog more often than not. Still, I strain to make out the ridgeline every time I pass by on the road below, watching for the silhouette of a particular triangular rock.

At first, I wasn't sure it was entirely wise to bury Dr. Mondo beneath that rock. I'd heard horrible tales from friends who buried pets only to have the ground later ripped apart by bulldozers — condos erected on the moldering bones of their best childhood friends. That didn't seem likely here.

The misty mountain was the familiar backdrop for many rewarding hours afield. Once, it overlooked a horrifying chase . . . five bald eagles after my gyr.

An eagle had actually grabbed him once, and ever since he had been fussy about chasing quarry in the presence of the big birds. Mondo usually chased eagles out of the area before settling down to serious hunting, but this day, he apparently missed one sitting in a huge old Sitka spruce. The eagle bailed out of the tree and barreled straight toward my partner. The gyr saw it coming and dodged aside, but that maneuver caught the attention of two more eagles, and then another joined the chase. As the parade passed a stand of trees, yet another eagle charged out and met the whole works head on. Eagles scattered in all directions. Dr. Mondo headed for cover.

When the gyr disappeared from sight, the eagles had recovered and were hot after him again. I envisioned what came next: a sleepless night, a long radio search in the morning, the discovery of a pile of gyrfalcon feathers. I stood in the snow, swinging the lure, blowing the whistle, hoping against hope, and it was well past sundown when he scurried back to me, just inches off the ground. Our mutual relief was palpable.

Typically, we began hunting just out of sight of ducks sitting in one of the shallow creeks that wind across the tide flats. I'd unhood him and let him assess the situation. He'd rouse immediately, bob his head and inspect the horizon in all directions. Maybe a mute, maybe not, but we always waited for that second rouse. Whether superstition on my part or idiosyncrasy on his, fewer difficulties arose if I let him rouse a second time before turning him loose.

Once off the fist, he quartered away from me, climbing all the way. No fooling around with endless circling; this bird always just did what needed to be done. He'd cut back across my path, always flying from right to left, sometimes a half mile or more away, still climbing. By the time he closed the last leg of his aerial triangle, he had emerged from the dark background of spruce, hemlock and rock and climbed out into the sky above me. He set his wings in a glide that let me know he was ready.

Success depended mostly on whether he really felt like catching a duck or not. If he was motivated, there weren't many ducks that could evade him. But what motivated him? Bottle it and we could be millionaires. Always the well-trained companion, I'd charge into the water to flush the ducks from their skimpy refuge. He'd learned to wait until the rattled birds were away from the safety of the water and out over the beach grass, then plummet into them with reckless fury. His terrible, determined swiftness always stopped me in my tracks for a few seconds. One needs time to appreciate the descent of a beast that catches its dinner — another animal nearly as large as itself — by crashing into it at high speed.

I marveled at his willingness to share the hunt with me, too. The flights were always different, always challenging, always exciting. Neither of us ever tired of the chase. Never did I head for home at the end of the day thinking, "Now I have done falconry, and it's time to move on to something else." The longer you practice the sport, the more you realize how much more there is to experience.

I think about him every time I drive past that mountain. I don't have any scars from him — at least not any that you could see.

Common sporting gear doesn't have to *want* to do anything to be useful, but not so for trained falcons. They need a reason to fly. Raptors aren't overwhelmed by their masters' sluggish terrestrial plodding, but they deign to return for food when it's time. Some of them even seem to enjoy it. Raptors are more specialized, more highly developed than mere humans. They shouldn't be impressed by us, and they aren't. Masters? Hell, we're just apes with car keys in our pockets. The occasional slash of taloned feet or stab of a sharp beak is a gentle reminder of who's really in charge here.

But the eyes of a trained falcon make it worthwhile. The bird stands tall on the glove and looks right through you. She gazes at the horizon and beyond, then glances back

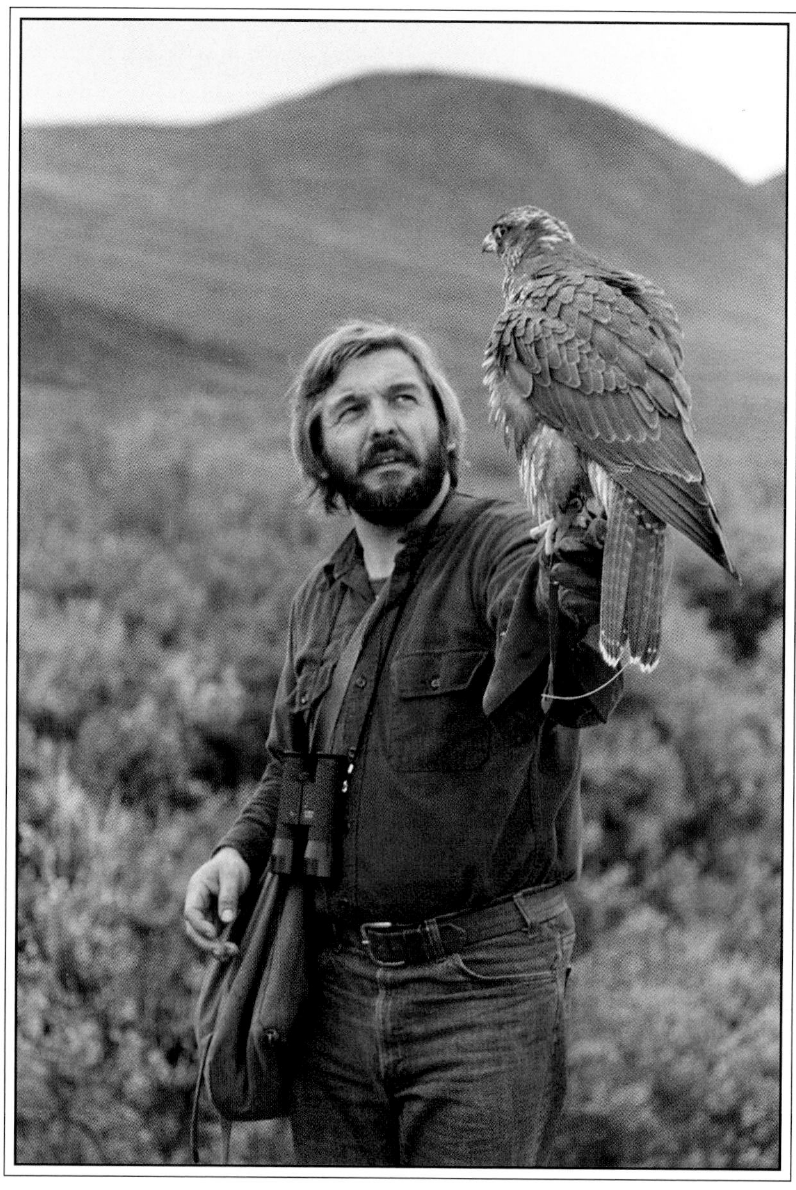

photo by Ronald G. Clarke

to you with the confidence that comes from knowing she could fly as far as she sees and humble anything that happens to show itself along the way.

Those eyes — polished brown jewels — conceal a benevolent schizophrenia. She'll tolerate you, maybe even develop a rudimentary fondness for you, and sit calmly on the glove. But cast her into the sky over a grouse or a duck and she transforms into a purposeful missile, hurling herself at frightful speeds toward meals that weigh as much or more than she does. Momentary ferocity behind her, she allows her trainer to pick her up with her prize, and she eats her fill back aboard the familiar gloved hand.

Then there's always the possibility that birds return to their scarred and earthbound human partners just to taunt them. Why else would an essentially wild creature float off to play with the wind, climb hundreds of feet in the air, fold up like an arrow, streak straight toward the earth and then, at the last possible second, flare her wings and settle gently on the glove, if not to say, "Don't you wish you could do that?"

Savage Beauty

by Joseph Vorro

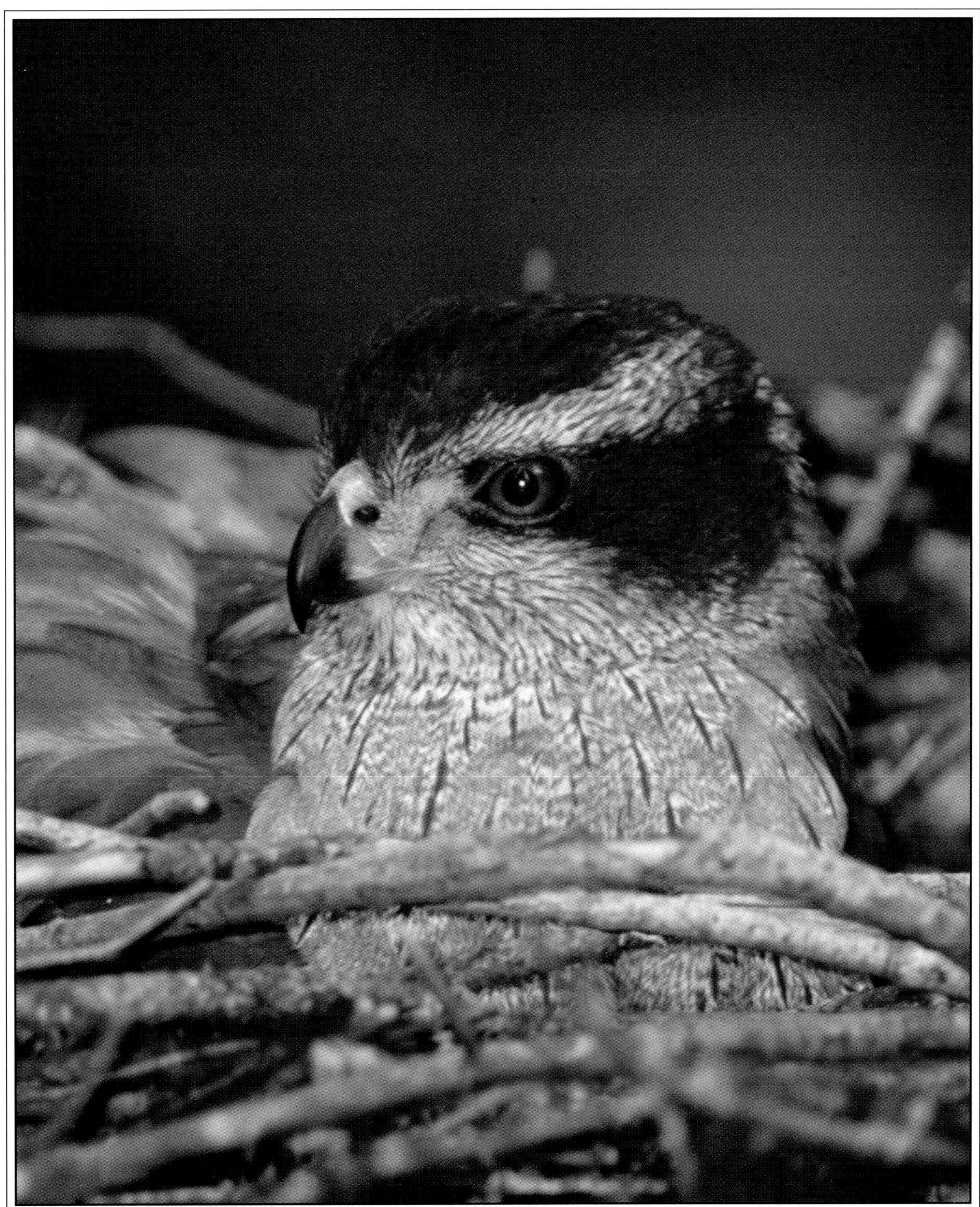

photo by Rick Kline

This year's quest began months ago. That first journey to the north country occurred when the snow was just about gone. Spring floods from the melt-off had begun, and waterfowl were starting their return. Timberdoodles, engaged in their dusk-time sky dance, accompanied the emergence of that strange harbinger of the grand thaw – skunk cabbage. Since childhood, the appearance of this acrid wetland weed had told me nature was about to undergo its annual renewal. As a kid who spent most of his non-school time investigating the outdoors, I was compelled to kick those emerald spathes when I saw them. For me their sour smell verified the onset of spring. Now, they also signaled the goshawk nesting season.

Yesterday, while my son Alex and I passed the final seven-hour journey to the nest area, I explained to him why a goshawk meant so much to me and why a large, female eyas would be my hard-earned gift for all the work and trips to find an active nest. At twelve, Alex had begun brief forays away from his black and white world of childhood into the grays and diffuse colors of early adolescence. Although my excitement was much like his at the prospect of fun and games with his friends, it confused him that my stories moved easily between descriptions of the singular beauty of goshawks, and tales of their predatory savagery and violence. To Alex, any coupling of beauty and violence was incongruous, although for me they aptly describe the natural order that embraces the life of a predator.

Once we were settled at the camp, I telephoned my trusted companion of the north country. Jim agreed to meet me at his cabin early the next morning before setting out for the nest.

Goshawks seem to possess an aesthetic faculty to select the most beautiful woods to call home. They live throughout the upper latitudes of North America in areas with elk, bears, mountain lions and deer. Here in the Great Lakes region, they nest in dense forests sharing the vast area with only a few other worthy predators: great horned owls, bobcats and the "magnum mink" called fishers. Searching for such a habitat and discovering a gos nest takes a long time, and I covered hundreds of miles of logging trails and two-track roads just to locate a likely area. When a promising site is found, it's time to hike it until the full extent of the woods is covered and every tree checked for a nest. This may sound arduous, but it isn't. Actually, it's a search for one of nature's most beautiful scenes.

My crusade to take a goshawk began last year as I knew I'd have to start the search well ahead of time. Jim had accompanied me on a number of those reconnaissance journeys. Unlike the small-town, coffee-shop types, Jim is a real backwoodsman, a trapper and hunter who lives very close to nature. He's in his seventies, and has never lost his love and fascination for the wild. Although he isn't a falconer, he appreciates goshawks for their ability to thrive in the north country. Jim was tough too, hardened by his lifestyle, still capable of chopping wood, climbing trees and hiking through the woods for hours. His knowledge and experiences fit with my needs as the pursuer of goshawks. Our conversations always centered on my quest. He often cautioned me about the harshness of the local environment and the vulnerability of a nest, warning me to be very careful when I found and inspected the site.

"It's those damn coons," he'd bark. "They'll follow your scent right into the nesting area if you don't do something. You oughtn't to walk right up to the tree either . . . lest your scent linger there. They'll climb the tree and eat the eggs or kill the young. Better to watch from a safe distance."

At times, and this was one of them, I wondered about my obsession with goshawks. Because of their difficult nature, other falconers had turned their backs, the ancients: caliphs and khans, Europeans; and even new world hunters, all preferring alternatives. But for me, the attraction of falconry was singularly tied to finding, raising, training and hunting with this noble bird. I'd care and provide for her earliest needs myself. This would be a more complete and satisfying experience than other contemporary ways of acquiring a hawk.

I also knew that many aspects of this intimacy would be short-lived. Once she fledged, gained strength and started killing for herself, our relationship would change significantly. At that point, my role would be as a participant as she honed her craft. I was certain she would thrive in my care, growing strong and healthy. It was similar to my relationship with Alex, who gazed at me from the other side of the campfire with wonder and maybe even some confusion. I can well remember my ambivalence at Alex's early steps toward independence. On one hand, I experienced tremendous comfort having him come to me for support and nurturing. However, at the same time I knew I'd have to take steps to insure his development and independence. It was going to be the same with the goshawk. After months of training and playing the role of nature's surrogate, I'd be obliged to release her to pursue wild quarry. I had to cope with thoughts of her possibly flying away or being injured in the chase or by the quarry. But that was the essence of the sport, just as it was the essence of a child growing up.

The ancients, of course, would never have handled a hawk this way. Traditionally, they waited instead to trap a passage bird in the autumn. These birds had successfully negotiated nature's lessons by this time and were experienced and efficient. I wanted to do it differently. I'd have only one chance at intimacy and nurturing with the gos, just as my one chance with Alex would be during his formative years.

With the darkness settling down around us, I couldn't help but tell Alex more about goshawks. The words came out with the same awe as hunters in a western deer camp telling stories about mountain lions and grizzly bears. Alex's coal black eyes widened as I told him that goshawks, the superior woodland aerial predators, are endowed with a resolute fearlessness resulting from their keen predatory instincts. In the wild, they catch avian quarry, anything from robin-size birds to grouse, nor are the smallest voles or the largest jackrabbits spared. In most places, however, their lives are intimately linked to catching the ghosts of the dark, tangled, conifer swamps — snowshoe hares. It's no small accomplishment to have a dependency on hard-kicking hares that can be twice the goshawk's weight. Goshawks sometimes choose to stay the winter in the mountains and in the boreal forests. The courage, stamina and confidence necessary to contend with such harshness are ample evidence of their uniqueness. Lesser creatures migrate, hibernate or die from these winter conditions.

Just as the beauty of a rose is guarded by the sharpness of its thorns, the goshawk is carefully guarded by her pointed and nervous temperament. The price I'd have to pay for her imposing predatory nature was the very thing that made her so attractive. I don't know why goshawks take life so seriously. They seem driven by an inner fire. Where other raptor species thrive in a hunting relationship with humans, the goshawk maintains her insular nature. Is it that any creature so perfectly endowed with spectacular hunting and survival abilities has very little room, so to speak, for social contact? Her unrelenting bent seems to have replaced her ability to forgive even the most minor mistakes of a falconer; her versatility for varied quarry supersedes any patience or tolerance for all but the most efficiently designed hunting situation; her tremendous courage seems to have stolen away those brief moments with other hawks and falcons when you actually feel that they look forward to associating with you. Like her talons, her beak and her spirit, the goshawk is too sharp and precise to adjust to the mere human condition. No wonder an

photo by Rick Kline

Elizabethan hawker, to emphasize that a gos fiercely resists anything that doesn't suit her, wrote that we should court the gos like a mistress rather than treat her with the authority of a master. The hunter's only reward would be to bear witness, in the most intimate way, to her lightning-bolt reaction, her maniacal pursuit, her singleness of effort and her savagery.

Following our first arrival in the north country this spring, Alex and I ventured out with Jim to the scene of last year's goshawk nest site. We were devastated to find the area logged and slashed by chainsaws and heavy equipment. The beauty achieved by many decades of self-organization had been significantly altered by man's purposeful and destructive activity. These denuded hillsides now issued scrub brush instead of mature oak, maple, beech and pines. Burned stumps, wood scraps and brush piles occupied the ground instead of ferns, trillium and morels. The goshawks were gone too. My only hope was that they had relocated nearby and that we could find the new site. The search continued, but more solemnly than it had begun. It was then that I found myself entertaining the idea that by taking an eyas from a nest I would be doing, in effect, something very similar to what the loggers had done.

During a mid-morning search, I spotted what appeared almost as an apparition. We were traveling on a sandy truck trail that paralleled the Lake Superior shore, the sun was high overhead and the windows were down to let us soak in the warmth. A goshawk was also sunning itself, but on a branch overhanging the side of the road. I continued slowly past the hawk hoping not to disturb it, but it startled and took flight immediately. I pulled the truck over and jumped out. There was no need for a plan or conversation. Alex and I headed in the direction of the hawk while Jim, figuring to cover additional ground, took off in the opposite direction. For the next hour or so, we walked in a series of circles trying to sight the hawk or find the nest.

It was too early in the season for the leaves to emerge and I could feel the unimpeded heat of the sun surrounding me. I clearly remember hiking up a hill where I could see a wide area of forest silhouetted by the clear bright sky. There, almost at the crest, was a large stick nest in a pine tree. My heart knocked wildly at my ribs as I ran to within a few yards of the tree. In a mixture of emotions, the instantaneous recall of Jim's words of advice about coons came to me from a recess in my mind and stopped me from getting too close. At the same time I recalled that moment on the Chippewa Flowage when a huge muskie, up from the depths, followed Alex's bucktail back to the boat. This waterwolf eased up, as though to study us with his piercing eyes. Then suddenly, the water boiled and his huge, broad, dark back disappeared under the boat while his tremendous reddish tail broke the surface for just a moment. Close enough for a phenomenal rush . . . but no contact. After hours of fishing with nothing to show for it, this whole situation was sudden and surreal. It took a while for us to compose ourselves, and Alex and I wondered if it had really happened. Just as at the Flowage, the wind had stopped at the nest site and the forest was silent. I couldn't tell my heartbeat from the drumming of a distant grouse. I thought I was close to an active gos nest, but as with the muskie, there was no proof yet.

I walked around the area, Alex by my side, trying to find evidence that the nest was occupied. The first sign of success was an isolated goshawk dropping on the forest floor. Then, from a different angle, I could see the long, slender tail of a female gos sticking out just a few degrees above the rim of the nest. An overwhelming feeling of exhilaration and satisfaction came over me. However, mostly I recall the awe with which I witnessed the serenity and beauty of the sight.

Back at the truck, we discussed the situation. Given the date and fact that the female sat tight to the nest, we felt sure she was on eggs. All I could do now was to leave the area and return home. "Nature," Jim said, "has to take its course."

Like locating the nest, it was no easy accomplishment during the two-and-a-half week wait to be satisfied that nature would be sympathetic and kind. This time I knew the tiercel would have to hunt successfully for the female and for himself. For her part of the bond, the female would have to incubate the eggs, taking care to turn them periodically. She also had to be careful not to break them with her huge feet nor crush them with the weight of her body. She had to modulate her maternal sensitivities with the ambient temperature, not allowing the eggs to chill. Neither could she expose them to excessive heat or rain. This nurturing couldn't even be relaxed once the eggs hatched and the eyases developed.

My next pilgrimage was timed to coincide with the hatching of the eggs. The woods smelled different than before, drier, not as fruity, and the deciduous trees had burst into leaf. Jim and I approached the nest carefully, maybe even overcontrolled and certainly anxious. We looked at each other with a sense of relief when the female's tail could once again be seen sticking out of the nest. She had performed dutifully and I was prepared for the climb.

Jim inspected my climbing spurs, making sure I was using the right ones for softwood. At first, the climb was slow and difficult. The old pine was very wide and didn't yield any branches for the first thirty-five feet. I used a waist harness until I got to the first branch. From that point to the nest, many branches spiralled out from the trunk. From

photo by Rick Kline

there I found it easier to climb from branch to branch instead of using the harness and spurs. It was easy, that is, until the gos could no longer tolerate my presence. She flew from the nest uttering an anguished *kak.* I remember seeing her steel-gray form and her blood-red eyes highlighted by that thick white blaze. She flashed down and away from the nest making a tight half circle, then headed straight back for me. Earlier I had thought my hat and light jacket would come in handy for the mosquitos, black flies and everpresent no-see-ums. But I was terribly underdressed for the wrath of that hawk.

She feigned the true depth of her passion with the first few passes, only coming close to my head and back. Then, when I failed to retreat, she turned up the attack, and using the rear talon of her left foot, ripped a long gash into the shoulder of my jacket. It wasn't the actual contact that frightened me so; it was the blurring speed, the rush of air and the thought that I was clinging to a tree more than forty feet in the air and out of my element that worried me and made me lose concentration on my footing and grip. On another pass, she hit my hat but failed to knock it off. Next, she came so close to my head again that I felt the tip of her wing move up against me. It was then, with that last measure taken, that I envisioned the needle-sharp point of her rear talon actually raking across the skin of my back and neck.

Luckily, however, with that last barrage completed, the gos flew off to a nearby tree only to utter the occasional sound of dissatisfaction. She chose not to face me as she took her perch. Instead, I could see the broad expanse of her back as I continued to climb. Better that sight, I thought, than the closeness and passion of her attack.

I finished the rest of my climb as fast as I could. Once I got to the nest, it was exceedingly difficult to maneuver up and over in order to be able to peer inside. However, the reward was certainly well worth the effort. There on a bed of branches, lined neatly with small pieces of bark and fresh hemlock and cedar sprigs, were three healthy downy goshawks, two to five days of age. All of my training and self-admonition about being anthropomorphic ended temporarily with that sight. The eyases were beautiful. It was like looking at babies in a maternity ward. As I stared at them, some tropic mechanism caused the nestlings to turn and face me. They screamed with their mouths agape as though to demand food and attention. Instead, with that scene imprinted in my memory, I started my descent.

The gos didn't bother me during my climb down the tree. At one point, she quietly flew off deeper into the woods and out of sight. Once on the ground, I babbled incoherently about the scene at the nest. Jim listened but was distracted as he dutifully spread mothballs around the tree to dissuade the coons. He also wrapped the tree trunk with a burlap and mothball invention. We left the area to get back to the truck, but I just needed to calm down.

I had to be content with another wait while the nestlings developed. Figuring at least one of the youngsters would be the female I wanted to take, I could do nothing but return home for another measured wait. This was much more agonizing than the previous one. Those beautiful little downy goses were much more tangible and evocative than the eggs, and the wait was more like the anxious hours I had spent in the hospital waiting for my son to be born.

Finally, this was the day I'd been waiting for. I was afraid Alex might incur the wrath of the gos and not wanting him hurt, I asked him to stay at the camp. Jim and I chatted nervously as we drove the final miles on the warm, dusty road to the nest. It was midmorning when we arrived. Expectations and anxiety levels were enormous as we headed into the woods.

There was too much solitude in the woods. The tiercel we had happened upon by the side of the road was nowhere to be seen; however, he had been obvious only on that chance sighting weeks ago. The usual crowd of squirrels, robins and blue jays could neither be seen nor heard. It was too quiet, too still. Things felt quirky. We didn't talk and I could sense the same strange aura from Jim that I was experiencing myself. When we got to the tree, I strapped on the climbing spurs and readied the waist harness. As I climbed, I expected the gos to leave her nest to attack me again. She never appeared. I was drenched with sweat and gasping for breath as I neared the nest. It too was still. I stepped out on the branch to clear the bottom of the nest and lifted myself up to peer over into it.

It was empty.

photo by Rick Kline

I know that I stared into that void for quite a while. My mind had come to expect a scene with three well-developed robust young goshawks. They would be getting too large for the nest and almost ready to leave its security for a temporary life on the branches. What I saw instead didn't fit my preconception. The nestlings were gone, their neatly arranged home was now disheveled and the evergreen sprigs were old and withered. My dream had faded to a moment of truth. It was an empty sight and my emotions swelled with grief as if to fill the void.

Jim knew something was terribly wrong, especially when I lowered the empty basket. My descent was difficult and precarious, but now just a few hours later, it hardly registers. I reached the ground, and just as I was about to explain what I had seen, Jim uttered one word, "Fishers."

I was depressed, exhausted and confused. Jim saw the vapid look in my face.

"Fishers," he said again, pointing way off to the right at a hollow log. "I just spotted two of 'em over there while you were climbing."

I stood silent and numb.

"It had to be them that robbed the nest," he went on. "The adult goses either abandoned the area or they got killed too."

We hadn't even considered this mustelid to be a threat. A variety of factors had wiped out many of the furbearers decades ago. In the meantime, nesting birds and other potential quarry for fishers didn't need to contend with this type of predation. I recalled that the state Fish and Game Department recently traded wild turkeys to the neighboring Canadian province of Ontario in exchange for fishers. They were then translocated in an attempt to restore them to their historic range. However, not even Jim with his knowledge and background could have expected fishers in this area. In the incipient stage of this restoration program, no one could have anticipated the creation of a new imbalance and the damage it would cause.

The ride back to camp was solemn. I felt completely alone with my thoughts. Amidst my sadness were the all too obvious contrasts and comparisons: my need to hunt with a predator versus another predator's conquest of my prize; man's interference with the natural order resulting in the loss of a species, followed by the further imbalance once we sought to reintroduce a species. Our mark of humanity is certainly everywhere.

I paced around the campsite trying to clear my mind. As I attempted to put things together, the murmur of a small brook feeding the lake drew my attention. There, scattered about the banks, were cowls of purplish-green skunk cabbage leaves, standing out as if to reflect the spirit of the moment. For an instant, I returned to my childhood, wide-eyed and excited, anticipating adventure behind every tree in the forest. I kicked those bitter-smelling weeds again, more in an attempt to return to reality than for nostalgia.

All I could do was to absorb the wonder of nature by drawing in a deep breath of that sour odor. Spring would come again and after all, back at the camp I had another growing eyas to tend to.

Not Just a Game...

by Bill Girden

The frost of night remains now only in the morning's shadows. Even in winter, the desert is too hostile for so delicate a form of water to linger, but it's a treat while it does. Its icy whiskers mimic the spines of the cactus, and occasionally it will even form there. For a time then, the wicked points and angles of that plant are softened, until the sharp orange sunrise sends its crystals trickling away.

We step from a dry river bed, which I have used to enter an area often rich in quail, without being seen. This much, at least, of the hawk's nature has become mine. The sun, risen only moments ago, lights an impossible pair — Sharkey and me. Sharkey is a once intermewed tiercel Cooper's hawk. Though his blue-grey back is dulled by the orange sunlight, his eyes and breast, orange by nature, capture the light and blaze with its color. I will lay claim to no such beauty. I am a middle-aged man, camouflaged as an unmade bed. My boots are aged, my clothing a bit ragged, my hair thin, and I have been a falconer most all of my life. I have cared to do no one thing for as long, nor struggled to do anything else as well. I feel absolutely no shame in admitting this. When Sharkey and I hunt, my body feels all of the twenty years I have spent thrashing through brushpiles in search of quarry, and my intellect remembers how often frustration has come from trying to understand thoughts from a mind so alien to my own. But throughout the decades, my spirit has never tired. Indeed, it races with boundless delight when a hawk rides my glove. Why? Because I have asked this wild thing to take me as a partner in free flight, and have exchanged with that creature gifts of trust and goodwill. No struggle, scars nor weight of task would be too great for this reward.

Reminiscence, however, belongs more with a comfortable chair and a warm fire than in the hunting fields at sunrise. My thoughts spring to the here and now, and I let my awareness of the drama-to-be expand around me. The wash and surrounding area we will hunt today occupy the northern end of the Sonoran desert. Several million years ago this land was the bottom of a shallow ocean, which waxed and waned more than once. Volcanic activity and climatic change, too, altered this land time and again. A scant two centuries ago saw here a marshy wetland, rich in mesquite and cottonwood forests, but they are no more. The land is now much warmer, much drier. The geologist will feel awe here, the botanist, perhaps sadness. I feel only mounting excitement—for here abide quail, the Gambel's quail. Dressed in colors of cream, black and rich coppers, they are as fleet afoot as they are swift in flight, a challenge to my predator who seeks them. The gently-sloping sandy valley before me has refuges in abundant hackberry thickets, woodrat nests and wicked cactus patches. All may hide quail in abundance, or not at all. I have no dog to give advantage today, and I probably never will. When my hawk and I are closest and I wish nothing to disturb us, a dog would do just that.

Sharkey's flight jesses, necessarily of snag-proof Teflon tubing, have been on since he left his mews. His persona during the car ride to "our" area has been that of granite.

photo by Les Oxner

Gone is the exuberance of immaturity. He knows where we are and he knows what we'll do. His every move is that of studied efficiency. He leaps from my truck with wings tightly shut, finds my glove and is in place before I stop moving. As I remove his tail protector, his wiry toes and talons flow into the creases of my ancient glove. Once settled he fluffs, then rouses explosively, as if he were an orange fireball, barely contained. The sun warms his back, and he lifts those feathers slightly, accepting the meager warmth. His long, barred, elegantly mobile tail twitches, then spreads fully.

We walk into the desert, the sun to our rear. Sharkey has been on my glove only minutes, yet, from the self-possession he shows, he might have sprouted from the leather itself. At this I smile and, relevant or not, I feel pride. I'm careful not to jostle him as we thread our way, although inevitably a rock will trip me, or a branch will reach out to sweep Sharkey away. But he will ride with the stumble, or dodge the intrusive branch as only one with the reflexes to strike from ambush can. With the smallest of movements, he sees and takes the measure of everything. I, claiming only a human degree of senses, and with no concern to being invisible, search for quail with a fervor. As we work across the valley, a wonderful feeling grows within me. I feel a joining, a bonding of two different beings toward a similar goal. Satisfaction warms me. To know of a different blood, sharing some — WHOOSH! Quail flush behind us and Sharkey is gone, just that fast. We walked within feet of two quail. It is likely that Sharkey saw them even before they moved. As a younger

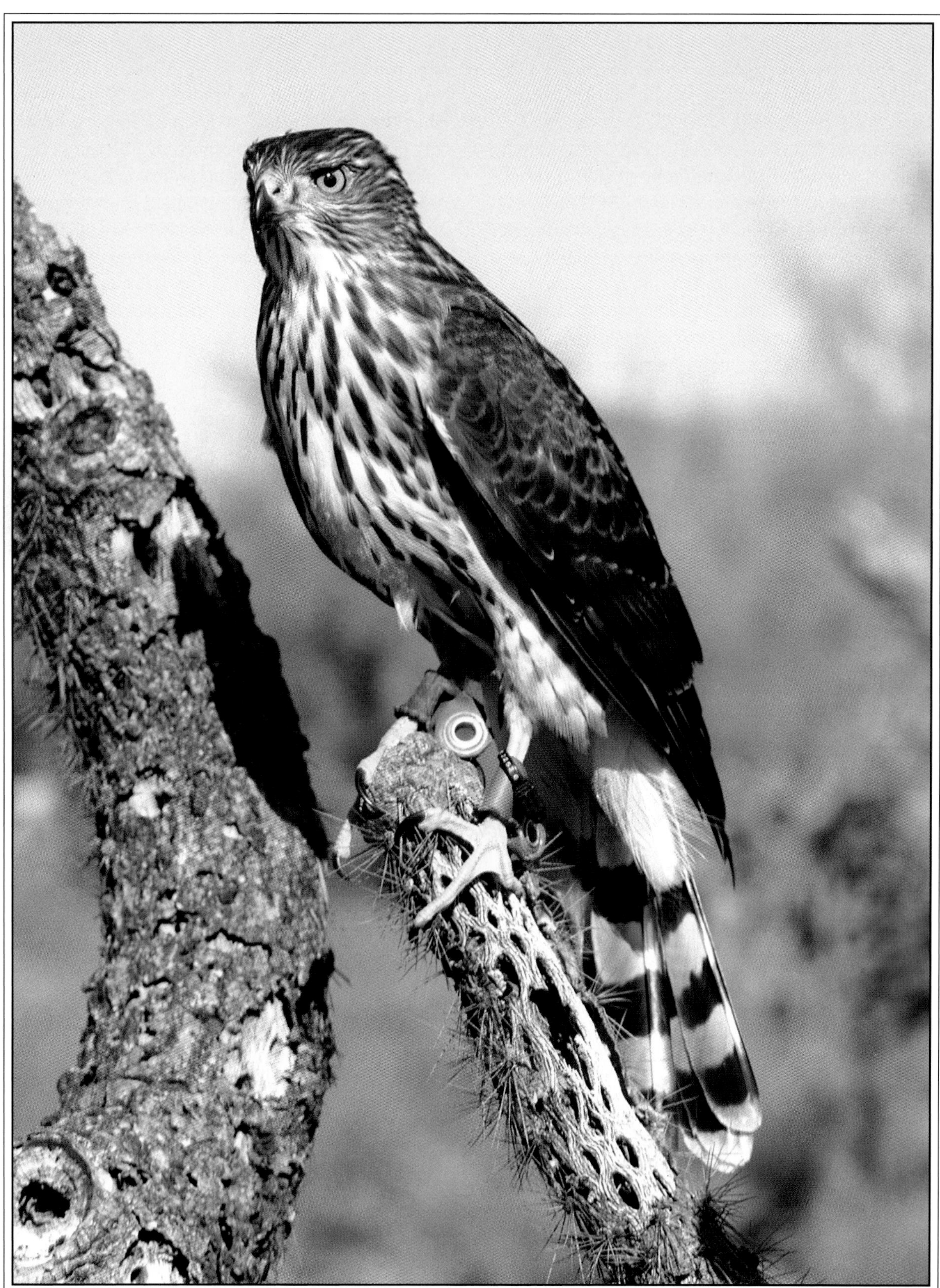

photo by Bill Girden

bird he would have revealed himself and his intentions at once, but he has learned. He now plans, in ways I don't pretend to understand, and waits for them to move first, to commit. He knows. I, however, reveling in our "unity," had no inkling of the hidden prey, nor of my "partner's" anticipation of the flight. *I did not know.* First flights on quail are fast, direct and quickly gone from sight — no exceptions here. I stand, flat-footed, dumbfounded, and alone. I begin to realize things. While I was "bonding," Sharkey was hunting. The bonding I felt probably I felt alone. Yet we remain partners. The problem? I sought to homogenize us, to shape him to my ideals. Social animals that humans are, we need to find similarities before feeling we belong. Often, we do this without realizing it. Accipiters are the essential loners. They do not "bond" by human definitions — they cannot. This is hardly a "flaw"; it simply *is.* They live the now, now, now of a life painted in dashing colors and vibrant strokes. Rather than seek (and imagine) a type of bond which might never be, falconry can add something to our lives obtainable nowhere else — wildness. Purity of design, of being, of intent. A way to partake of true, raw life, a drive unpolluted by politeness, civility and flavorless monotone to mire our spirits. Is that so bad?

Somewhat humbled, if not clearer of mind, I engage "the voice in the wilderness" — my telemetry receiver. My Cooper's may not fly miles when in pursuit, but he is as good as lost nevertheless when on a kill in an acre of concealing brush. I would never fly him without it. The signal is there (always a welcome sound), distant but readable. I head off with determined steps, as Sharkey is not alone in hunting these hills. The Harris' hawk is common here, and would certainly hunt him. I go seeking my — friend? Yes, my friend.

Two rocky, saguaro-dotted hills come and go when suddenly the signal reaches overload. I am within fifteen feet of him. He is invisible. Before me sits a large brushpile, or more precisely, a dead, fallen palo verde tree. Often a woodrat will build its cactus-laden nest within such a heap, and it is into these concealing tunnels that a quail will vanish, sometimes for good. In his first year, so would Sharkey, occasionally so deep I'd have to literally dig him out. But no more. He shuns such antics now, instead taking stand on the pile to await my arrival. I have trudged in, but see only a scattering of quail feathers at the edge of the pile — a close call. Of the quail's location I have no doubt, but where lurks the demon who tattered the quail's cloak of grey? A twitch of neon yellow throws everything into focus. Often, as now, I locate my eight-ounce raptor by the movement of his half-ounce, bright yellow transmitter. So — there he is. In plain sight. Twenty feet away. *Right there.* Well, well. Camouflage, they call it; plain spooky, I call it. I try to read the situation. Sharkey's on stand, one foot pulled up, his crest fully spiked. This should be easy. Habit has me extend my glove, yet I pull back as if burnt, before Sharkey can jump to it. Easy. The way that word sticks in my mind sounds — wrong. One fact of falconry easily glossed over is that, in such times as these, a life hangs in the balance. The efforts of the falconer here will surely tip the balance — won't they? To me, this question is a burning one. Suddenly, I have to find out — and I will. I retreat to the skimpy cover of a palo verde tree some twenty feet uphill. The morning sunlight has lost its orange and even the shadows are now bare of frost. Soon it'll be warm. Far downhill is a new apartment complex, having sprouted with mushroom-like suddenness last summer. From there, a dog barks warning as a truck and driver rumble into the chilled morning. An indignant human voice screams the dog into silence. We wait.

We wait, Sharkey, the quail and I. Five minutes, six, ten. A cactus wren, cheeky but not stupid, scolds the hawk from its hackberry sanctuary. All at once and no one part first, Sharkey comes to life. His feathers tighten, his eyes focus, and after several seconds of scrutiny he delicately works his way into the tangle beneath him. My breathing becomes ragged. What does the quail think now? Could I ever know — or understand? A minute passes, then two. I no longer see Sharkey. Whatever awaits him, he goes to it alone. Suddenly, frantic scrabbling erupts. Sections of the pile shake, and wisps of dust appear. I become aware that I am not breathing, but a gasp is all I get. With a snapping of twigs the squealing quail is airborne! Sharkey too is free of the pile, and with the quail so fast he seems tied to it by a two-foot string. The fifty-foot-wide wash is crossed by the pair in seconds, and into the top of a hackberry they plunge, forsaking flight for the footrace. I stay put, but crane hard to see. The hackberry is twenty feet across and roughly circular. Downward through it they scamper, across every inch, into every nook. Not much more than quail-sized himself, Sharkey keeps pushing and the quail finds neither rest nor sanctuary. Every one of the four laps through the bush nearly nets him his prey. A sudden break! The quail (I see now it's a male) risks all with a return flight across the wash, back to the brushpile, straining, shrieking with fear — safe! Sharkey hurls himself in, but will not stay. His finesse evaporated, he kicks and forces his way up and out, back to the branch from which he launched. He is no longer the same bird. Even from here, his eyes look black, so dilated are the pupils. His slate and orange sleekness is so no longer. Broken twigs poke from his back feathers, and he is more than a little dusty. His tail is spread, his primaries are fanned downward like spread fingers, and he pants furiously. As he regains his wind, I sheepishly shake loose the sand and gravel clutched in my right hand. I am excited — thrilled! But for whom? For which was my silent cheer? Do I care? Damn! Again, I am thinking too much. Let go, I admonish myself. I am here, I am now. I watch a drama like no other, decided in spite of, rather than because of, me. I may never see something less "human" and more "real" than this. To me *this* is falconry.

Soon recovered, Sharkey begins to circle the pile with quick, agile steps, peering from so low to the ground at times he actually lies in the sand. I begin to believe the duel is done. The quail is quite safe, and Sharkey will not risk entering the pile again, possibly to lose all. Still, he does not leave. He knows I'm here, and at his beckon we will hunt elsewhere. But his attention is on nothing but what hides amongst the branches.

He has not shifted his gaze in some minutes — staring it to death, I muse. If it could ever work, it would here. Then, something changes. Instantly he snaps erect, really snaps. His head swivels wildly, and what little calm remains in him is gone. Adrenaline pours into his system, and his blood begins to fizz. I have seen this before, and I know what is coming. "Explode" is the only way to describe what he does next. In a scattering of sand, he is airborne. The quail had escaped, and he did not see it! Against my promise, I stand. From the rear of the pile it had crept unseen, but "escaped" doesn't mean gone. A dozen wingbeats take the predator high enough to relocate the prey, and a sharp wingover thrusts him deep into a prickly pear cactus. Frenzied quail clucks and hawk bells blend. Out vaults the quail. Only a second behind is the hawk, but that second is a long one. The quail knows this is the last chance, and perhaps the hawk does, too. As one, they burn the air directly at me!

Time becomes slow, syrupy. I see their individual wingbeats, and I see Sharkey's glowing orange eyes. The gaze of a predator is, above all else, unnerving. Just for a moment, I too feel fear. The quail, flaring at the last possible moment, whips around me and dives for the few dead branches to my rear. I am not Sharkey's target: I know this. His reflexes are magnificent, and he will not collide with me: I know this. But I blink. In that instant his every feather strains against the air. I feel the barest pushing touch of his feet, the nick of his talons as he runs across my ribs and plunges after the quail. The quail bolts from behind me, now running without thought or goal, exhausted. Spent too is the hawk, who lashes

photo by Bill Girden

out with a long yellow leg, but pulls only feathers. The quail stumbles, almost staggering. Sharkey again grabs, and takes the quail's wing. They tumble as one, wholly twined in violent struggle. This is the flesh, blood, fear and need which give truth to the polite words "balance of nature." It is powerful, heady stuff. Their struggle takes them to a small hackberry. Sharkey braces against the branches with spread wings to keep from being dragged into the tangle. Anchored thus, he will wait out his prey's struggles. It does not take long. The quail's time has come; for him, there will be no tomorrow. His rhythmic flapping weakens, slows — stops. Sharkey's feet grip convulsively. The quail dies. Sharkey seems to realize this. Gradually the poisons of fatigue clear his system and regaining his senses, he slowly draws his feathers in tightly. He then crouches so low over the body that he lies upon it, and he disappears. His outlines blend so well with the branches and scattered wash debris that it becomes difficult to separate him from it. He has scarcely moved, yet he is gone.

I am moved by this drama, this tragic adventure, both in depth and in ways which surprise me. Few among us would not be. I am sad for those with whom I share falconry, who know nothing but the lust for blood, the triumph of the kill. As a species, humans can take a life with ease — sometimes too much ease. It's not merely a sport if a life is at stake. Nothing preys on humans, we have seen to that. Predators no longer stalk us from hiding to end our lives so that they may end their hunger, we have seen to that. While I hardly favor a return to such times, I feel its lack has lessened us somehow. We are not prey, yet we believe we still understand the hunted, and perhaps we do, though certainly not easily. But experiences such as this can give us a taste, small but potent, if we let them. We should.

Some minutes pass. Sharkey remains still, waiting for me. To complete this hunt, I must rejoin it. My legs, stiff from tension, move me to within ten feet of him. What happens next is not of the Cooper's hawk's wild world, but that of its certainty. I crouch and lay my gloved hand, palm up, in the sand between us. Held in the fingers is a small piece of meat. Breaking his stony stare, he glances first at his kill, then at my glove. Pulling the quail's body free, he scrambles/hops to me, prey in tow. I remove my glove, and trusting his motives as he does mine, I open the quail's warm body for him. Blood stains both his toes and my fingers. With eagerness he swallows the heart and liver, all the while perched with almost comic gentleness on my bare hand.

We are partners. We have done this countless times before, yet now is different, for, briefly, I cry. The mix of emotions within me is considerable, but whatever I feel, none of it is shame. However, it is private. I will examine it further one day. But in feeling it, I am happier now than perhaps at any other time with hawks. To share such a moment with such a creature! To know that I am a falconer — that is enough.

photo by Pamela Ensign Wollam

The Rage of Knowing

by Alan Schauer

After my physical, the new company doctor asked me to wait in his office. I was looking at his golf trophies when he asked from the door, "How many Valium do you take a day?"

"None. What do you mean?"

"You have the lowest blood pressure I have ever seen in a living person who could still walk."

That sounded like me. "Thanks," I said.

"Any other medications? Drugs?"

"No."

"Are you awake, do you think? Hypnosis? Anything like that?"

"Oh no," I replied. "I'm awake as I ever get, I guess."

He pressed on. "How do you feel?"

"Fine. I feel fine. No problems."

"I can't find anything wrong with you except the blood pressure, and that's not particularly dangerous. But it's not good for you, you know."

"It isn't?" I asked, confused.

"I mean being so far removed from the rest of us."

He had actually noticed my attitude. Still, I found the statement unusual coming from a doctor — the ultimate, dispassionate technician of human degeneration, disease, and death.

"Somebody has to stand back and take a look," I replied. I was not worried.

That was me — laid-back, lazy, uninspired and uninspiring; an observer, not a participant; cool and calm, watching and waiting; uninvolved and proud of it; detached, icy; intellectual and scientific; knowing that in time, an explanation will be found for everything; certain that getting excited about it won't help.

That was before.

He ran harder than ever in his life. Had to. Anger and loss were pushing — anger because it had been his fault, loss because his fanaticism had become real to him. The wintering southeastern forest, a jungle's skeleton, rushed at him, thorns tearing his legs, rotten wood surprising some of his panicked strides. Down into a hollow, up the other side into a jail of pine trunks that swayed to the hissing music made by their high needles in the cold wind. Up further onto a flat ridge where oak and hickory limbs weaved under their empty canopy. (Her world, those towering architectures that survived the ancient struggle for light.) He was panting now, coughing, staggering. And there, a brown movement in the distant leaf litter. Was it she, the hawk who allowed him to hunt with her? No, wind. More running, pursuing the memory of her flight path. But . . . a clear cut. And somewhere the angry scream of a resident hawk. He stopped, hoping she wouldn't have dared cross the open under the owner of this air. He tried to be silent, but no; gasping, coughing, and the wind. Would he hear the tones that were a part of him, the bells, her bells, his salvation?

Yes? He turned, hands behind his ears. Where? The slightest ting. Up? Yes. Another. Up? In a pine. There!

He collapsed, sickened with exertion, into the forest floor's quilt of leaves. Could be the end of us, he thought. He lay on his back gulping air and watched the clouds, through the high nervous fingers of the trees, slide across the setting sun. Time, he thought. How much time?

That was after, in another world. The beginning? Lost. Best I can remember, awareness of the planet grew slowly from nothing as I matured. When young, I didn't notice because I had no past with which to compare. Anyway, I was technological and had to elbow out a place in that world of goodies and people in which I could survive. Back then, we worried about the nuclear war that hadn't yet happened and the other wars that had. The "environment" was an even more occasional item than it is now. Certainly it wasn't home for me: home was a house, a school, a car, a town, a city. But life expanded as I lived it and watched people madly trample more and more of everything and learn nothing.

One day I wanted to know that other part, I thought, the part unmanaged, where the edge is only one cold night away. Did I want to pay the price? Was anything out there that wasn't already in a book somewhere? I roamed some libraries and happened upon a few falconry books. Falconry still alive? People writing books about it? Those people must be analytical. That was just my thing.

And my problems had begun, as I discovered later when it became clear that fanaticism was the actual motivation for the books.

The wind rose and fell on a cycle of minutes. The uncaring power and scale of it made him feel insignificant in a way he had never felt even in the largest crowd. The leaves, crunchy as cereal, had made a small drift on his downwind side. Synchronous with the chilling, killing respiration of the wind, he was in turns calm, then nervous, as his own mammal-sized breaths returned to normal.

Up in that pine forty yards away, she seemed undisturbed by any of it. She saw him, of course. He was probably her scarecrow against the resident hawk. She ate.

He plotted. Probably twenty minutes to plan her recovery. He thought about psychology — hers, his, theirs. That and the place, weather, time of day, history of the hunt, what she had eaten two days ago — all must be accounted for. Place: don't call her toward the clear cut; she doesn't want be exposed to the resident. Wind: makes birds unreliable, too much stimulation. Too late in the day, dark soon, she gets unnerved as dark comes on, owls and stuff. Small quarry, much too small, big mistake. She should be plenty hungry, only advantage.

He exposed a hand to bite his fingernails.

She is a red-tailed hawk weighing two pounds plus with a wingspan of four-and-a-half feet and a lifespan of twenty years. Perched on my fist held at belt level, she is tall enough to bite my nose. She doesn't bite; biting would risk her eyes. Like most raptors, she addresses the world with her feet. They are taloned, talented, and on long, powerful legs that disappear into that free-form feather costume and actually end at her wing roots. She can step, not jump, but step up at least fourteen inches. She has a wild, intense, and challenging yellow stare that makes me avert my own gaze in cowardice; when I look back, she is looking elsewhere, the winner.

I never named her; no name seemed to capture her regal wildness nor all that she has taught me as we've lived together. I whistle through my teeth and she responds or not, as circumstances move her. The falconer carefully arranges those circumstances.

The bird evaluates them just as carefully. I have imagined that red-tails are at the top of the cerebral scale in the raptor world. They exude confidence and lack, except at the terminal stage of an attack, the maniacal disregard of consequences of some of the other raptors. They seem to do things chess-wise, calculating many moves ahead and probably

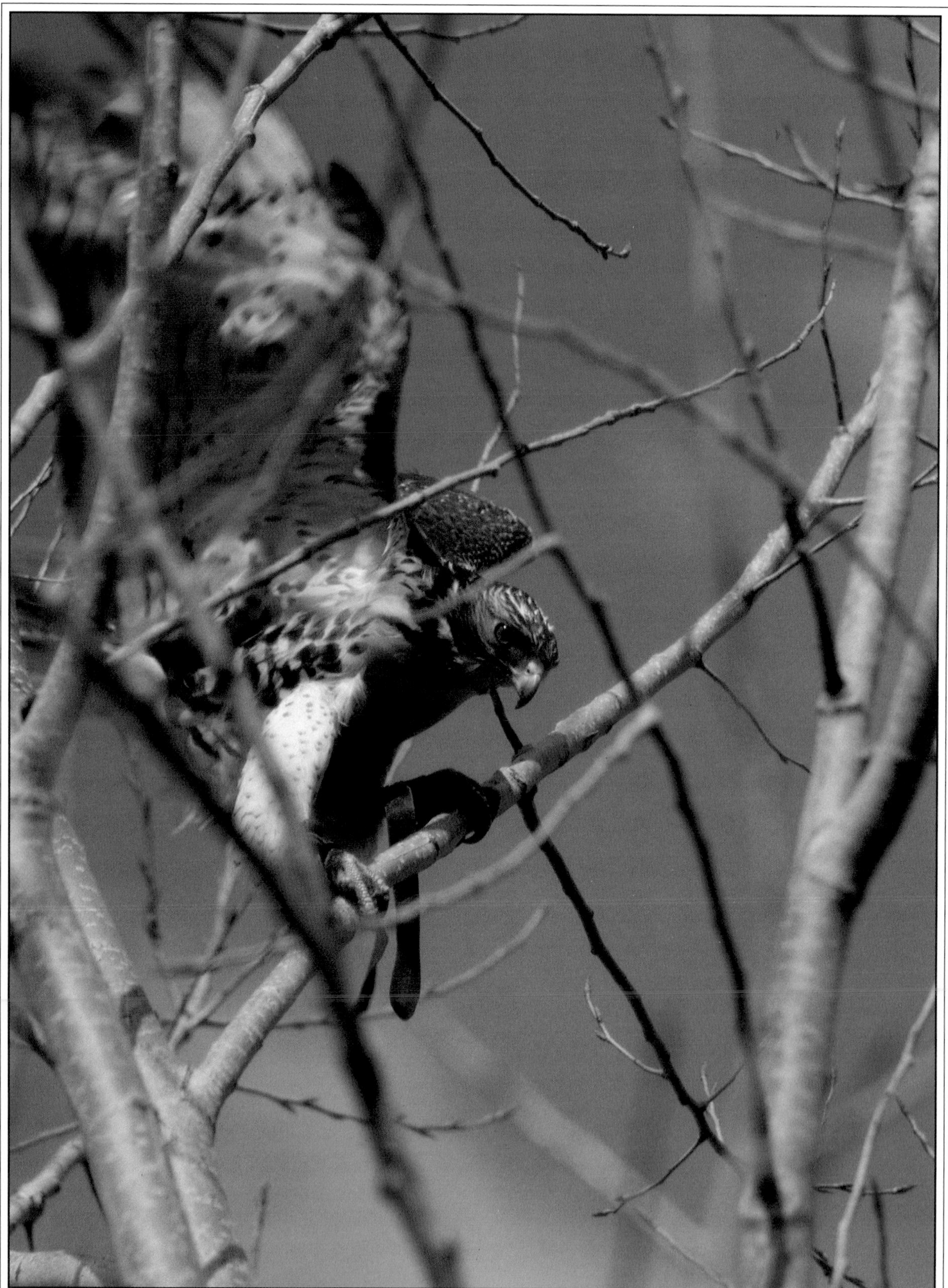

photo by Paul T. Schnell

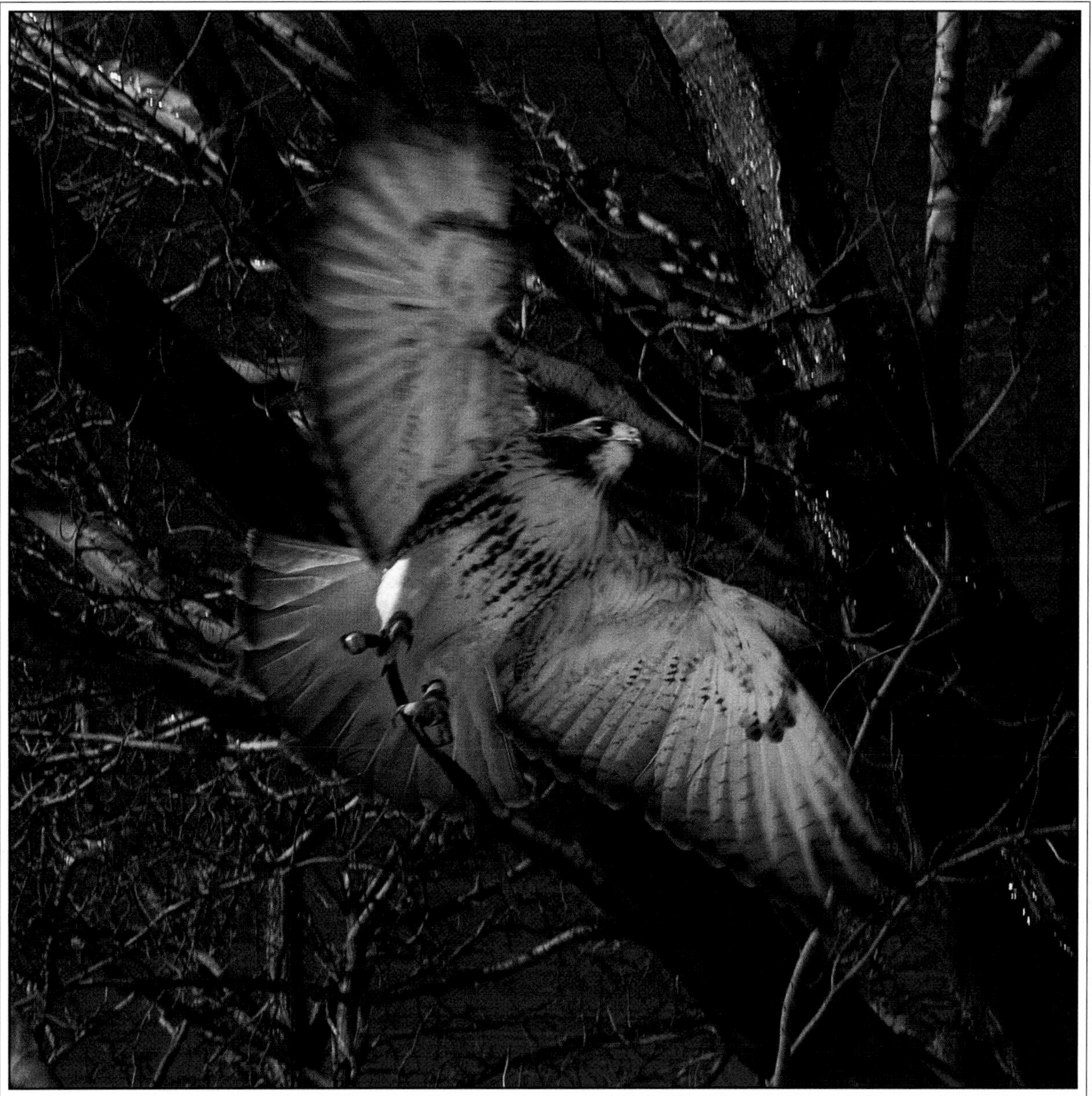

photo by Paul T. Schnell

getting headaches from all the decisions they must make.

In field or forest, she flies; I flounder. She chases and captures; I lurch along behind. She sees edibles; I look at wood. She is swift and elegant; I am clumsy and crude. She is to me as insect-eating birds are to the grazing herds that inadvertently kick up food. I stir up the forest in a most untargeted and ignorant fashion, plowing through the leaf litter, hitting trees with a stick, shaking vines. The forest animals, squirrels especially, are uncertain about me, and sometimes disdainful. They know well the danger of the bird, but they don't know the horror my kind brings. We haven't been around long enough to etch their genetic code. Though I don't see them, they are checking me out, moving slightly in their trees to get a better look. They are still learning, in the usual and evolutionary senses, and the bird gets an advantage.

It is enough to make a partnership work. There is a wonderful moment in the training of a red-tail when the bird realizes the slight edge, that the madness means meals. She has learned to love blundering.

In spring she will be back in the wild. A process called hacking will insure her successful reintroduction to the hard life. Trained to hunt by her parents in the wild, captured and taught falconry, ferried hither and yon for fanatic fancies, she has taught me much. I will gratefully return her to independence and, I'm certain, to the raising and training of more excellent red-tails. For me there will be other birds; for her, perhaps dreams of a strange winter with the enemy.

The paper-white sunlight aged slowly to gray. Behaviors in the forest shifted. Feeding gave way to hiding . . . from the cold, from dark stars of the unknown and unknowable. On her way to a secret night-perch, an adult female cardinal, only beak and feet in Vatican red, twitched with an annoyed chirk each time she stopped to look at the hawk.

The falconer pulled his mind, distracted now by his chilling body, back to a review of the hunt. Embarrassing as it was, there might be a key to her recovery there somewhere.

It had been falconry follies for sure. Mister Sporting Life, in a minor miracle, had found something. It was a meal too small — possibly a flying squirrel — in an old oak. He insisted that she come take a look because that was his job, to move fur. As if she knew where foolishness would lead, she attacked after a long, reluctant pause, but with her usual efficiency. From high in an open sycamore, she wheeled into the cramped, arthritic spaces of the oak, bounced off the trunk and one limb, and she had the flyer which, unaccountably, didn't. Maybe it was a rat. She carried it off downwind without one look back at her poor falconer in flailing, swerving pursuit.

She had educated him again — don't serve quarry she can handle with one foot. Two-footed captures, he realized, force her to the ground with no feet remaining to grip a limb.

His shivering body reasserted control. It said he was ready as he'd ever be. He willed her to finish. His body curled from the cold.

Enjoying classical music and challenging literature, and fine dining, and intellectual pursuits, and urbanity, I've never been a hunter. In fact, my wife buys the groceries; I don't even hunt the supermarket. Until falconry I was enthralled by the invented systems that we think free us from the earth and from the plant and creatures that have made us possible.

I still don't like hunting as, say, sport. I do like watching the bird work and the feeling of being a temporary auxiliary in the unmanufactured food chain. I like thinking that perhaps I could be a hunter if I had to be, and I have the conceit that uncivilized humans have always hunted with reservation — in need, not in greed — and that the storied reverence in which "native" peoples hold nature is real. I have that reverence myself, but whether real or an overreaction to the excesses of my species, I cannot say.

That the bird allows me to help her find her food is the greatest honor I have known. I have fallen prey to the vice of pride in being able and allowed to consort with a wild creature as she makes her living. I know what few people know; I know also the hedonism, elitism, pain, and rage of knowing.

The tree trunks slowly blackened in winter's blowing dusk. He could lose her to darkness, wildness, wind, attack of the resident, a comfortably full crop. It was safer to hack her back to the wild, he thought, but she'd be all right out here if she decided to bug out now. He refused to think about how he'd be.

He was in a cold, tight ball now as she cleaned her only tooth — that wicked, hooked beak — on the limb. Beak cleaned, she used it to clean her talons, scraping each from toe to tip underneath its curve. She would clean her beak once more now.

It was time. He stood.

It is an old problem, often religious — how to transfer the unbelievable from the anointed to the uncomprehending. In the United States, the master/apprentice system for falconry is law. Falconers demanded it. The three-thousand-year-old literature of falconry, a tribute to the fanaticism the birds inspire, is insufficient. The literature raises questions; the birds and the master (sponsor in the U.S.) answer them. I owe my sponsor more than I can say, so I won't. He knows.

The books, birds, and sponsors try to teach. Then there is what the apprentice learns. And that is much more, things that have not been, and may never be, contained in language. What medium could my sponsor have used for these things? Music struggles free of language. Rock, baroque, classical, Rodgers and Hammerstein, whatever, music is a way to think, be, or feel outside language. It frees us from the need to symbolize. There is so much that the symbols in our heads don't cover. The bondage of language. If language can't do it, what medium can? Our music doesn't seem to fit in the forest, which plays its subtle symphony.

The medium, I believe, is me. I only really learn after the fact of the detail and the larger experience of my life come together. My sponsor knows this. He may have said it explicitly, though of course I didn't comprehend. A simple thing, I suppose, but it seems I have come a long way to get here. Teachers cannot teach, but they must have the passion.

Darkness was a definite factor now. He had difficulty seeing her in detail. He showed her the meat on his glove. He thought she looked at it briefly, but then her head was in profile again, eyes apparently on the horizon. He quickly walked a constant diameter arc from her until he was directly upwind. His sponsor's words recurred. "Give her an easy approach." He stopped and turned into the wind, away from her. "Your eyes and face are a threat. Be a post." He shot his glove straight over his head and whistled over his shoulder. The wind rose a bit. He might not hear the bells as she launched. "Don't panic. She's got to do her thinking." He waited in the wind, moving the meat slightly with his fingertips. Those big feet didn't hit. A post for a few more seconds. He twisted around to look. She was gone.

I wouldn't recommend it to anyone. It is the life of a fanatic — odd, troubling, risky, painful, and hard work.

There is a dense layer of reasonable, but still burdensome, federal and state regulations. They are just the beginning of an infinite list of details. You don't trip on down to your local shopping center for the facilities, equipment, and leather gear. You build it, make it, borrow it, or order it from some who-knows-where place in, like, Idaho. This work never ends.

There is the killing. I'm civilized. I hire people indirectly to kill animals so I can have my beef, poultry, pork and the rest. But falconry is real life. It is about eating, which means something must die, which means I frequently have to kill it, either to assist the bird with unreleasable quarry or to prepare feeder animals. This is not amusing. But for the bird, eating is all that it's about. She doesn't seem to know about "hunting." (Why do we?)

Expense? I'm afraid to add it up. Don't ask.

Half-hour days are rare; sixteen-hour days are also. But I estimate the overall average at three hours per day, 365 days a year. It's non-deferrable, like the attention required by small children: it must be done when the bird needs it, not when the fancy strikes you. Much of it is road time. You can't hunt the same place all the time; the game gets bell-wise.

Want a friendly, loving relationship with a wild animal? Falconry is not your gig. Wild-caught hawks don't worship their falconer; they tolerate the falconer because of the better food opportunities. They merely tolerate, nothing more.

There are the aches and pains. The physical ones heal quickly. But each instance of habitat destruction adds to my shame that I belong to the species responsible. And there is the guilt that all I can bring myself to do is appreciate nature, not go to war for it. Abandoned portions of cities disintegrate into rubble, rust, ash, poverty, ignorance, and crime while developers ignore the cities and instead destroy natural areas so that humans can continue to overpopulate and overuse the planet. The latest shopping/office "park" near my house cost one hundred acres of forest. The woods were totally destroyed down to the sterile strata upon which they had struggled to life. "Terra"-forming followed. Two adjoining signs erected on those lifeless plains advertised the advance of culture. One said, "Coming Soon — Wildwood Center"; the other, "Site Preparation by AllWaste." The wild, big mama red-tail that used to visit my yard doesn't anymore.

The wind died slowly, a pause in the heartless push toward the edge. The sight of that empty pine had pulled a brief shock of anger through his head and chest. But the work wasn't over, and the continuing requirements muted and delayed emotions. "Many a bird has stayed out all night and come to papa in the morning." He needed to make sure he could find this place in predawn darkness; he couldn't stay the night without building a fire that might drive her off. He looked around at the unusual sight, for this day, of peaceful trees awaiting the night. For him they were full of tension, as if making ready for some diabolical giant's next frozen laugh.

In that spring-loaded calm, he heard a bell.

And there is the transition problem. After the forest and a hard hunt the evening before and driving home in the dark and washing the bird's feet (the bird's disciple) and putting her down to sleep while I, into the night, dress the quarry and cut it into hawk-snack portions and stow it in the freezer and clean up the mess and clean up myself and feed the feeder rats, the dog, and myself and . . . the next morning in suit and tie in a suburban office complex constructed at the expense of squirrels, raccoons, foxes, insects, trees and up and down the food chain, and standing, disconcerted, wondering which is real — the woods and the bird or the office and the telephone. The office with the glass and plastic is inescapably simply geometries, nothing ecological about any of it except perhaps my desk — a true mess that only I can clean up. Not like some kill sites. After eating there are leavings, but it will be cleaned up, nothing wasted, and be born into a million different forms. Not so the stuff on my desk; it will be forgotten, even by me.

At the office I often ask myself, "Why am I doing this?" The answer is somewhere in a past I wasn't smart enough to control. I never ask myself that question in the field. It is a consolation.

She was high in a hardwood, facing away, looking at the horizon. He whistled and ran toward her, spitting on the meat to make it the shiniest, bloodiest red it could be in the accursed twilight. "Show it to her, then take it away," his sponsor's calm, smiling voice-memory said. Almost under the tree he stopped and held the meat out. She looked first at his face — over her shoulder, haughtily — then at the glove. The feathers on her back ruffled as the wind rose. He let her have a good look, hoping to turn her around. She didn't turn, but she looked. So he flipped the glove over to hide the meat and walked rapidly upwind away from her, bulldozing a jumbled track through the leaves as he went.

He walked as far as he dared and turned. She was still there. He couldn't tell whether she was looking. He whistled, turned into the wind, and shot his arm up. He couldn't hear anything but wind. The leaves on the ground were moving now, a brown foam washing past him. Despair tensed his throat. He wanted to blame her for playing with him this way. "To train a dog, you've got to be smarter than the dog." He couldn't blame her; it was his fault. He waited in the cold.

And then it was too much. He half-turned. Her tree was empty.

But as he lowered his arm, there she was. She had converted all of her altitude in the tree into speed. Pulling out of her glide to the glove, she was a dark sliver of head-on hawk less than a foot off the ground and twenty yards out . . . and moving. Leaves spiraled in her wake. He had less than a second to catch the end of her ascending flare-out. Arm up and turn away. She hit lightly. When he felt her shift her feet to hook the meat with the two inside talons, in eating configuration, he slowly brought her down to waist level and secured her to the glove. He cursed her softly so the wind would drown his words, so she wouldn't hear.

He walked toward the other world; she dined. She rewarded him every so often with her fierce, malevolent stare.

The only contact between the two worlds is at the point of domination, or "dominion over" in Biblical parlance. The forest seems to try to insulate itself with dense thickets along roads and around clearcuts. And people teach their children myths to insure that nature will be feared, and thus the abuse of it ignored, even valued. The cartoon images of the wolf in *Little Red Riding Hood* and the humanoid trees in *Alice in Wonderland* are still vivid in my mind. And of course only the most evil people — like the hunter that kills Bambi's mother — actually go into the woods.

I am a potential point of contact, but I am not Moses with convincing stone tablets. When I speak to people at work about being out in the field, they make jokes, or their eyes glaze over.

Worse, I have begun to flirt with the notion that the earth with humans is incompatible with the earth before humans, that the environmental cause was lost the day the first chimpanzee used a stem to prise termites out of a mound, or the day the first australopithecus hit something by throwing a rock, or the day the first homo erectus struck two rocks together to form a cutting tool. Human technology and inventive talent seem to have reduced hallowed evolution to a plodding artifact — a horse on the freeway. Wildness may become a niche market for the overly sensitive, a set of private enterprises without any public support whatsoever. Maybe we are too selfishly individual now to spread the "costs" of wildness. Governments seem to be losing their grip anyway. Is the Sierra Club ready to do the coordination? How soon? Will some president's final gift to the American environmental movement be privatization of national parks and forests?

Homo sapiens probably can survive indefinitely with a limited set of controlled species, and seems more than willing to try. Folks would rather plant a tree than save one. People flock to cities and cities sprawl. Agriculture continues to stress nonindigenous species and biotechnology will take it further. Stimulation, invention, and newness mean more than the structures of nature with their boringly slow rate of change. The trouble is that I can understand that; it scares me that I can.

And I can't resist it. Even if I really wanted to, the chainsaws would find me. There is no Nirvana. There is no place to hide from the dark stars of consciousness. There is only temporary escape from the invention of a million unknowns every day.

He felt rich, walking through the wind with a creature of the wind. There was a sadness too, for he wanted the other world now. His truck was just over the next rise. He needed to see it. The wind was too cold, too lonely.

Falconry has brought me to the edge of lunacy. It has made me hate myself and others. I rant and rail. I wonder about mass sterilizations and tax disincentives for human procreation. It has raised more questions in my life and brought me to yet another turning point. Just what I need.

For now, I dance in two different worlds. I use one dance to find the other. I knock on the wall between the worlds. No one knocks back.

That's what falconry has done for me.

"Your blood pressure is up a little."

"Good . . . I guess."

"Are you doing something different?"

"Hunting."

"Aha."

"With a hawk."

"And?"

"Do you know what that means?"

"No, do you?"

"I've got some idea. I wish I could tell you."

"Well . . ."

And he left, so that he could continue his real life.

The Near Horizon

by Doug Pineo

photo by S. Kent Carnie

Before we get too far into this, you should all know that things have changed awfully fast from my perspective. Middle age is in my face like a panhandler. I've tripped awkwardly into the ranks of the other post-war "kids," all of us utterly stunned to face creaky knees and exhaustion at 10 p.m., just when the party's getting started. And do I have anything to complain about, really? The pundits and scholars are now rubbing their collective chins about the declining middle class in America, while I've industriously dug my way in, at least to the lower rungs.

With all those years I spent studying ecology and learning to make falcon hoods, or read the *baetis* hatch, I could have become a CPA. No, a doctor. Wait a minute, they're like me, always putting restorative pursuits behind a great burlap-covered ball of obligation and commitment they insist on pushing or pulling around. Anyway, I hedged my bets, and here I am, my profession as a landscape ecologist carrying the back beat and paying the mortgage, and making hoods when I can get to them after family and work, providing the resources necessary to fly hunting falcons. But not all, or even the principal resource.

A great and senior friend of American falconry observed to me recently that most falconers only worry about where their next falcon is coming from, and where their next flight is going to be. The principal resource of falconry is not the falcon, not the sky, not the little electronic toys and leather trinkets we fuss over like matrons in a milliner's shop. And though it isn't hard to argue that falconry is really an excuse to see good dog work, your setter isn't the principal resource either. The principal resource of falconry is the land. Without the land and its *profits à pendre*, the game we seek with our dogs and hawks, there is nothing.

And that's what has changed awfully fast for me. It's understandable that most falconers focus on the falcon and the quarry. It is a struggle indeed to marshal the time and other resources to put yourself in the right place at the right time often and regularly enough to succeed at hawking. After the collective effort to overcome the inherent difficulties of domesticating hunting hawks in order to ensure their availability as wild stocks were declining, can we be blamed too much for looking up into the sky at the peregrine (born in a barn), in her place of pride high above us, instead of the encroaching fences and warehouses? Prevailing above the evils of a bureaucracy and its private sector courtiers who had lost their sense of mission, but not their stomach for mendacity, has certainly distracted our tiny group-which-is-not-a-group from realities in the troubled land. Collectively, hunters, particularly falconers, are in a state of denial. Anger and denial are the first stages of grieving, and most of us grieve because we know what's happening. Yet now, even as urbanites, alienated profoundly from all natural things and natural cycles, call for an end to hunting, it is time to get off the dime and act on behalf of the land.

No need to quote Leopold here. If you haven't read *A Sand County Almanac* yet, put a marker in this story and go do it. Then come back and I'll finish. The point for every hunter and other conservationist is that as a culture, we have reached a watershed. We're standing at the top of the ridge and have choices to make. The average farm kid in the Palouse now doesn't hunt like his dad did. His dad gave it up when his last bird dog died. When I experienced the Palouse behind a dog and a falcon the land was depauperate of wildlife compared to primitive times. And it was richer and more diverse than it is now.

The price of one B2 bomber would buy more wildlife habitat than has been purchased by all the wildlife agencies west of the Mississippi in the last 10 years. But if bureaucrats and politicians won't face up to it (sage grouse don't vote, but B2 bomber factory workers do), then the average hunter must.

Sometimes all of us need a mentor, a teacher. Our greatest guide, in the end, is our own accumulated experience, influenced by the mentors and opportunities encountered along the way. I now am convinced that sport is as worthy as anything a person can pursue. It is certainly on a par with any sacred or prosaic profession, and far superior morally to many. So with matters of the superego instilled in my military youth, it has fallen to mentors in sport to inform my actions and attitudes as an adult. But not all mentors are human. And if you will let go, and listen, you may find mentors which we honkey white people call inanimate, but white people, men in particular, don't like to let go. It's threatening and somehow seen as effeminate. Falconers have an advantage here because we quite literally let go of the treasured focus of our passion, in order to experience it at all.

In the Palouse I found a beautiful, abused landscape, and memorable people, some of whom were very wise in the land, and from all of whom I learned. It was in the Palouse that a dog, a hawk, and the land taught me about clarity of purpose and the real meaning of survival.

Before I ever saw one in the field, the gray partridge fascinated me. *Perdix,* the old world partridge in a pear tree of the Christmas carol, is a stout, rotund game bird, classical in European falconry and now a mainstay of American hawking. At home in grain fields, pastures, and rangeland — it was introduced in North America in the late nineteenth century.

Half again as big as a bobwhite, partridge seem confident of themselves feeding in sprouting winter wheat hundreds of yards from cover. Foraging in a field or skittering down a dusty harvest road, they are archetypal galliform birds, plump and rounded like daphnia in a drop of pond water. A hun covey is the fat of tamed and fertile land, all its ripe vitality expressed in trim, earth-toned avian bundles. In late summer of a good year, family groups of ten to fifteen can be found along the roadside, one or two to the mile, in an evening's drive. Later, these amalgamate into big coveys of thirty birds or more, until winter snows split them into smaller coveys again. Finally, in late winter coveys evaporate into pairs. March finds squabbling trios not uncommon, as two cock birds scrap for the favor of a disinterested hen.

Grey or Hungarian partridge ("Huns") afford American falconers from Wisconsin west across the northern tier of the country an opportunity for excellent upland game hawking. Much of their range lies east of the Rockies in open, relatively flat country. The Palouse, where I hunted partridge for a number of years, lies on the west slope of the Rockies. Tucked away in southeastern Washington, it is a hilly landscape, though the hills are of a peculiar nature, resembling big seas or a river's standing waves. The north slopes are usually steeper than the south slopes, and on the steepest areas, patches of native vegetation sometimes grow in lens-like or airfoil shapes, called "eyebrows." Above and below these elegantly shaped patches of cover, the plow and combine do their work. In the eyebrows, grasses and shrubs provide nesting, thermal, and escape cover for huns and pheasants, as they once did for Columbian sharp-tailed grouse, before the plow and spring stubble burning eliminated this wonderful bird from the region.

I see the sharp-tails' ghosts out of the corner of my eye in this Palouse country, sometimes in spring when the pink and white phlox, yellow balsam root, and blue lupine are all blooming on a rocky break tumbling down from the wheat-covered plateau, or in the grasses under an old hilltop locust stand. They remind me that grey partridge aren't the native inhabitants of these hills. But the hun is now part of the Palouse, like wheat and white men.

Naturally, for every hilltop in the Palouse, there's a corresponding valley, bowl, or draw, where the richest soils lie and yields are highest. These more sheltered depressions are often where a racing setter slams into a point, on a covey of huns or a pheasant. On the higher ridges, and from atop the ancient volcanic plugs of Bald, Kamiak and Steptoe Buttes, grand vistas in the western tradition greet one's gaze. In the foreground, always the hills march on from southwest to northeast. Almost any day, you can see the Blues and Wallowas in Oregon, or far north into Spokane County, and as far into Idaho as the cloud ceiling will allow.

Drop down a few rods into one of these bowls, though, and suddenly the open landscape becomes intimate. All around, the near horizon makes the longwinger apprehensive, queasy. This is some sort of arena, or colosseum, not a rolling prairie put to the plow. I'll lose any falcon I put up in this place, won't I? Surely she'll fly away over the surrounding edge, never to return. Well now, that depends.

Abe returned to Bald Butte for good in the late seventies, when his mother became too unsteady to carry on by herself. The family place spreads down the northern slopes of the butte to the south fork of the Palouse River, the better part of a square mile of deep, brown loess soils. Abe grew up in these Palouse hills, then ran pack strings into the Lochsa and Bitterroot wilderness for thirty years. Early on, he'd come back in spring and summer to help his father plant peas and barley, and bring in the winter wheat, but while September was still young, he left for the high country. Abe never married, and now the place needed constant attention. The horse string went to a younger partner.

Through the seasons these undulating, voluptuous hills seem to parade in a procession of hues and patterns, but not as variegated and spattered with color as in Abe's youth, before aerial application of herbicides became common. In spring and early summer, the vivid green of peas, winter and spring wheat, and barley relieves late winter's tired grays and browns, covering the open wounds of massive erosion. In high summer the pea harvesters rumble over the hills day and night, like green dragons gobbling up the fresh pods, disgorging them into waiting flatbeds rigged with side boards, to be rushed down the Snake River breaks to Clarkston, and the freezer.

Later, the combines come, self-leveling marvels transforming tawny velveteen slopes into corduroy. Finally in autumn, the stubble is plowed or chiseled, and the season's pea ground is planted to winter wheat: somber tweeds. In winter snow comes and goes, remaining only in the weakly lit shadows of steep north slopes. Scattered stands of locust, ponderosa, chokecherry, hawthorn or cottonwood look black in the distance, though they are fading from the landscape like old people. Only a rich burgundy of patches of wild rose travels very far to the eye, through the cold haze of a midwinter afternoon.

In the eastern Palouse, near the Idaho border, enough rain falls to crop annually, without the need for summer fallow, when soils are kept bare and sterile to store moisture. And in the eastern Palouse the wild rose and chokecherry, ninebark and snowberry, and the county weed board's dirty half-dozen noxious villains explode agressively out of the ground in every gully, roadside or rocky place the plow can't reach. Even after one hundred years of erosive farming, this is still fertile ground. The region's productivity, chemical fertilizers and pesticides, and high-yielding wheat varieties combine to mask the destructive effects of some of the nation's worst erosion.

The Palouse, then, is a paradoxical place, in summer and fall a beautiful, dream landscape from a Thomas Hart Benton mural, without the extruded aluminum detritus of irrigation equipment, rumpled trailer houses, and wire fences that blight so many agricultural regions. Yet to be in the Palouse in late winter and spring when cold rain and melting snows rip the hills down with them to the valleys toward the Snake River is to be shocked, saddened. As more thoughtful and thrifty farmers have observed, it won't go on forever. Chemical applications, cropping, and tilling practices which characterize this diesel-powered postwar farming are collapsing under the weight of their own short-term productivity. Before the Hungarian partridge and pheasant are gone, and maybe while Abe is still farming the tide will turn.

On Abe's place it's still tough to find the erosion that chokes the Palouse River every spring, and leaves clay bones pushing up through hilltops and north slopes. The top of the butte is still in native pasture. Small stands of ponderosa and fir rise up in the draws. Wildflowers still bloom, as almost nowhere else in this sea of wheat, peas, and lentils. Abe at sixty-plus is the embodiment of the tough people who homesteaded this land, but he recalled for me one day how there aren't nearly the number and different kinds of wildflowers in the Palouse that there once were. This extraordinary landscape, no longer wilderness, has withered and hardened.

Abe is a hunter, beginning with pheasant and partridge around the butte, and elk and deer in the nearby mountains. He is sure the game bird numbers are down in the

Palouse because flowers, forbs, and the little insects that used to live on them, and in turn were crucial to newly hatched birds, have declined. However, "down" is a relative thing. The highest gray partridge densities ever recorded were observed in the eastern Palouse, a measure of the region's productivity. When I first met Abe, I was prospecting around the Palouse at the end of harvest, when things are pretty relaxed. I was looking for places to fly my falcon at partridge over my setter. As I drove from farm to farm seeking permission for future hunting, I saw many huns and pheasant.

As often happens with farmers, I found Abe that first day in his shop, tinkering with an old Caterpillar tractor. He was able to farm his 550 acres comfortably enough by maintaining the old D-6, rather than borrowing for a new, massive, articulated wheel tractor. I asked him if he would mind me running my dog on his ground, and hunting with the falcon. I was prepared for the usual questions about falconry, or the disinterested murmur of approval that emanates from laconic old bachelor farmers. But Abe must have been looking for an excuse to ease out from under that yellow cat, because he slid onto the seat of my old Dodge pickup, and directed me up the hill, to show me where the hun coveys on his place were this year. During the intermittent, motorized stroll (a lot of it happened in compound low), I received the grand tour of Bald Butte, and his exposition on the changing natural history of the eastern Palouse. Our ramble was punctuated by discovery of several coveys of partridge and a batch of late pheasant poults.

When I asked Abe if he cared to walk with me, to watch the setter cast across the lower skirts of the butte, and the falcon stoop on partridge over a point, he laughed and said he just might do that. I didn't start flying at Bald Butte until a month after our first meeting and Abe usually had something else going, or wasn't home when I stopped by to ask him along.

Bald Butte was one of those spots you want to hunt on weekends, even when huns could be found closer to home. The twenty-minute drive gave me and the setter, Willie, curled up in the wheat straw in the bed of the truck, time to settle into the hunter's attitude of quiet, disciplined anticipation. The falcon, Sage, riding quietly on her perch in the truck canopy, always lived within that state of being.

There are two ways to hunt partridge with falcons, broadly speaking. You can cruise the roads slowly, looking for coveys as their heads poke above the stubble, and when they're more obvious, digging through several inches of snow for green blades of winter wheat. The dean of Palouse partridge hawking is Les Boyd, who was born and raised on a wheat farm near Pullman. You would be forgiven for suspecting he had every dirt clod in Whitman County numbered, given his legendary ability to spot huns in plowed or chiseled stubble.

I bought an old pair of huge, 10 x 60 Leitz binoculars to spot huns like Les, but realized soon that more was involved than driving slowly along past his uncles' fields, stopping periodically to scan with the glasses. The real key was a quarter century of hawking the same quarry on familiar ground, experience not quickly duplicated. Boyd knows the value and use of a good bird dog, and is never without one. Still, he always seemed to spot a covey on the way to some good ground or other I'd rediscovered, where I thought we'd both find flights in quick order.

Another way to hunt partridge, the one I prefer, is to walk into your hunting ground behind a good pointing dog. Apart from any impatience or distaste on my part for creeping along dusty back roads squinting into the slopes and flats for some small glimpse of partridge, I like the dog work, and the quiet walking. Because of the mud and plowed furrows it's more work than you'd suspect. Trying to keep up with a three-year-old setter is a lesson in pacing. I used to swear I'd train the next dog to stop on command, so I could catch up with him at the ridge line, and watch him as he plunges down the other side. When Willie was young, I struggled to the top of endless slopes to search with heaving breath for a distant white streak. It would be pure bullshit to claim he ever got much better, but I think he got a little more tired a little bit quicker, and, he would check back now and then.

I'm not sure why the best hawking often occurs in solitude. Most falconers claim hawking alone as their most treasured time. Maybe it's because acuity is heightened by the absence of banter and chitchat. No one to correct as the point is approached; no praying that company will keep their heads, drink in the spectacle, and do as they're told! Alone, a guy can park the rig, heel the dog, take up the falcon, and head into the field. Roads and cars disappear behind a stubbled slope, sounds are reduced to the tinkling of horned larks, the raven's call, and the panting dog. Yet more of it is simply that time is short, falconers are spread pretty thin across the country, and you just end up hunting alone a lot. Also, with advancing age patience with the perceived shortcomings of other guys and their dogs and birds declines.

Whitman County can be damn cold in January. The sky is often a pale gray with a thin, high overcast. I stopped by Abe's place on a Saturday afternoon, and asked him if he felt like taking a brisk walk behind the dog with me. He was ready. His mother smiled from her chair by the front picture window as we crossed the road and headed up a draw of spring wheat ground, which had been chiseled rather than plowed after harvest.

Chiseling breaks up compacted soil, creates deep fissures which trap runoff, and incorporates some of the stubble, but doesn't destroy the soil profile. Moisture is stored without triggering massive erosion, and most of the stubble is left standing. Chiseled stubble poking through a few inches of dry snow hides the huns well, and they're almost always found in it in winter, gleaning wheat kernels left by the combine, and volunteer wheat sprouts.

I leaned down and touched Willie lightly on the back of his head, whispering "all right." He was off, moving swiftly up the sloping sides of the draw, back down, and across to the other side. Even at two hundred yards, his panting was audible in the dense air, between the sounds of our pac boots squeaking in the snow. We moved a quarter mile up the slope of the butte, when the draw shallowed out, still without a point. Willie stopped and looked back at me, and I waved him on. Our breath was deep now like his, our insulated overalls unzipped a foot or so. Sage rode with feathers relaxed on my fist, which was aching from the cold, even as we were getting warm from the climb.

The sun was trying to penetrate the quilted sky, succeeding seconds before the setter, loping along, drew up instantly into a point. He skidded perpendicular to the direction of his cast, snow flying up, sparkling in the sun. My little tricolor weather vane! I don't know how many times he has found birds like this, but the same excitement surges every time. Abe was the perfect partner on a day like this, if there was going to be one. Quiet and steady, his pace matched mine. He smiled at the dog's point. Willie was farther up the slope than us, setting on the point, which he would do sometimes. His tail was almost tickling the top of his head. Bad form, I thought to myself, smiling too. He would hold that point as long as necessary.

We walked slowly across the cold breeze a hundred yards or so, then upwind past the setter. From our vantage point, the Palouse in winter spread out before us. Willie's head was angled down just a little. He was a sphinx. I gathered my breath, and gently removed Sage's hood. In her third season, she was splendid, waxy yellow feet and cere, feathers perfect. One of the best times to really appreciate a falcon is on the raised fist, just as you present her to the sky. She had seen this scene many times before, instantly fixing her gaze on the dog, then bobbing her head intently. Every feather on her body rising erect, she shuddered in a tight rouse, loosing a little cloud of powder down. Wings outstretched and tail spread momentarily, suddenly she was off. She flew directly toward Willie, daring him to break point, but he was always a focused dog with a clear mission, and he never flinched. She had certainly pinned the huns to the ground, passing a few feet over them as she buzzed the setter, then climbed up abruptly, reaching for altitude. With snow on the ground and a pearly sky, falcons quickly become difficult to see, even when they are directly overhead. I could just see her, and faintly hear her bells as she waited on above us.

We began to walk into Willie's point, pausing a few times to note Sage's position, moving again when she was upwind. The ineffable essence of hunting was distilled in the ensuing moments. No value lay in hurrying. We were a few yards from Willie's nose when the partridge exploded from the stubble between us in a cackling whirr. Sage threw herself into a stoop, stroking hard, then tucking her wings. We'd tried to flush the huns uphill, by angling somewhat down slope from the dog's point as we walked in. Knowing the advantage of flying downhill under a falcon's stoop, the partridge banked around and down, hellbent for cover. In the whipping beats of her greatest speed, Sage's parabolic trajectory leveled out behind the covey. Fifty yards from a rose patch, she took her chosen bird, landing in the stubble with her prize near the cover where the rest of the covey had escaped.

Abe and I walked down from the light on the shoulder of the butte, into the draw where Sage stood plucking feathers from her dispatched partridge. The near horizon rose up, closing around us once again. Willie had found the rest of the covey, and held them. I secured Sage, offering her the hindquarters of a pheasant she'd caught the day before, warmed in an inside pocket of my coat, in exchange for the partridge, and eased over to Willie. It seems to disappoint and confuse a dog to pull him off a point, so I quietly walked in to flush the birds. They went out the back side of the roses. He held, watching with longing intensity as the birds disappeared over the ridge.

Now we could return to relax a little near Sage, while she finished eating. As we stood in afternoon's shadow, the cold began to seep in. It came to me that we'd just participated in a hunt which had occurred many times before, here in the Palouse. In winters past, if we've pieced the past together accurately, gyrfalcons, prairie falcons, and goshawks lived on sharp-tailed grouse. Where sharp-tails still occur in North America, they are pursued by these wintering hunters. The wild falcons hunt the Palouse country now, preying instead on easy game, huns and pheasant.

We'd killed a gray partridge, an old world quarry of classical falconry, introduced not long after the wheat and barley replaced bunchgrass and wildflowers. We'd flushed the covey before a setter's point, as it has been done for centuries. Sage's stoop hissed through her bells. The steep, rolling terrain was a challenge not common to partridge hawking everywhere. It was a good flight.

Contemplating the denouement of a successful hunt, there is that pensive moment. After the covey's noisy rise, and the falcon's furious burst of focused power, I heard the beating of other dark, great wings. It wasn't so much the death of the partridge, which was clean and fast, and part of an ageless cycle. A hunter owes his quarry respect and good use, and I would always see to that. Maybe it was the ghost of the sharp-tail, always with me in the Palouse. It was more, something else. As I knelt in the thin snow near Sage, the old question came again What would these hills be like, covered for miles, as far as I could see, with a pelt of bunchgrass the draws filled with chokecherry? Would it make the solitary death of bird or man any easier to contemplate?

I chose not to kick these ruminations around with Abe. I didn't know him well enough to discuss my peculiar perspectives on floral and faunal diversity in the working landscape. But the old guide and horse-packer could tell that what the falcon had made look so easy was really more than met the eye. He saw in Willie's casts that the dog knew how to look for partridge on this ground. He even observed, like a seasoned falconer, "If we hadn't pushed those birds uphill first, they'd have all hit the roses before Sage got down to 'em." He was right, of course.

Abe, who'd been witness as sharp-tails and wildflowers disappeared from the Palouse, nevertheless knew how to appreciate what we'd seen and done that day, while acknowledging the irony that not partridge, or stubble, or white man, or hybrid falcon was native to these hills. Falconers like to hunt alone, but hunting with a good dog and falcon is something worth sharing.

Sage finished her meal, and jumped up to my fist. Predation being what it is, no ironies, paradoxes or contradictions marred her evident satisfaction. It was an easy walk back to Abe's house. I thanked him for his company and hospitality, and gave him the partridge. Willie curled up in his wheat straw. Sage stepped up to her accustomed perch under the canopy.

Steering the old Dodge back to Pullman at dusk, I flipped on the radio, and tuned in "A Prairie Home Companion," on the local public radio station. Garrison Keillor whispered the news from Lake Wobegon, then introduced Chet Atkins. The heater's warm roar let muscles relax, as I reached over and turned up the volume.

Homecoming

by Bruce A. Haak

The undulating hills of the Piedmont stretched to the horizon as our jet banked on its final approach to Dulles International Airport. Flaming red and gold forests shimmered in all directions, icons of another glorious fall along the Eastern Seaboard. From above, the outline of the cyclone fence defined the border between airport and suburbia. An avalanche of buildings and asphalt rushed to devour the natural beauty of the landscape. Tiny, undeveloped parcels winked up at me like distant lights, precious remnants of a land continually besieged by a metropolitan area hungry for space and construction.

This journey, in October of 1989, was one that I both dreaded and relished. I longed to see again the hardwood forests in their autumn splendor. Emotionally, I needed to see my family. As surely as autumn leaves are plucked by winter winds, my relatives were growing old. Suddenly, I felt a hollow intestinal chill, the fear of losing loved ones. More than just a visit, this must also be a time of closure.

In September, 1963, the vibrant colors of the Appalachian foliage stood in stark contrast to the sun-bleached beaches of San Diego and the lush rain forests of Puget Sound. It was another patented Navy move: no warning and only two weeks to pack everything you own, drive nonstop across the country, and start life over among strangers in a totally new environment. In those days, civilians might have moved across town or perhaps to another city, but Navy people had the dubious distinction of regularly swapping residences on one coast of North America for the other. The spasmodic move from Puget Sound to southern California in the spring, and now the relocation to Virginia, had left me disoriented. My family and I settled in Alexandria, across the sullen Potomac River from Washington, D.C.

Over the past three years, I had become interested in falconry. By age thirteen I had raised and flown a kestrel, but lacked any practical knowledge of the sport. At this time, falconry was undergoing its most fertile growth in centuries. Most would-be falconers were trying to learn falconry through books or long-distance correspondence with falconers. In a few population centers, among them Philadelphia, Chicago, Los Angeles and Washington, D.C., there were practicing falconers who were willing to guide and counsel beginners. It was during a chance encounter with a keeper at the National Zoo that I mentioned my interest in falconry and gained a valuable tidbit of information: the name of a local falconer. The man's name was Alva G. Nye, Jr. Of course, I had no way of knowing that Al was being deluged with calls from youngsters yearning for a start in the sport. Quite unintentionally, he found himself in the anomalous position of having to eliminate the less motivated from among a sizeable crop of suburban "baby boomers" aspiring to become falconers. In my case, Al simply put me under the tutelage of one of his young proteges, Allan Cline, an arranged friendship that has lasted for thirty years.

For me, life in Virginia was an internment, a test of will and mental stamina. Not six months before, I had been a free-roaming creature of the beaches and bogs of Puget Sound. My domain had been a captivating island of duck marshes, trout lakes, pastures and rain forest. To my way of thinking, the rural Northwest, with its abundance of outdoor experiences, was still home.

There was no doubt about it, I suffered from culture shock. The previous fall I had attended a small junior high school in Oak Harbor, an island town on the coast of Washington. The students didn't actually ride horses to class, but many could have with little prompting. My fellow students and friends were a mixture of local residents, farm kids, and service brats like me. It was an outdoor-oriented community focused on active pursuits like team sports, boating, fishing and hunting. The town was middle-income, middle-class America. It was real, unpretentious, and I fit in.

Back then I was a Boy Scout. For one of our overnight adventures, we had camped along the beach and gotten a tour of the naval aviator survival training camp. Until that time, I hadn't actually considered eating snakes, impaling deer on sharpened spikes, or catching tree squirrels with snares fashioned from salvaged aircraft cable. But then, I'd never been starved or stranded. These are not skills that everyone necessarily needs to know. And even then, I related to this in realistic fashion. I'd killed enough game and fish to know that creatures didn't volunteer to die and fresh meat didn't come wrapped in cellophane. From firsthand experience, I also knew that game and fish were good to eat. The idea that some things must die in order for others to live has always seemed to me the most basic of principles.

The Washington, D.C. metropolitan area was a world away from the Pacific Northwest. It was a grim realization for me that the closest thing to a big, open field from my house was Arlington National Cemetery. We lived in the midst of urban sprawl, surrounded by asphalt and concrete, and I had unwittingly entered a completely controlled environment. It started when I became a slave to mass transportation. The bus carried me back and forth from high school daily. It was not the familiar yellow school bus that can yet be seen rumbling through pastoral settings. This was the fume-belching monster that whisked its capacity of business-suited commuters to their daily pursuit of legal tender. To me, the bus was a constant reminder of purgatory, the daily penitence of people who made the wrong decision with their lives.

Most of the time, I got off at school. It was an expansive maze of concrete wings and levels that conscripted almost 3,000 of my peers between the hours of 8:00 a.m. and 3:00 p.m. This was where I would first taste the stinging lash of conformity. It started upon learning of the student-imposed dress code. Heck, I already knew the unwritten rules of dress: start pressed, never wear the same shirt two days running, match your socks, and avoid green and blue unless nothing else is clean. My peers were, however, looking to ensure that our illustrious student body would not be denigrated by the wearers of the devil's fabric: blue jeans. It was un-American! I'd just rolled in from Marlboro Country and the first order of the day was to change my wardrobe. These suburban twits and I were not getting off on the right foot.

The most important aspect of student life in Virginia in 1963 was to look "collegiate," whatever that was. Our student body came from diverse backgrounds: upper level military, diplomats and government workers, comfortable middle class types, and low-income black and white kids from some of the rundown sections of central Alexandria. From what I gathered, most of them had never camped out or baited a hook. Nor did they care. The few who did have a passing interest in animals and nature gleaned everything they knew about wildlife from television. Student government and mores were dictated by the more affluent types who were under strong home pressure to attend good colleges.

My personal revolution was not a conscious effort. I simply rejected the values of industrialized, urbanized society as I knew it. No big thing. My adolescent response was fairly typical. I checked out mentally from my surroundings. Although I tried to fit in, it was largely a wasted effort. Offsetting this alienation was the cultivation of my interests in wildlife, the outdoors and falconry. I was biding my time for a change that I knew was coming.

My first hawk house or "mews" was not a flattering end for plywood and stud lumber. In fact, it would probably be safe to characterize it as one of the eyesores of the neighborhood. Conspicuously located in our driveway, adjacent to a major intersection, it looked out upon the world with a disdain equalled only by that of passing motorists. To be fair, its function was to keep the hawk in and potential predators out. Within the framework of that limited definition, it served its purpose. While it was located close enough to the house to discourage accidental arson, this structure fairly begged for a match.

I was wholly unprepared to be a falconer. But come to think of it, I was unprepared for just about everything else in life at the age of thirteen. My shortcomings were particularly obvious when it came to building the facilities necessary to house hawks and pigeons. It wasn't bad enough that I had normal teenage phobias, but these were compounded by an acute obliviousness to two rather important topics: construction and automotives. It would get worse as I got older, especially when I needed jobs and became dependent on cars as a mode of transportation to out-of-the-way places.

It was true that I, along with many of my friends, suffered from a relatively recent cultural phenomenon, inherent in the post-World War II "baby boom" generation, known as SCDS (suburban capability deficiency syndrome). Long before I was born, Americans migrated in mass from the country to the city. Almost immediately, they lost that Jack-of-all-trades ability to improvise with the materials at hand. Handicrafts, the stock-in-trade skills of the hinterlands, were replaced by specialization. Formal education, usurping the practical elements of knowledge, worked great until you broke a chair leg or stalled your car in traffic. Then you were at the mercy of a specialist. Through falconry, I would learn that personal endeavors, including art, sport and craft, in many ways preserve the best of the human condition.

I always thought that my problem was mainly environmental; my family didn't fix, build or repair anything. While many of my friends grew up hauling lumber and hand tools, or pointing flashlights at greasy car chassis in dingy garages, my family never had more than two screwdrivers, a dull hand saw, and a hobby hammer. Power tools and timing lights were not topics discussed around our dinner table, nor were they of interest to me. But later, I would know that such things could save you time, grief and money, keep you from getting stranded in some godforsaken place, or provide a sense of pride and personal satisfaction that can only be earned.

Falconry is also like that. In the old days, we made most of the gear we needed. I was taught that a falconer needs to be resourceful and self-sufficient, capable of constructing a passable hood, jesses, leashes, and perches when needed. While there are a good many falconry items on the market today, they aren't exactly stock items at the neighborhood convenience store. With falconry, most of the time you are on your own. When you fly hawks in the middle of nowhere, and live hundreds of miles from the closest falconer, you often end up living with your mistakes. This, unfortunately, may mean living without your bird. Falconers are a culturally isolated lot. But it is by design, a conscious choice, and they are the richer for it.

I have to wonder if society has really done us any favors. We go to great lengths to learn career skills, like operating computers, but are at a loss to fix a blown fuse. Most people don't give these notions a second thought. But then, most people don't drive all over creation looking for birds in desolate reaches of the continent or try to redefine a 4,000-year-old sport using modern technology.

"Hi, Tony, we've never met but my name is Bruce Haak. Years ago, I lived in Alexandria and I'm back here on vacation. Earlier today I spoke with Al Nye about ridge trapping and he told me that you still worked the blind up at Paris. I used to spend some time there and wondered if I could tag along? . . . Thanks, I really appreciate the invite. On the flight out, I was trying to remember when I was there last. It must have been the fall of '66. A lot of water under the bridge since then, eh? I'll get directions from here and unless they've moved the mountain, I'll be at the turn-off at 7:30 a.m. Yep, the weather looks great for the morning. See you then."

Pop's Store stood at the base of Paris Mountain in 1963. It stands there still. I'd always thought these tacky, back-woods roadside attractions were part of a low-budget franchise scheme. You know, something to perpetuate the crass American image among the sightseeing dignitaries from D.C. But in reality, few, if any, dignitaries ever pulled into Pop's. Maybe it was the herd of ceramic deer that lined the parking lot out front. Or

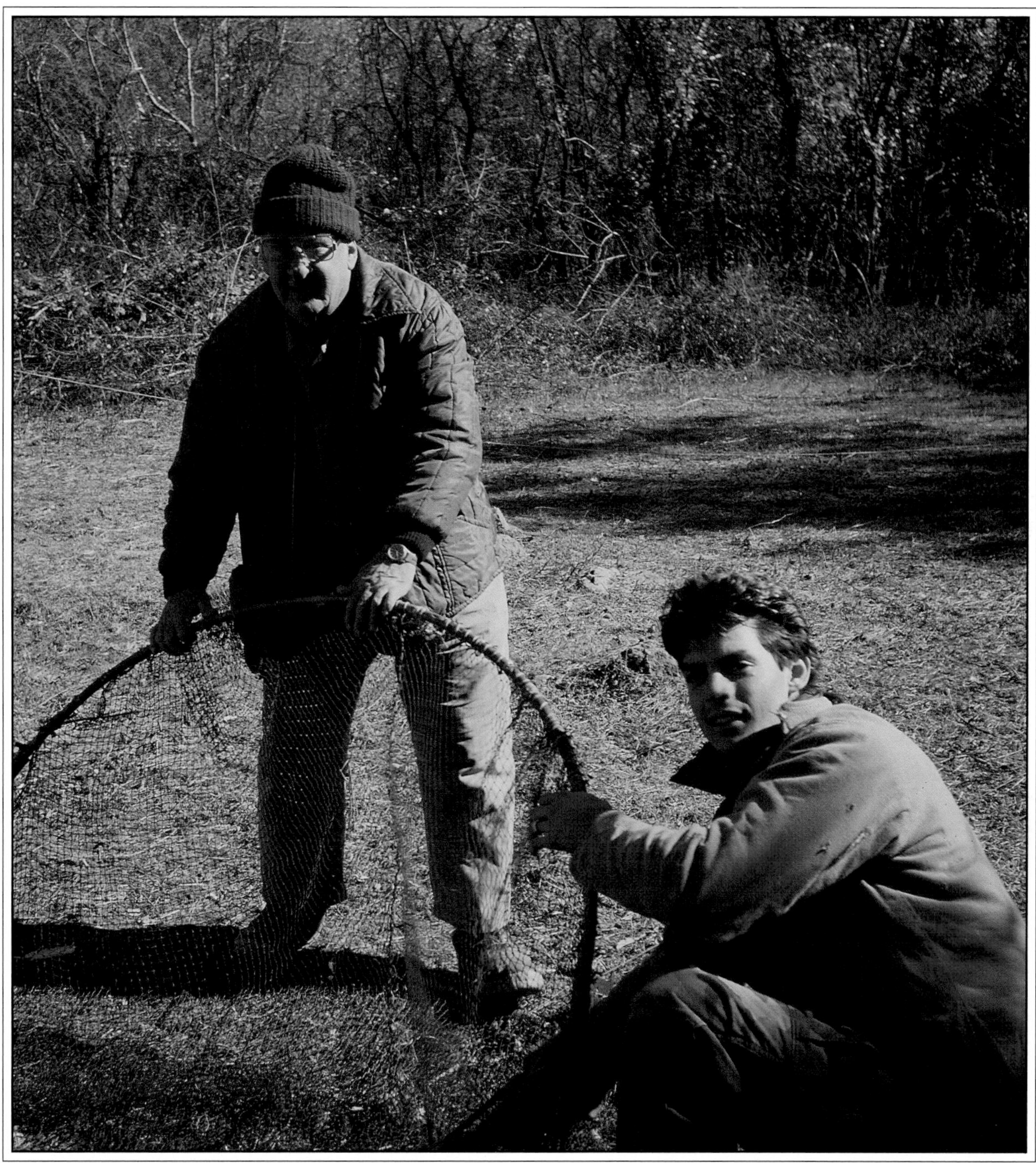

photo by Bruce A. Haak

perhaps the Smithfield hams, hanging from the porch rafters like moldy cocoons, were a deterrent. A sortie inside revealed Li'l Abner's personal potpourri of tasteless postcards, Indian tomahawks made in Japan, and every scent of car air-freshener known to man. A true "Americana" experience.

Strange as it may seem, we didn't come to Pop's for the Early Redneck decor. Off to one side was the kind of facility that could prompt boys to walk for miles off a wind-swept ridge in the dark of night: a snack bar. The food of choice was always hot soup. And Pop's could crack a can of Campbell's with the best of them. To my knowledge, hot soup or a stiff tug of "red eye" are the only cures for the bone-chilling cold that permeates hawk trappers confined to a flimsy burlap blind for hours on end. My pals and I were far too young to buy hooch, so soup it was. I guess Pop's had heat too. That was important for someone facing the prospects of a brisk autumn night under the stars in a hand-me-down summer sleeping bag. But we were tough. Well, tough enough.

For a time, Paris Mountain was the focal point of my existence. Each autumn, I became physically gripped by "zuganru," an ornithological description of the fervent unrest of migrating birds. Chilly nights, decreasing daylight, and changing leaves still trigger this physiological and emotional effect in me.

In the days before I could drive a car, my parents made the two-hour trip from the suburbs to the mountain ridge where two or three hawk trappers would rendezvous for the weekend. It wasn't much of a mountain by western standards, but the fall colors were never prettier than on the ridge. I always felt a mental sigh of relief whenever we cleared the city congestion and motored along the rural highway through the Virginia countryside. Later in the season, roadside stands with fruit, apple butter, Indian corn, and pumpkins would herald the coming of Halloween in uniquely eastern fashion.

Like all good get-away places, this one was guarded by a hidden entrance. A path led the short distance through the trees and brush that camouflaged the blind from the road. It probably wasn't a 100-yard walk of straight distance, but that inconspicuous deer trail had the magical property of transporting me back to the freedom, with that spark of wildness, that I had left out West.

Those were glorious days and nights. We were actually using a method of trapping devised hundreds of years before by Dutch hawk trappers to waylay raptors migrating down the coast of Europe. We rose early to rig bow nets (these looked like large, spring-loaded rat traps with netting on the inside) that were pegged to the ground about thirty feet in front of the blind. We then harnessed our baits and began the slow, methodical rhythm of catapulting the lure bird into the air, causing the wing flutter needed to catch the eyes of hawks aloft. The blind wasn't a hot spot by anyone's standards, but it did serve as the proving grounds for many young falconers. Experiences there laid the groundwork for a variety of future endeavors in life. We learned lessons, like the importance of having good equipment when you are miles from home and the neighborhood hardware store. Actually, there were just enough hawks coming by to show us the errors of our ways.

It was always entertaining to have some lovely passage red-tailed hawk suddenly appear in your bow net. The outcome of such shock was always in question, but knee-jerk reactions were predictable. On a good day, you might pull down half the blind in front of you while reefing too hard on the wrong end of the trigger line. Another "smooth move" was when somebody managed to release the bait bird from inside the bow net while simultaneously twanging the trigger line. The eruption of the trap adjacent to the hawk, now outside the circumference of the net, inevitably caused its hasty departure. Then there was the situation when a really big hawk bound to the lure bird at about the same moment that the lure line from the blind broke. It's amazing just how long a hawk will hang upside down off the jacketed lure bird, trying to figure out what to do next. We, of course, were helpless to influence it one way or the other. Another favorite time was when a hawk was down on the net and everything was cool and calm. You'd slowly draw the trigger line taut, feel the spring of the trap through your fingers, and see the net stop in full arc, halfway over the hawk. With the net hung up on some overlooked root or twig, you could only shake your head as the hawk flapped its way out over the valley, caught a gust of wind or kettle of rising air, and continued its long journey south.

Trapping from a blind put a new twist on the challenges of bird identification. Just spotting hawks in the clouds, much less categorizing them as to species and age, is pretty tough while peering through mosquito netting or holes in burlap. We developed a number of unusual upper torso contortions to keep up with a bird moving quickly through the limited field of view. Bugs passing nonchalantly in front of the blind ports caused more than one calamity, and we learned quickly just who among us had the "spotter's" eye. Picking specks out of a cloud bank was never my forte, and I've come to respect the ability of others in this regard.

Paris Mountain and October came to be almost synonymous in my mind: crisp weather and radiant fall colors of the hardwood forests in full splendor. Fall signalled many things, but for me the most important was that another sweltering, humid summer in Virginia had passed. It also meant that the hawk migration was going to peak soon. Depending on wind and weather conditions, precious few days were available in which to trap a passage hawk, a young malleable bird of the year, to train. Time was of the essence and a few classes might have been skipped in the rush to reach the mountain. But education, the real stuff that stays with you for a lifetime, often happens far from the halls of academia.

I could not have reached the ridge from Alexandria without a map and good directions. Considering the nonstop construction that had taken place in my twenty-two-year absence, it was predictable that I would be turned around in the wake of massive urban sprawl. For my entire life, road work has been ceaseless on the highway that surrounds the Washington, D.C. metropolitan area. A dramatically changed landscape was inevitable. In years past, the drive to Paris Mountain was out a two-lane highway through sleepy farmland, past older colonial homes built along the gracious lines of Southern pride. Now I found that beyond the malls, high-rise apartments and planned communities, a vestige of the past remained. The facade of gentility was there, but the substance had changed considerably. Many of the village houses were national historic sites and had become shops and specialty stores rather than homes. The farmland was now top-dollar real estate owned by the wealthy.

Years ago, along this quiet stretch of highway just east of Paris, I came upon a real chain gang. Manacled prisoners glistened in sweat as they labored cutting brush along the road under the watchful eyes of armed guards. The merciless late-summer sun fried them to a crisp while they earned nothing but strange stares from passing motorists. It was a scene devoid of humor or hope. It was also a time to reconfirm in my young mind that a career in crime was not my calling.

The stretch of highway is now four lanes, carrying travelers to West Virginia in record time. I reached the turn-off ahead of schedule and looked out over the valley to the east as dawn broke over the Piedmont. Living in high desert as I now do, I've become acutely aware of humidity (or the lack of it). Not only does humidity influence the feel of our surroundings, but it alters the view like a filtering system. That view, that feel, and the ever-present forests stretching from horizon to horizon were an unaccustomed yet strangely familiar experience for me. A dappled corona topped the vista of woods and fields. Then the tedious expanse of deciduous forest, just recently past its artistic autumnal prime, began to close in. For a moment, I was afflicted with claustrophobia. I closed my eyes, imagined the vastness of the Snake River Plain, and the constricting sensation was gone.

I had come a long way, styling a life on an all-consuming interest in raptors. It carried me through graduate school, directed my career, and motivated me to move West. In essence, these personal decisions had caused me to abandon my parents and grandparents. I could not have lived happily in the East; they knew it and I knew it. Yet now, the people closest to me were aging and dying in my absence. Despite our bonds, I was not an integral part of their lives. Time passes so quickly. My thoughts were overtaken by a flood of emotions.

In my rearview mirror, a vehicle approached slowly and came to a stop in front of my car. Who else would be on the lookout for a blue Buick along this road at dawn on a Saturday morning? As I approached to introduce myself to Tony and his son Anthony, a familiar face exited from the passenger side. Smiling, Brian McDonald extended his hand in greeting. Talk about kismet. In the old days, Brian had earned celebrity status for his high-quality hawking equipment. Much of his gear is now considered collectors' items. He was also one of the most innovative and successful peregrine trappers of his generation, helping to pioneer the trapping techniques which would enhance North American falconry as we know it today. Of course, I knew none of this when I first met Brian. All I knew was that he, like many of his "gentlemen falconer" colleagues, had paid me the great courtesy of answering my questions and inviting me to see his birds. It was Brian who gave me my first red-tail (a lost eyas that kept ending up on his doorstep) and who trapped the first passage goshawk I ever saw captured.

My host, Tony Meyer, was, as it turned out, perpetuating a long-standing tradition at the blind. The property was posted "no trespassing," but Tony had established an excellent rapport with the owners that enabled him to trap whenever time allowed. One must experience the camaraderie of blind trapping, even among relative strangers, to appreciate it. The elements are basic, the qualities simple. In that blind, we could have been back in the 1960's; I could have been thirteen again. The jokes might have been shaded a slightly different color, but I would have been treated just as well. The ribald humor and trappers' talk recreated a forgotten comfort.

Much of the day was spent getting to know these men. I queried Brian about mutual friends still living in the area and did my best to update him on those who had migrated West. We talked a lot about trapping, equipment, and peregrines. Brian was a wealth of information on all three subjects, and he warmed visibly when discussing the glory days of the tundra falcon. Early on, Brian had explored the Eastern Seaboard and Gulf Coast on his fall excursions. I tried to visualize him as a teenager, hiking up and down the beach at Assateague Island toting a pack with pigeons, a basket, a shovel, food and water. He and his pals actually caught peregrines on foot in the old days. It was a far cry from the air-conditioned four-wheel drive Blazers, the large rings of access keys, and briefcases full of federal permits needed by the trappers on Assateague who can only band peregrines now.

One of the things I have come to value most about my early falconry teachers was that they practiced what they preached. This point was driven home to me when Brian retrieved his bow net from the back of Tony's car. As if it were yesterday, I remembered purchasing a circular cotton dip net from Ed's Bait and Tackle for all of $5.00. It was perfectly suited for bow nets and my friends and I each bought one back then. Mine got carted all over the country until it eventually died of

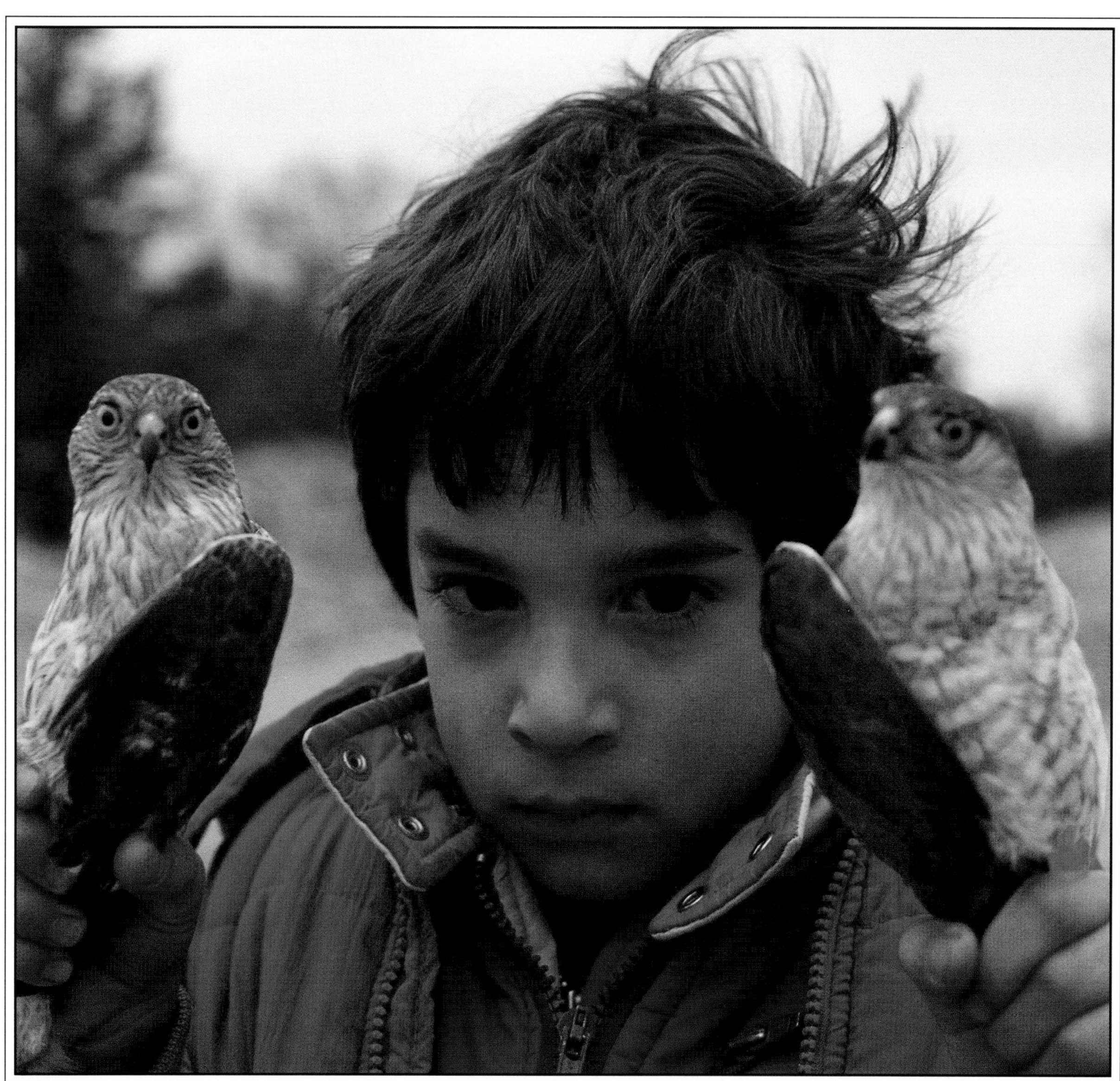

photo by Joseph Vorro

neglect. But here, attached to Brian's bow net, was the very same net that he had when I first met him. How many hawks had it trapped over the past three decades? A poignant lesson about care and concern for belongings was driven home, telling me much about the character of the man.

Between Tony, his son Anthony, Brian and me, we sighted well over twenty migrating accipiters before noon. I marveled at the abundance of short-wings as compared with the 1960's, and learned that sightings like this were now the norm. During one lull, a spunky sharp-shinned hawk came in low over the brush in a playful strafe at our bait bird. The diminutive hunter must have found the pigeon too large for its liking as it shot over the trees in front of the blind and continued southward. However, the mental trigger of a stealthy short-wing jetting into our rig at low level took me back to the fall of 1965.

Allan Cline was a senior in high school and two years older than I, and he had a pretty firm grasp of falconry for a young man. He made it a point to pass the fundamentals, as best he knew them, on to me in a pointedly direct manner. He was a stickler for details, resourceful, and well-organized for our weekend expeditions to the Virginia outback. Despite his seriousness, and the fact that he was crazy when he wasn't hawking or trapping, we shared an interesting youth. I learned a lot from him. Unfortunately, I wasn't at liberty to share most of it with my parents.

One Friday in mid-October found us camped out on the mountain, passing the long evening with a creative collection of horror tales and recounted shark attacks. A popular local story told of the blood-crazed moonshiners preying on "city folk" who accidentally stumbled upon their stills in the dark. The stories made the five-mile walk down to Pop's store on a moonless night a vivid experience.

The following morning dawned clear and cold, typical for the time of year. We busied ourselves with setting up the blind just so, and wrapped in sleeping bags against the cold, we began to advertise our lure pigeon into a perfectly blue autumn sky. Usually, the excitement began about mid-morning. Warming air masses deflecting off the ridge created lift on which hawks could float effortlessly by on outstretched wings. One reluctant haggard red-tail came in and was promptly caught and released. Others followed, but by noon we still hadn't drawn in anything exotic beyond a flighty sharp-shinned or two. We had no sparrows to attract the smaller raptors that routinely gave our pigeons a wide berth. After lunch, we hit the doldrums. The hawks appeared to have quit flying and things were getting downright dull. Around 3:00, Allan and I exited the blind to stretch and perform the necessaries. True to form, it was about this time that we spotted a red-tail soaring nearby (never fails). On a lark, Allan suggested that we sit quietly in front of the blind and try to lure it in. Our rumps barely hit dirt when a passage female Cooper's hawk came swishing in over the bait bird and landed in a spindly tree on the edge of the clearing. We were wholly exposed and very close by. In my right hand, I gingerly held the trigger line to the bow net. Allan was manning the line to the bait bird. "You blow this and I'll kill you," Allan hissed between clenched teeth.

For a full thirty minutes, we sat immobile: eyes forward, cramped and trying not to tremble. The pigeon in the middle of the bow net was catatonic and didn't even blink. Millimeter by millimeter, Allan took up the slack to the bait bird; he wanted to make the line taut in an effort to center the bait in the trap. The Cooper's hawk stared off into space, recognizing our forms neither as a cause for concern nor alarm. Suddenly, the pigeon was off balance and fluttering. With barely a perceptible flick of its wings, the hawk did a sailor dive out of the tree, straight at the trap. This was it. The choice was clear. Either I was going to catch this hawk on the first pass or outrun Allan down the mountain to preserve my life. The scene is still framed in my mind:

the zippy little hawk with the rudder tail fanned wide as its feet came forward to clutch the pigeon. In the same frame, the lightning-fast bow net covered the silhouette still suspended in mid-air. Perfect. Our howls of glee were deafening.

I cannot recommend this rather unorthodox method of hawk trapping. In order to fully appreciate this accomplishment, one needs to remember that during the 1960's, Cooper's hawk populations were greatly reduced by DDT poisoning. They were rarely trapped in northern Virginia. It was ironic that this native raptor species was nearly impossible for the average falconer to acquire. This fact was brought home to me by the number of phone calls Allan got from falconers trying to trade him for his hawk. At least three tundra peregrines were offered in exchange from people as far away as Kentucky. It was a strange perspective then and now.

My father started me fishing and hunting at an early age, so the progression to falconry seemed natural enough. The passages I'd read describing high-flying falcons attacking game in "stoops" from the heavens must have hooked me. It didn't seem to matter that I had never actually seen a falcon do that. In fact, it would be years before I actually saw peregrines fly and kill in the classic style. So what carried me? Escapism? Faith? For some unexplained reason, I was willing to accept these written descriptions as truth and I had faith in the knowledge that such exciting things were possible. This falconry fantasy would eventually take me from a high school library in Virginia to the high desert plains of Idaho. My initial fascination became an overwhelming desire to see falconry in action and to do it myself. Ultimately, I would travel many miles and meet many falconers in this quest for knowledge.

The apprenticeship concept was much in favor among the D.C. area falconers. To my mind it was, and still is, an excellent way to learn the mechanics of falconry. The surprising number of my cohorts from those days who still fly birds is testimony to the fact that the system worked well for us.

I'd seen Allen bite his lip before. It happened first when he, Ben Elliott and I were car trapping around the new Dulles Airport being built out in the country. The roads near the airport took us through some of the most open country I'd seen in northern Virginia. Unfortunately, most of it lay behind an ominous cyclone fence that encompassed the airport and served quite well to keep us and everyone else out. However, adjacent to the perimeter road were woodlots, power poles and fences, home to many kinds of raptors in winter. It was here that we plied yet another level of our inexperience as hawk trappers. We searched for kestrels and red-tailed hawks mostly, with the occasional broad-winged, red-shouldered or rough-legged hawk making an appearance. Besides learning how to spot and identify any number of birds from a moving vehicle, we practiced the presentation of ancient and modern trapping devices, mainly variations of bal-chatri (noosed cage) and pigeon harnesses, to a variety of unsuspecting subjects. This was real outdoor school and we took full advantage to savor all of the sensory experiences of subadult freedom. This included indulging in all of the "guy" foods we wanted, like chocolate sodas, pork rinds, and pepperoni sticks, for those early-hour breakfasts. There are times when life is good.

One Sunday morning at the airport, we came across a red-tailed hawk perfectly situated for some unnecessary experimentation. More advanced than Ben and I, Allan knew about the "dig-in" trapping method, a method where a person was buried with hands free to grab an unsuspecting hawk by the feet when it attacked the bait. As the leader, Allan made a spontaneous, unilateral decision to trap this hawk by emulating the "dig-in" method with an old canvas tarp that had spent a quiet life in the trunk of his parents' jalopy Dodge. Yes, it was a pretty macho idea.

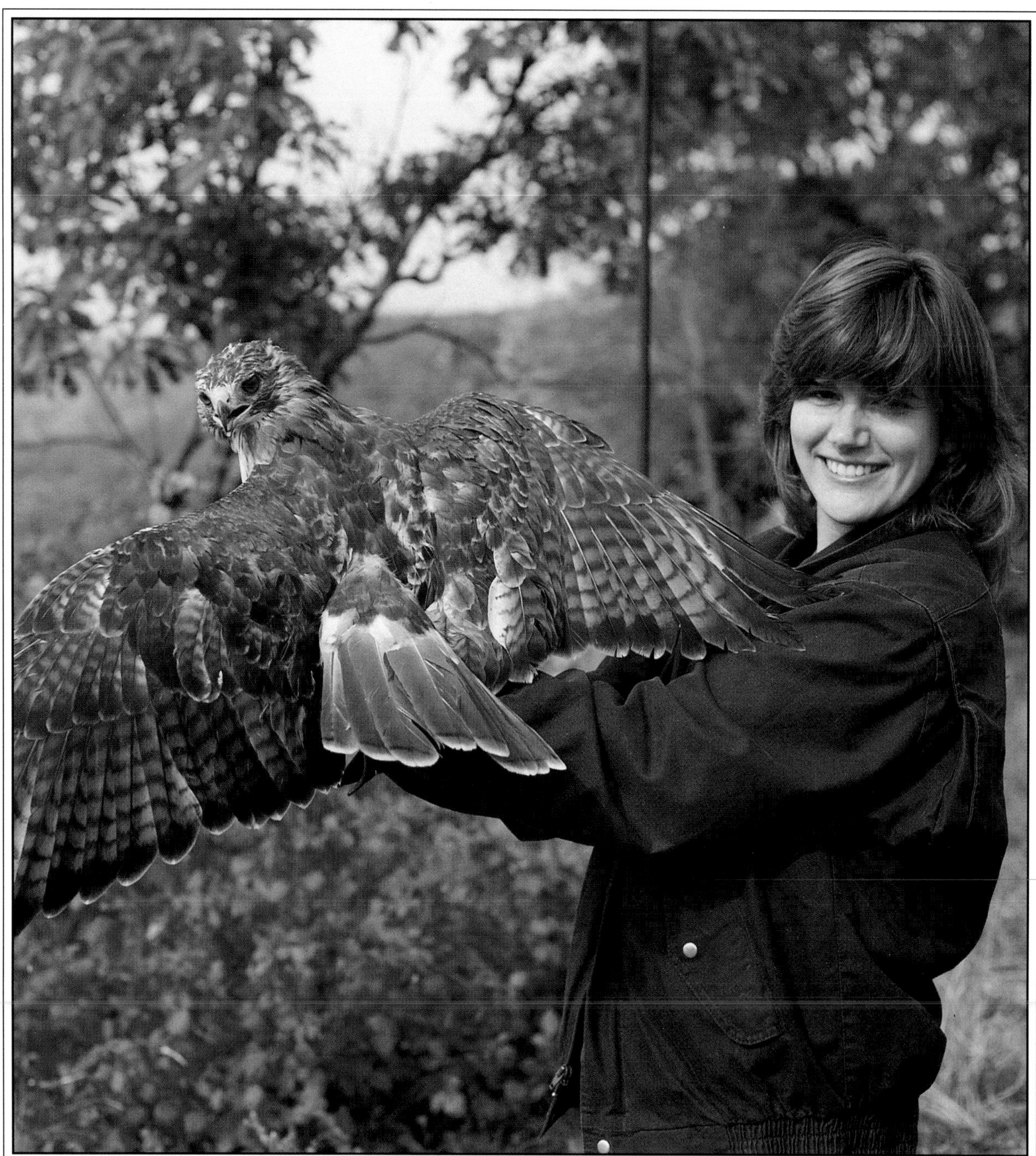

photo by Mike McDermott

Since only he had the requisite skills needed for this technical task, someone else needed to drive the car away while we waited for the hawk to strike. Naturally, a short but heated argument ensued as Ben and I vied for the privilege.

I didn't lie when I told Allan that I knew how to drive a stick shift. It was true in an elevated awareness, cosmic-connectedness sort of way. I'd just never done it in a car. But with Allan hot to try something heroic, he took my word for it, sneaked out the driver's side door, and covered himself in the faded tarp. I slid into the driver's seat, pulled myself up to the wheel, and levered down the clutch pedal. At Allan's signal, I depressed the accelerator, released the clutch, and jerked down the road. We'd gone about 150 yards when Ben started slapping me on the shoulder and yelling at me to stop.

I remember looking back over my shoulder and seeing Allan stomping down the road. Trailing from the right rear wheel was the fully extended ball of string that Allan had used to secure his bait bird. He was walking but his face was going through a kaleidoscope of contortions. He was visibly biting his lip. It made me nervous. He arrived at the car red-faced and heaving for breath.

"Did you ever look back?" Allan asked.

"Well, not actually," I replied.

"Then you didn't see all the smoke?"

"Well no, I guess not," I said. This was not sounding good.

Allan continued deliberately. "Oh, I thought with the deafening noise of a floored engine, you might have been curious if it blew up!"

He was starting to get emotional. I hated it when Allan got emotional.

"Sounded okay to me," was my response.

His right eye started to twitch uncontrollably and he clenched his right fist. I was getting a real mortal feeling, like when your car starts sliding on ice, heading straight for a telephone pole. Ben and I were both cowering behind the safety of the car door.

"Then you clowns couldn't hear me screaming or pounding on the fenders?" he continued.

"Well, no. Like you said, it was a little noisy."

"A little noisy?" he shouted. "Well, it wouldn't be so goddamn noisy if you hadn't popped the clutch! All I could see through the smoke was the rear end of the Dodge swerving at me, it almost had me pinned to the fence. The only reason I still have legs is that the tires were spinning too fast to have traction. You left a helluva skid mark on my old man's tarp, right before it got sucked up around the wheel!"

After the adrenaline quit pumping and the mask of panic subsided, Allan began to calm down. About a year later, I took a driver's training course and got my license. I used my parent's automatic Oldsmobile to take the test.

One of the benefits of aging is recalling all of the good times you've lived through. Over the years, Allan and I have covered thousands of miles of the American West between the Mexican border and the Columbia Basin in Washington. While ostensibly looking for birds of prey, we saw many novel sights. We even may have pioneered the combination of weekend binges in Tijuana, Mexico, with hawk trapping in southern California. But I don't bring up the old "dig-in" trapping story around Allan. Despite the passage of time, he's still prone to exaggerate the negatives of the situation.

During my vacation, I had driven from Virginia to Maine, visited most of my relatives, and trapped hawks in the mountains and on the beaches. It was a great experience, tempered only by the frailness of my two ninety-year-old grandmothers and the prospect that I might not see them again. It never dawned on me that my telephone conversation with Al Nye during that trip would be our last; he later lost his battle with cancer.

The jetliner rumbled down the runway, accelerated to speed and powered into the air. Amid the deafening noise and thrust of the engines, I visually tallied the price of progress. From the window of the plane, the familiar fence that edged the airport was again visible. This once-powerful barricade now functioned less to keep airplanes in than to keep the city out. As the jet banked, I could see no respite from the edifices of civilization. City land is seldom, if ever, reclaimed from asphalt for the purpose of nurturing nature. Here, like other places where man leaves his mark, there is no environmental reversal of fortune.

While flying back to the Northwest, I pondered the state of American falconry. Without question, most future falconers will be products of suburbia. More than likely, these young people will grow up without an outdoor orientation and will lack the most rudimentary understanding of hunting skills. They must be strongly motivated to overcome these handicaps. Who will guide these youngsters eager for the challenging outdoor experiences of falconry? Without a helping hand, future falconers may never witness the marvel of migration from a blind on a brilliant autumn day; learn to transform leather and metal into artistic falconry furniture; or experience the meteoric fall of a falcon across a treeless plain in pursuit of game. The reality is that future generations of falconers will judge us not only by our merits, but also by the quality of the falconers we leave behind.

Half a Metaphor

by Dan O'Brien

All day I had been in one of the great canyons that run east from the Teton Range. It had rained on and off, and we were wet for most of the ten or so miles we walked. The couple with me had been hired to make observations and take care of four eyas peregrine falcons for the summer. That morning I had helped pack them into the area where they would spend the rest of the summer, then taken them up to the top of the cliff and down a rope to explain just how the wooden box, cabled to the ledge, would function as a base for the young falcons. The falcons would be flown into Jackson Hole in two days and I would bring them up in a wicker basket and put them into the box. These young people had two days to make themselves at home and get ready to take on a great deal of responsibility.

I was thinking of that responsibility when I pulled the pickup into a restaurant parking lot in Jackson. I was just getting to the part in my reasoning where I ask whose responsibility it really was and does any of it really do much good, when I saw the sign advertising the meat loaf special. I lost interest in thinking. It was not quite dark and I wasn't sure where I'd be sleeping that night; I was still wet and cold. I was also very tired and could feel that nagging catch in the small of my back, but the idea of the meat loaf special was like a tonic. I guess I was mostly hungry.

I sat down and ordered a cup of coffee and the special, then, thinking again of responsibility, I slipped out of the booth and went to the pay phone just down the hall from the rest rooms. I had not called into the office since the night before and knew that people would be wondering what was happening. The phone rang only once. It was Bill Burnham, my boss, the manager of the Peregrine Fund's Rocky Mountain division, and a long-time friend.

"Glad you called," he said. "Where are you?"

"Jackson," I said. I could hear that he was untypically excited. "What's up?"

"Well," he began, "we got a report of a pair of peregrines in the northern Rockies." I listened for the usual skeptical tone that we used when we talked of such reports but heard a hint of hope.

"What's the deal?"

"It's up in that tri-state area," he said. "I've looked at the general location on the map and we've released a gang of birds up there in the last four years."

"Who says they saw them?"

"That's the best part. Terry McEneaney."

My interest picked up. "Did you talk to him?"

"Yeah. He was up fooling around on a glacier and says they were a long way off but he's pretty sure. Heinrich called in from Salt Lake and thinks it's worth a look. He's on his way to McEneaney's right now."

I could see that my dinner had come. "I'm about five hours away," I said. "I was going to check out the third Teton site tomorrow and get ready to put the birds in on Wednesday, so tomorrow is not critical."

"Good," Burnham said. "Call me when you get in tomorrow night."

By the time the waitress had scraped

photo by Ronald G. Clarke

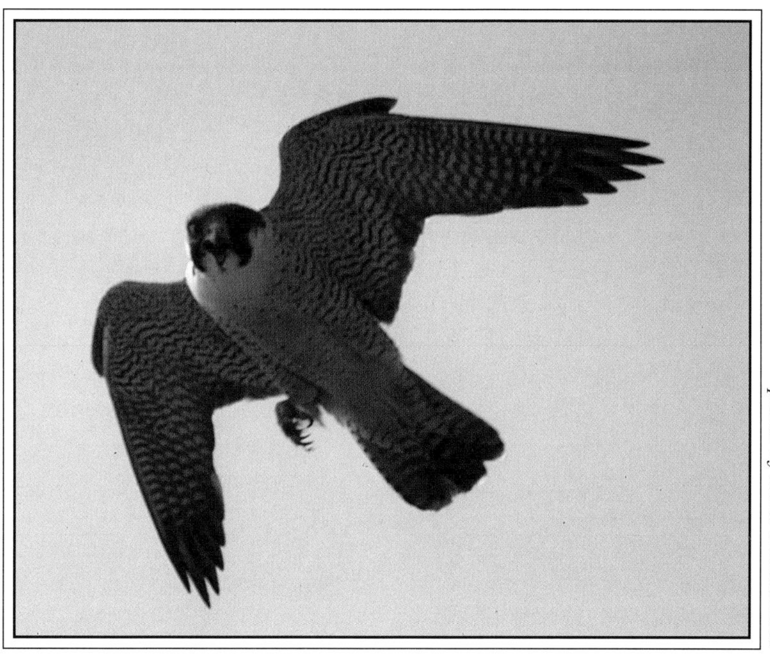

photo by Alberto Palleroni

my meat loaf and instant potatoes into a styrofoam box it was ten o'clock. I had a tank and a half of gasoline and the traffic was dying down, so I decided to go up through Yellowstone Park instead of going over Teton Pass and into Idaho. At that time, McEneaney was the trumpeter swan biologist at Red Rock Lakes Wildlife Refuge. He lived on the refuge which was at the western side of the area where Wyoming, Idaho, and Montana meet. This area includes the Teton Range, the high country of the Centennials, and is dominated by the Yellowstone ecosystem. It is an area like no other on earth, with great quantities of good marshes, meadows, and mountains with huge sheer cliffs. At one time it was inhabited by many peregrine falcons. But because of pesticides and possibly other reasons, no peregrines had been known to nest there for at least fifteen years. It was the area where the efforts to bring the peregrine back to the northern Rockies had been concentrated.

Luck was with me that night. I had good weather, plenty of gas, a styrofoam box full of food and an excuse to drive through Yellowstone Park without much company. It was dark by the time I passed Jackson Lake, but I could see the moon hanging up there with the Grand Teton. Its white reflection shattered on the lake and spread out for five miles in my rearview mirror. It was nice to see the moon; it would make the night come alive.

I had made that drive many times and had learned that the dead of night was the perfect time. The tourists were tucked into their motels and Winnebagos by then, and often I made the run from the south gate to Madison Junction without passing a car. I had also come to realize that the fatigue that was always a part of traveling during the time we were releasing peregrines was a sort of asset on this trip. It could keep you calm and let your mind loose while you drove the road that winds up and crosses the Continental Divide several times in twenty miles. When the moon is right, like it was that night, you can see white-water rivers below you at impossible angles. You pass meadows with tall dark moose standing at the harsh edges and run along the Firehole River where the steam from the geysers refracts the moonlight and contorts shadows into shapes so fantastic that you can forget that you are in a pickup truck. The night, and fatigue perhaps, allow you to see this country as John Colter might have seen it. Every shadow takes on importance.

You see the land as mystic and sacred, until a Great Gray Owl slides through the steamy moonlight over the road and you remember why you are there.

You are on your way to a rendezvous called to check on the authenticity of a report that peregrine falcons are once again nesting in this high country. If it were true, I thought, it would be the most wonderful news I'd heard for years. And then I smiled at myself. More wonderful than the artificial heart? The personal computer? MTV? Was a single pair of birds significant at all? Was a reprieve for a whole species significant? I thought about that all the way from Madison Junction to West Yellowstone. By the time I crossed the Divide into Idaho, I had still not decided if a pair of peregrines was more important than an artificial heart. I was very tired by then and imagined I was dealing with apples and oranges.

When I turned off the asphalt for the thirty miles of gravel to the refuge, I began to think about peregrine sightings. We had chased hundreds of them. In the northern Rockies they always came to nothing. Nesting peregrine falcons in the American West have a way of turning into prairie falcons. They can also turn into merlins, red-tail hawks, owls, even crows or ravens. The record was so poor on this sort of thing that we seldom responded anymore unless the sighting was made by a person whose expertise and reputation were very solid. Even then, a strange array of birds have come cackling from cliffs where peregrine falcons were guaranteed to be nesting.

But this sighting was different. It had been made in an area where we had been releasing captive-bred peregrines for several years. The time was right, and it had been made by a friend who had seen a lot of peregrines.

It would be a sort of reunion. Bill Heinrich, the head of the reintroduction effort in the Rockies, and I had met Mac on a peregrine banding expedition in Greenland four years earlier. We had gotten to know Mac well on that trip, the way you do in remote places, and had only been all together a few times since.

It was almost three a.m. when I pulled into Mac's driveway. Heinrich's truck was already there. There were no lights on in the house, so I took my sleeping bag and pad from the back of the truck and rolled them out in the lawn next to the driveway. It was a cold night at that altitude, and the stars were bright and close. I was familiar with the refuge and had always felt it was a special place. I thought being that close to the trumpeter swan, for which the refuge was established, would make my mind race. But I was too tired. I breathed in the cold air and felt it against my face, and in seconds I was completely asleep.

Three hours later I opened one eye when I felt someone nudging my leg with his boot. The sun was just coming up over the marsh and the backlighting would not let me see Mac's face. I hadn't seen him for six weeks but all he said was, "Breakfast. You going to sleep all day?"

Mac's wife, Karen, was cooking sausage and eggs and Heinrich was drinking coffee at the table. He smiled and I knew he was excited. Behind him, the remnants of a fire burned in the fireplace and a large picture window framed the upper lake of the refuge. Mac had a spotting scope set up in the main room between two full-sized mounted trumpeter swans. From his living room he could keep tabs on part of the refuge's precious population. The sausage and eggs were delicious. Karen did not eat, but was kept busy bringing more food to the table. She was going to Great Falls for a couple of days after we left and was happy, pleased about the chance to get to town.

We joked and talked about everything except the peregrine sighting. No one was sure and we didn't want to jinx things. There was a strange tension in the kitchen that morning, and it persisted in the pickup as we drove at a right angle from the rising sun.

Heinrich was in charge so, finally, he brought it up. I was driving and looked straight ahead as they talked, but I heard the way Heinrich said "the peregrines." He said it firmly, as if there was no possibility they were anything else.

When we pulled off this road at the drainage up which we would walk, Heinrich seemed to know where he was. He asked if this was the creek that ran under the cliff. When Mac said that it was, Heinrich's features slumped. As Mac climbed into the rear of the pickup for gear, Heinrich took me aside. "I surveyed this drainage two years ago from the air," he said. "There were prairie falcons in the lower part and most of the rest is over 9000 feet." He raised his eyebrows. "Pretty high for peregrines."

We carried light packs: rain gear, an extra sweater, lunch, binoculars, ropes, and ascenders. I took the big spotting scope and tripod. There was a good trail for the first few hundred yards, but it faded into a game trail as it wound its way along the river. We walked in single file and talked at first. But as the trail headed upward, the conversation slowed and so did we.

Sometime after my thirtieth birthday I noticed that there began to be an awkward stage to every long hike. The first mile or so goes as it always has, light and exciting. But the next few miles, before I hit a rhythm (or is it a numbness?), are difficult. That period of a hike is hard in many ways, but my attitude seems to suffer most. It is during that time that I think of southern California and condominium living. Visions of hot tubs and reading novels on the beach at Puerto Vallarta float through my head. I find myself wondering what I am doing still wandering the high country. Then I think of the older men who set the example I'd followed, and I remember how they finally would walk only a few steps at a time, when the going was steep, and breathe in the thin air through a gaping mouth in a red face. That day, going up that rocky canyon, I wondered how long it would be before young people would see me like that. I wondered if they already did.

But those first few miles purged these thoughts, and by the time the snow came into sight, the moving had become smooth. We walked for two hours without a rest, but when the cliffs were close enough to study with binoculars we came to a halt. The river had dwindled slightly but had become more wild. It tumbled ten feet wide and made a good opening through which we could survey the cliff top. It was still a very long way to even the base of the cliff, and we knew that to identify birds at that distance would be reckless at best. In a way, we were lucky. We did not see a sign of anything from the river, and so did not have to grimace and shake our heads and say that it was just too far to tell for sure. We ate some fruit and headed up into a snow chute on a route that Mac had pointed out.

It was a nice day and the snow was soft and very bright. We put lotion on our noses and dug into each other's packs for sunglasses. The snow was actually in two chutes. One started at the river and went between two small granite faces to a large flat area at the bottom of the upper cliff. The other went up alongside the upper cliff to the top of the gorge. It was our plan to get above the first cliff and onto the plateau. That is where Mac had made his observation. I would set up the spotting scope in the hope that if they were peregrines and landed somewhere on the cliff, I could get a clear enough view of them to see if they wore our bands, that is, if they were birds that we had raised and released. Mac and Heinrich would start up the second snow chute with climbing gear and try to positively identify any bird that came off the cliff beside them and, if I could determine a nest site, rappel down to see if any attempt had been made to nest. Since this sort of dealing needs to be done as quickly as possible, we had worked out a system of hand signals that could guide them to the right spot on the cliff if I could determine it.

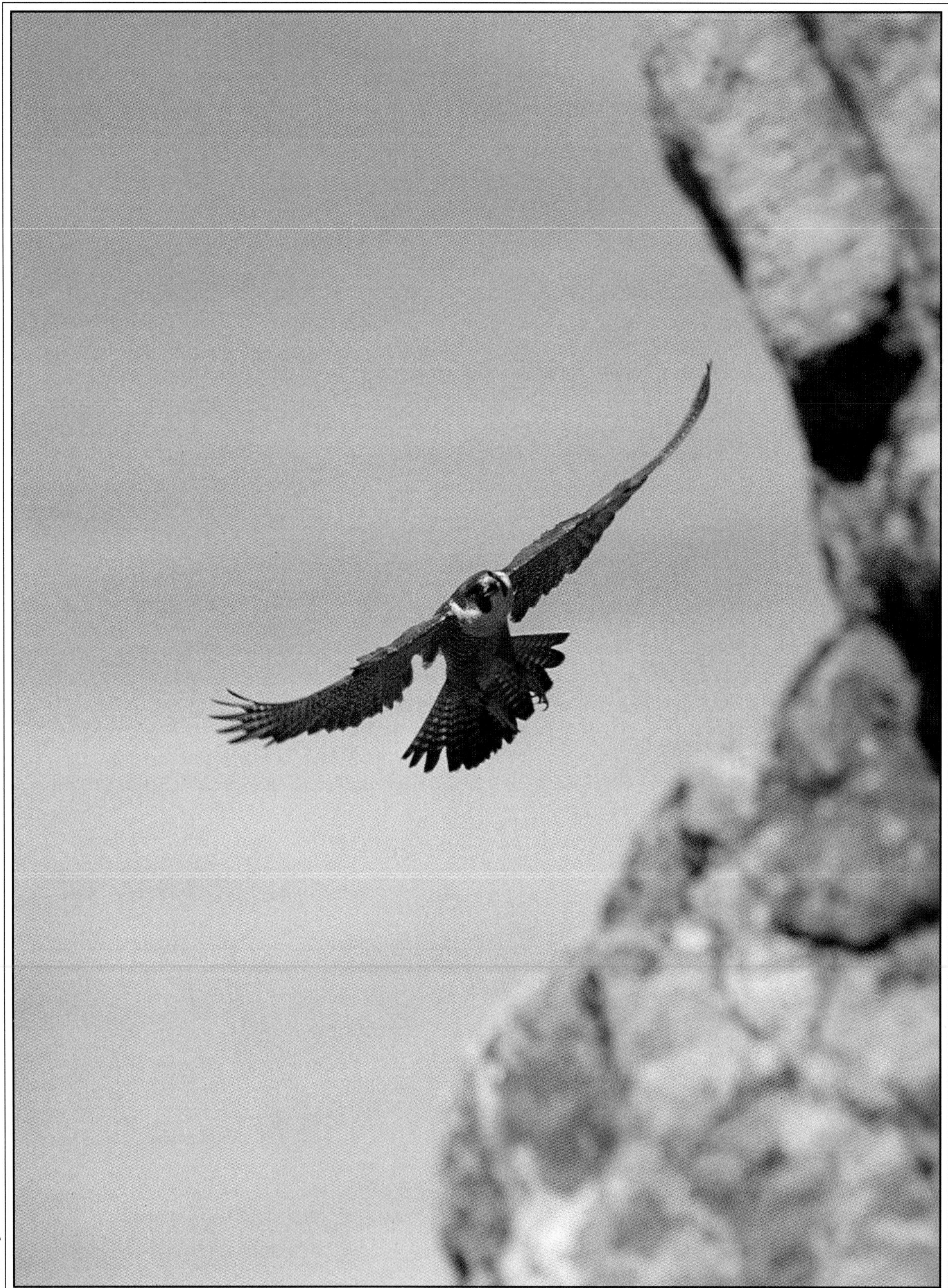

photo by Alberto Palleroni

The plateau turned out to be a dish, several hundred feet in diameter. There was no snow there and the blueberries, though not yet ripe, grew in abundance. There were plenty of large flat rocks on which I could set up the tripod. The wind was still and the sun warmed me to the point that a nap did not seem out of the question. But of course it was. Mac and Heinrich greased their noses again and started up the snow chutes. They moved slowly and carefully and as I watched them growing smaller on the snow, I found my mind going over it all again. The peregrine, a rare bird to be sure. But still, as so many people had told me, just a bird. So why all the fuss? Defensively I thought, because they fly like missiles, they rule the space above us. And it came to me that it was all in metaphor — feathered cannonballs, avian royalty — and I knew that it was not just the rareness. It was a sort of envy. Then I thought of the other rare ones, the rodents and the tiny fish, and knew that there would be no grand stay of extinction for them. I thought about the species whose ancestors mutated away from flamboyance and beautiful colored feathers or fur, those species who, for one reason or another, sought out the dark recesses of the earth and became slow and clumsy.

I looked back at my friends struggling in the snow and thought, yes, it could indeed be envy that drove us. It could be not our superiority that drove us to attempt to reverse an extinction that we had begun, but our guilt and suspicion of inferiority. Mac and Heinrich were just spots on the snow then, and I did not recognize them for what they were. I looked at the river below me and the mountains stretching out to infinity. It was all so grand that it was hard to believe. It was hard to believe in a sky that blue. I looked at the cliff and didn't believe it was real, and for an instant, I didn't believe in peregrines.

Until I heard them kakking.

In my heart I knew immediately that they were peregrines, though I had long before given up identifying peregrines until I had them solidly in a scope or binoculars. I cannot describe the sound that came down to me in that dish. It had the quality of the wind and the coyote and the loon, with a brittleness that made even the sound seem rare. Indeed, for hundreds of miles from that spot, it was the first time in fifteen years humans had heard that sound. It could have been the sound of migrating whales. No, the bugle of a unicorn.

And when I squinted in just the right fragment of sky I saw them, careening typically on the thermal above the cliff. My friends were near the top. I saw that they had roped together and were moving off the snow and onto the top part of the cliff. When I raised my binoculars an image of an adult peregrine falcon, wings stretched and black eyes scanning the canyon below, appeared perfectly framed. I lowered the binoculars as if to clean them. They were peregrines; and when I raised the binoculars again, both birds floated into the frame and I saw without a doubt they were a male and a female.

Then the female folded her wings and dropped and I remembered why I did this kind of work. Her barred under-wings became invisible and her bright orange feet tucked in, and everything flattened for a long stoop. She twisted, leveled off, adjusted her position, then plummeted almost too fast to follow. By the time the cliff came into the view of my binoculars, she had moved her wings away from her body slightly and started her flare to land.

It was a magic day. She flared her wings again and swooped upward, landing ever-so-lightly on the lip of a pothole in the cliff face. Without taking my binoculars down, I fumbled for the scope. I moved it blindly in front of me and, still through the binoculars, studied the pothole and the area around it. A small pine tree grew on a ledge just above the falcon, yes, and orange lichen in a horseshoe shape, and some very dark rock formed a star just below her. I breathed deeply and lowered the binoculars, being careful not to move my eyes. I located the general area of the cliff where she stood, because she was much too small to find with the naked eye. Then I moved to the spotting scope and, magic day indeed, there she stood, clear as the oil painting in my study. She ruffled her feathers, picked one foot up and tucked it away, then squinted her eyes and looked right into the spotting scope. She gazed haughtily through the optics and found me hunkered there behind the eyepiece like a depraved voyeur.

Her stare embarrassed me. Could she possibly know I was watching? It seemed impossible, with all that was below her, that she would even notice me – a slow, ugly, insignificant terrestrial creature – yet, there it was. With a million directions to look, she was definitely gazing dreamly into the end of my spotting scope.

I locked the scope on the falcon and the pothole. It was too much to even hope for, but she looked for all the world like a peregrine falcon about to have a snooze in front of her nest site. I directed my binoculars to the top of the cliff nearly two hundred feet above her. I could see Mac and Heinrich and could tell they had seen the birds. I could just make out their smiles with the binoculars. When they raised their own binoculars, I signaled that there was a likely looking hole below them. I directed them along the cliff about fifty feet and they threw the rope over. I switched my eye to the spotting scope just in time to see the falcon slick her feathers and take to the air as the rope skittered down within ten feet of the pothole.

Now Heinrich was moving fast. Both falcons were aware of the men and started stooping at them. I knew Heinrich well and knew that just then he was sick with concern that the adults were being stressed. He dropped in long bounds to within twenty feet of the pothole, then looked over his shoulder to me. I watched him through the binoculars and, when he looked, signaled with my whole body that he'd have to slide over only a few feet. He lowered himself carefully and jockeyed in the direction I'd indicated. The peregrines were taking turns diving at him. They missed him by only inches and I could hear the noise of the air through their wings even from that distance. But Heinrich worked steadily. He moved closer to the pothole and shifted his position. He peered into the pothole and paused suspended there at the end of that rope for only a few seconds. Then I saw him reach down for his ascenders and snap in. He moved quickly up the rope and was at the top for only an instant before the rope began to be retrieved. In less than five minutes from when Heinrich had started down, there was no sign of Mac or him on the cliff. The peregrines screamed a while longer before they went to perches on the cliff. Then it was my turn to go to work.

I located the general area of both birds with my binoculars as they came back to the cliff. Then I found first the female and then the male with the spotting scope. When I got one focused perfectly in the scope, I flipped the power up as high as it would go and tried my best to focus on the right leg of the bird. Powerful spotting scopes like that work backward. That is, right is left and left is right. It makes this type of observation difficult. The birds would sometimes pick up the leg I was interested in and tuck it away beneath their feathers. There were heat waves and wind to contend with and a couple of times the birds moved, so I had to relocate them. It took all my attention, so I was surprised when Heinrich touched me on the shoulder. I had been at it for an hour but I'd found out what we wanted to know. "They're both wearing our bands," I said.

Heinrich smiled. "And there are two youngsters up in that pothole," he said.

Then the three of us were quiet. I'm sure we were all trying to figure out what it meant.

The walk down went quickly. Now we joked and slapped each other on the back. We laughed and Heinrich told us he had put some beer in the truck, just in case. The beer was gone by the time we got to Island Park and we bought more along with six huge T-bone steaks. We figured that Karen would be gone and that there would be nothing but meat and beer. Mac and I got the charcoal ready while Heinrich called Burnham. When Heinrich got off the phone, he came to me and said Burnham was mad that we were drinking beer. I looked at him oddly and he slapped me on the back. He said we should have bought champagne.

We ate the meat rare and sat in front of the fire and talked about the Arctic. We talked about other mountain ranges and the Eskimo girl that Heinrich had never forgotten. We talked about how cold it had been that winter and the time Mac got chased by the moose. And then it was late and we knew that it was time for sleep. Heinrich was leaving for Boise in the morning to check another release site. Mac was trying out new floating swan nests and I had to be in Jackson by ten in the morning to meet young peregrines at the airport. It would be a long day for all of us.

We let the fire go out so it would not be too warm in our bags. Mac decided to sleep on the floor with us, and brought his bag in and curled up with no pad or pillow. I unrolled closest to the door because I would be leaving first. I set my watch alarm for four and guess I didn't hear any of the conversation after that.

When I awoke it was just beginning to get light. It was like Alaska outside the picture window. The cloudiness thinned before it dissolved into the surface of the lake and the peaks of the Centennials were gone. I was cold as soon as I got out of my sleeping bag and looked out the window. I thought of crawling back into the bag, but of course I couldn't. It looked miserable outside, a misty rain over everything, but the birds of the refuge didn't seem to notice. The willets were shrieking and lifting their wings in their black and white territorial posturing. A raven circled in the mist. The sandhill cranes crisscrossed the grasslands at the lake's edge. And the swans, Jesus, the swans! drifted effortlessly through the dawning dream of Mac's picture window. I looked at my friends content in their sleeping bags and tried not to notice the pain in my lower back.

Then came the same old question: How important was all of this? Was it a worthy thing to spend your life doing? And I decided in an instant that that was not really the question, that perhaps we had no real choice in the matter. Our humanity didn't insure such options and in spite of our oversized brains, we might only be doing what we had to do.

That thought seemed an optimistic one to me that morning. I wasn't in a mood for reason and accepted that we were dealing more with a matter of the heart than with science. The power to uplift the human spirit was the peregrine's ace in the hole. It was the ability to fill half a metaphor that could best buy a species more time, maybe even save it. But that was all too hard for me that morning. I had a full day ahead. I stuffed my bedroll into its bag and tossed it into the truck. I started the engine and let it warm up. Then I wheeled the truck out onto the gravel road and pointed it through the fog toward Jackson.

Photographic Credits

Cover Insert: *Ronald G. Clarke*

The Inspiration of Falcons: *Gary M. Cargile, Dave Boehlke, Norm Nelson*

E6: *Ralph Rogers, Scott Rogers, Joe Papp*

Perfect Birds: *Jill Graves*

Beyond: *Greg Hachigian*

Passagers: *Charles Schwartz*

Pursuit: *Ronald G. Clarke*

Gus: *S. Kent Carnie*

The Prodigal: *Gary M. Cargile, Alison Meyer*

Two Boys and a Turkey: *Keith Thompson*

George and Harry: *Paul T. Schnell*

Scars: *Ronald G. Clarke*

Savage Beauty: *Rick Kline*

Not Just a Game: *Les Oxner, Pamela Ensign Wollam, Bill Girden*

The Rage of Knowing: *Paul T. Schnell*

The Near Horizon: *S. Kent Carnie*

Homecoming: *Bruce A. Haak, Joseph Vorro, Mike McDermott*

Half a Metaphor: *Ronald G. Clarke, Alberto Palleroni*